PROFESSING IN THE CONTACT ZONE

Professing in the Contact Zone

Bringing Theory and Practice Together

Edited by

JANICE M. WOLFF
Saginaw Valley State University

National Council of Teachers of English
1111 W. Kenyon Road, Urbana, Illinois 61801-1096

Staff Editor: Tom Tiller
Interior Design: Jenny Jensen Greenleaf
Cover Design: Carlton Bruett

NCTE Stock Number: 37407-3050

Library of Congress Cataloging-in-Publication Data

Professing in the contact zone : bringing theory and practice together / edited by Janice M. Wolff.
    p. cm.
Includes bibliographical references and index.
ISBN 0-8141-3740-7 (pbk.)
   1. English language—Rhetoric—Study and teaching. 2. Report writing—Study and teaching (Higher) I. Wolff, Janice M., 1947–
PE1404 .P658 2002
808'.042'0711—dc21

2001054671

CONTENTS

ACKNOWLEDGMENTS

It seems a long time ago that Jeannie Weiland Herrick and I sat on her patio and selected essays from those that had been submitted for the contact zone collection. We thought that was the hard part. A couple of publishers and several years later, the project has found a home at NCTE. I have read many, many acknowledgments, and now that I write my own, I understand more deeply what writers/editors mean in their statements of thanks. First, I thank Mary Louise Pratt for providing us with a starting point for examining our own professional situations. Second, I thank Kurt Austin for taking our work seriously and for providing us with the opportunity to publish a volume such as this. I thank all the contact zone authors for contributing to the collection and for their patience and belief in the worth of this project. When I would hail them in their busy lives and ask for yet another draft, or follow-up, or query, they would put this work first on their list. I owe a huge thank-you to Tom Tiller, a tireless editor, an intelligent reader, one who has asked all the big and little questions about text and context for this book.

My friends and colleagues at Saginaw Valley State University have been a great support: Mary Harmon has been a strong advocate for the collection, Kay Harley has been long interested in the project, and Gary Thompson has given me advice about academic publishing. I must give a world of credit to Saun Strobel, Honors secretary and support person for faculty publications at SVSU. She said it would happen, and her work is in a large way responsible for that. Finally, I thank my husband Terry for his support and love throughout the process.

FOREWORD

PATRICIA BIZZELL
College of the Holy Cross

I vividly remember sitting in a large hall at the 1990 MLA Responsibilities for Literacy Conference in Pittsburgh and hearing Mary Louise Pratt deliver the keynote address. That was my first exposure to the concept of "contact zone," and it was an unforgettable "Aha!" moment in my thinking. Just the year before, Joe Harris had published his essay "The Idea of Community in the Study of Writing," critiquing the concept of discourse community that David Bartholomae and I had been advancing in our work. Harris's analysis had started me thinking about the limitations of the discourse community concept, and "contact zone" struck me as just the conceptual tool I needed in order to go beyond it.

In my earlier work on discourse communities (e.g., "Cognition, Convention, and Certainty: What We Need to Know about Writing," 1982), I had suggested that a "discourse community" was held together by shared ways of using language, and that people typically belonged to several discourse communities. I was most concerned, however, to explore the academic discourse community, since I wanted to redefine the problems of my basic writing students as problems of entering a social group in which the linguistic habits and customs and taken-for-granted knowledge were unfamiliar (rather than entertaining any of the then-prevailing "deficit" theories to explain their difficulties). But, as Harris had pointed out, my approach tended to mute the voices of the nonacademic discourse community allegiances students brought with them to school, seeming to focus only on the necessity of assimilation to academic ways of using language, and on methods of doing that more efficiently and humanely.

Pratt's concept helped me to imagine the writing classroom, and indeed, the academy generally, as a contact zone. The advantage of this perspective is that it emphasizes that multiple discourse communities are always present. Moreover, it emphasizes that they are present in relations of unequal power. Thus Pratt's concept enabled me to rethink my students' difficulties as not merely those of assimilation, but rather as those of negotiation between the pressure to enter the academic discourse community and the force of their ongoing, and perhaps competing, allegiances to other ways of using language. And just as important, I was enabled to see more clearly how conflicted such negotiations would typically be: that learning academic discourse might not be as emotionally and politically neutral for basic writing students as, say, the learning of French was for me when I was a Midwestern, middle-class, high school student, who even had some French blood in the family. In short, the concept of contact zone both subsumed the concept of discourse community—a contact zone typically being a social location in which several discourse communities mingle—and also posited intermingling discourse communities as existing in dynamic relations with each other, struggling for power in ways that mirror larger social struggles for political power and justice.

It's clear from the essays collected in this volume that Pratt's concept of contact zone has been equally generative for many other scholars and teachers in our field, illuminating our work in many helpful ways. Indeed, as will be seen in my 1994 essay reprinted here, I went so far as to suggest that the entire discipline of English studies be reorganized in light of Pratt's insights. What strikes me most about the contributions to this volume is the way in which contact zone theory, as I think we should now call it, following the lead of Janice Wolff in her introduction to this volume, allows us to talk about conflict and negotiation in our teaching and administrative work. Such discussions highlight issues of power and authority that have been under debate in our field for some time. Thus they are of supreme importance if we wish to foster social justice in the classroom, and in the larger society.

Works Cited

Bartholomae, David. "Inventing the University." *When a Writer Can't Write*. Ed. Mike Rose. New York: Guilford, 1985.

Bizzell, Patricia. "Cognition, Convention, and Certainty: What We Need to Know about Writing." *Pre/Text* 3.3 (Fall 1982): 213–43.

———. "'Contact Zones' and English Studies." *College English* 56.2 (1994): 163–69.

Harris, Joseph. "The Idea of Community in the Study of Writing." *College Composition and Communication* 40 (February 1989): 11–22.

Pratt, Mary Louise. "Arts of the Contact Zone." MLA Responsibilities for Literacy Conference. Pittsburgh. Sept. 1990.

INTRODUCTION

JANICE M. WOLFF
Saginaw Valley State University

The essays that make up this volume have had their beginnings in a variety of settings: some came from attendees of
the 1991 and 1992 NCTE Summer Institutes for Teachers of Literature (focused on critical theory and practice) in Myrtle Beach,
some from participants at the Rutgers Conference on Contact
Zone Literacies, and some from readers of Mary Louise Pratt's
"Arts of the Contact Zone," published in MLA's *Profession 91*.
Some of the essays had their genesis in Pratt's more fully articulated study of contact zones, *Imperial Eyes: Travel Writing and
Transculturation*. Regardless of origin, however, the essays collected here all share the project of clarifying, extending, or
problematizing the ideas of the contact zone as they are made
known to us by Mary Louise Pratt. The discourses of the contact
zone, whether they are called "theory" or "literacy" or "rhetoric," speak to composition teachers, literature specialists, rhetoricians, administrators, and literacy workers in extracurricular
locations, and they speak meaningfully as well to all those who
inhabit spaces where sociolinguistic contact is made. The contact zone arts, literacies, and pedagogies as taught by Mary Louise
Pratt allow for and compel teachers to write their stories, to elaborate their experiences with contact zones.

This compulsion to tell those stories continues for those whose
work is included in this collection. The contributing authors continue to be invested in the knowledge and critical view that contact zone theory allows them. Though the collection has been a
long time in progressing to press, the authors continue to be committed to contact zone pedagogies. And contact zone analyses
continue to have currency in academic journals and at academic

conferences. Imagine my surprise when, on an elevator at a recent conference on feminisms and rhetorics, I noticed a fellow conference goer acting a bit flustered. He had noticed my name badge and connected my name with my work on contact zone theory. I asked whether he was all right, whether something was amiss, and, in a slightly embarrassed way, he mentioned that his paper for the conference referred to my earlier work. He asked whether I was planning to attend his session that afternoon, and I heartily answered, "I am now." It is this ongoing and expanding attention being paid to contact zone theory that continues to energize the contributors to this volume, several of whom produced an addendum to their initial contribution, explaining their continuing use of the metaphor in their teaching and professional interactions.

This collection proposes to illustrate how contact zone theory and literacies play out in a variety of institutional settings and spaces: in the university classroom, in the community college, in the secondary classroom, in student texts, in programmatic spaces, in curriculum development, in extracurricular sites, in the writing center, and so on. We collectively thank Mary Louise Pratt for promoting such valid ways of knowing and assessing the cultural work we are committed to, and, with this sense of gratitude in mind, we lead off this collection with a reprinting of her landmark essay "Arts of the Contact Zone." Her insights, articulated in that essay and elsewhere, allow teachers to see their roles in new ways, to reflect on the multiple literacies that affect education and the educational mission. She situates teachers historically and culturally and asks that we reassess what we teach, how we teach, why we teach, why we privilege certain discourses while dismissing others. Pratt teaches the teacher to see the power differential in the classroom and other institutional spaces, to reflect and to theorize, to read the rhetoric of the classroom. She advocates a contact zone pedagogy that produces a rhetorical reading of multiple spaces, within the university and without. She teaches us, too, to bring disparate elements together—material practices in the classroom in relation to sociocultural situations of students and teachers, theories of community juxtaposed with the sometimes violent spaces within education—and to reimagine the already imagined spaces of the classroom. Pratt draws a geography of the metropolis, where metropolitan literacies come into conflict with indigenous discourses, where Creole languages are a necessity for communication or commerce. These metaphors open up new vistas for postsecondary educators and demand a new, democratizing move in our institutions and in our individual practices.

Those who contributed to this collection did so from a variety of professional perspectives. In the first section, Spaces, several teachers describe their own environments and the implications of contact zone theory in those contested spaces. In "First Contact: Composition Students' Close Encounters with College Culture," an earlier version of which appeared in *The Journal of Teaching Writing,* Paul Jude Beauvais uses contact zone ideas to elaborate students' first-year experiences at a residential campus and to illustrate the ways in which contact zone texts can, in Pratt's words, "constitute a marginalized group's point of entry into the dominant circuits of print culture." He outlines a program of writing instruction based on the notion of student as historian, ethnographer, and rhetor, a program of study which richly elaborates Pratt's ideas about what the arts of the contact zone might be when brought to bear on the teaching mission. While describing the course, Beauvais includes compelling examples of interaction with students and student texts.

While Beauvais explores contact zone theory as it informs writing pedagogy—both successes and failures—Patricia Bizzell works at the level of curricular concern and innovation. In her essay "Multiculturalism, Contact Zones, and the Organization of English Studies," previously published in *College English,* Bizzell advocates applying contact zone theory to disciplinary and structural concerns, suggesting, as she does, that "we organize English Studies not in terms of literary or chronological periods, nor essentialized racial or gender categories, but rather in terms of historically defined contact zones, moments when different groups within the society contend for the power to interpret what is going on." It is a bold step to suggest that the discipline reorganize itself around historically determined bids for power, but a step that reminds us of the unequal distribution of power that accompanies literacy. Bizzell illuminates the way that contact zone theory promotes the best kind of self-critique, the way to tell our history to ourselves through a kind of disciplinary autoethnography. It's clear that contact zone theory has implications both at the macro and the micro levels of educational and pedagogical structuring.

Katherine K. Gottschalk's "Contact Zones: Composition's Content in the University" is a kind of companion piece to Bizzell's, but it tells a slightly different story—in this case that of an administrator of a university writing program with responsibilities to students, teachers, and administrators alike. As an administrator herself, Gottschalk wants some consensus in the writing program she directs, and she treads the difficult path between the danger of losing common purpose and that of imposing sameness on those who teach for her. She suggests that writing program administrators need to realize that staff are not a homogenous group of people who will see writing instruction in a monolithic way. Contact zone theory allows Gottschalk to think critically about the diversity of teachers in her program; it compels her to allow them the discretion to design their courses and to carry out their teaching effectively according to their own mandates. Tom Philion, in "Frontiers of the Contact Zone," writes of the spaces inhabited by both the supervisor of teaching interns and the interns themselves as he relates his experiences as supervisor of student teachers in secondary schools in an inner city. He shares his own "thick description" of those teaching spaces and of his evolving ethnographic approach to a classroom situation in which a young Korean American student teacher struggles to teach a classic American text to a diverse group of tenth-grade students. He extends contact zone analysis to the culture of the high school classroom and does so by foregrounding the student teacher's experiences with "unsolicited oppositional discourse" as recorded in narrative form in his observer's log. Daphne Key goes beyond the traditional classroom and produces an essay that speaks about the extracurricular spaces where contact zones are found. In "Safe Houses and Sacrifices: Filling the Rooms with Precious Riches," Key tells the story of how contact zone theory changed her teaching of writing to a group of day-care providers. In a workshop course designed to bring literacies to women in extracurricular spaces, Key experiences the wonders of the contact zone, where exhilarating acts of literacy take place. Key worked with the women in the workshop to create a setting in which participants learned to write and value their own stories, to "go public" with their stories, to celebrate and validate the oral tradition from which those stories arose.

In Section II, Clashes and Conflicts, the asymmetrical relationships of power become apparent, and the grappling and the struggling within contact zones emerge. Clashes are evident in Richard E. Miller's provocative essay "Fault Lines in the Contact Zone," previously published in *College English*. Miller addresses what he perceives as "limits" in Pratt's notion of the contact zone. Focusing, as Miller stated in an abstract of the essay, on "a student paper that both sets out to examine a 'community' (gay people in San Francisco), and to disrupt a host of communities (the paper describes a series of violent acts against gay people and the homeless encountered during the study), I [Miller] have attempted to re-locate discussion of the classroom at its most problematic and challenging point—the voice that apparently deserves no better fate than to be silenced." But Miller does not silence the conversation, oppressive and hostile as it may be. Instead, "community" becomes the key term that compels Miller to look more closely at Pratt's and his own pedagogy. Though Pratt acknowledges that the idea of "community" is largely an imagined space, Miller questions the possibility of ever arriving at community. Miller's essay, coupled with Pratt's work, becomes a framework for another analysis of "unsolicited oppositional discourse. In "Reconstitution and Race in the Contact Zone," Robert Murray uses contact zone theory as a lens through which to view the ways in which racism insinuates itself into the classroom, and he suggests that students' ideologies, rather than being inviolable rights, are intellectual responsibilities. Murray examines student discourse in light of contact zone theory, which enables him to see that students sometimes speak the racism of their culture, that is, oppositional discourse that must be confronted.

In Diane Penrod's "'Can't We All Just Get Along?' When a College Community Resists the Contact Zone," she examines a classroom moment when students resisted engaging in discussion of bell hooks's views on white appropriation of black culture in the pop music industry. Students dismissed hooks's often-anthologized essay as dated, out of touch. It wasn't until Penrod saw the same kind of dismissive treatment in a faculty meeting that she realized what had taken place in her classroom. Contact zone theory allows her to write a critique of tolerance, even as she extends and problematizes Pratt's theory of the contact zone. In "Contact, Colonization, and Classrooms: Language Issues via Cisneros's *Woman Hollering Creek* and Villanueva's *Bootstraps*," Mary Harmon chronicles the linguistic points of contact and clash in a section of a Themes in Literature/Composition II class taught at a regional Midwestern undergraduate university. Within the space of the lit/comp classroom, many students behaved contentiously in the face of diverse texts—those by Cisneros and others—but once the class members began to speak authentically about their own contact zone experiences as colonizer or colonized, and once they heard a tirade by a student named Ter-Ri, students began to "get it," to read generously and interestedly. They came to "re-see Cisneros linguistically and rhetorically." Ultimately, contact zone discourse and terminology allowed for some real successes in the classroom: celebrations of Mexican American heritage in music and poetry and drama— the exhilarations of the contact zone.

Cynthia Lewiecki-Wilson leads off the third section, Community, by recognizing the possibilities for community. Her essay, "Teaching in the Contact Zone: Multiple Literacies/Deep Portfolio," an earlier version of which appeared in *Teaching English in the Two-Year College*, tells the story of Lewiecki-Wilson's evolving pedagogy, and elaborates the way that contact zone theory has led her to develop the notion of "deep portfolios" wherein students use their own writing as the basis for more writing for different audiences and purposes. Her essay argues that a multiple literacies and "deep portfolio" approach best serves the needs of two-year college composition students. Carol Severino takes contact zone language and strategies out of the classroom and into the writing center in "Writing Centers as Linguistic Contact Zones and Borderlands." Originally published in *The Writing Lab Newsletter*, Severino's essay deromanticizes the writing center's role in the university as she tells how the metaphors of "borderlands" and "contact zone" "do and do not apply to the writing center's place, space, and mission in the academy."

Her text becomes a compelling linguistic analysis of the terminologies of the contact zone.

My own essay, "Teaching in the Contact Zone: The Myth of Safe Houses," previously published in *Critical Theory and the Teaching of Literature: Politics, Curriculum, Pedagogy* (edited by James F. Slevin and Art Young), employs contact zone theory both to analyze the reading of the novel *Beloved* and to explore the pedagogy involved in teaching and writing about such a novel. The contact zone ideas and the reading of the novel are mutually informing practices. The essay analyzes contact zone theory and its implications for reading imaginative texts such as *Beloved*, and for reading the classroom conflict that arises out of teaching/ reading a novel that is problematic insofar as it treats subject matter that pushes boundaries for students. Though the concepts of "community" and "safe house" remain imaginary, the essay poses the possibility of creating some safety in the midst of clash and conflict. Carole Yee applies contact zone theory to the institutional reading of assessment and shows how an ethnographic methodology can apply to "the description of institutional cultures, specifically academic programs and departments." In this case, contact zone theory permitted a creative, descriptive approach to assessment, a new avenue for assessing outcomes. In another ethnographic account, "Telling Stories: Rethinking the Personal Narrative in the Contact Zone of a Multicultural Classroom," Jeanne Weiland Herrick reenvisions what is at stake for nonnative students when they are asked to write a "personal narrative." Herrick wisely draws out the implications of making such a demand when students operate with competing cultural ideologies. When teachers assign this kind of writing, they need to know that students may be compromised. Contact zone theory allows Herrick to reconsider the cultural terrorism inherent in such an assignment, when students from diverse backgrounds may resist divulging intensely personal moments in their lives. For Herrick and for others, stories came to mean in surprisingly different ways, and a contact zone approach to teaching values them all. Contact zone theory compels us to understand that ways of knowing are culturally specific and critical to our approach to pedagogy.

And so goes the story of the contact zone: authors have written essays, developed pedagogy, revised curriculum, interacted with colleagues—and done all of these things differently given contact-zone approaches. Several contributing authors have reviewed their own earlier work and submitted postscripts representing their most recent views on the values of thinking through contact zone theory. They continue to pay attention to the principles set forth by Mary Louise Pratt; they continue to develop pedagogy that is attentive to the power inherent in academic environments; they continue to view the world through contact zone lenses. Readers will find these follow-up comments immediately after the respective authors' essays. Richard Miller's reflective comments, however, are found at the close of the collection, for they suggest a future for contact zone thinking. He has made an inventory of clashes of the contact zone; he has become disheartened by his collected data—that a planned sequel to his essay included here "never got written." But though he mourns for the change that he may not be able to effect, Miller nonetheless rightly tells us to take our small victories, to know that "when we devote our energies to the curriculum, to better understanding the funding of higher education, to taking control of testing at our home institutions, and to plunging ourselves headlong into the technological revolution," we are engaging in substantive change. He rightly tells us that we are moving "from studying the contact zone to creating a zone of effectivity, a pragmatic space where our actions have discernible consequences." It is my feeling that this book may help bring this desire for change closer to fruition.

Works Cited

Pratt, Mary Louise. "Arts of the Contact Zone." *Profession 91.* New York: MLA, 1991. 33–40. (Originally presented as the keynote address at MLA's Responsibilities for Literacy conference in September 1990 in Pittsburgh.)

———. *Imperial Eyes: Travel Writing and Transculturation.* New York: Routledge, 1992.

Arts of the Contact Zone

MARY LOUISE PRATT
Stanford University

Whenever the subject of literacy comes up, what often pops first into my mind is a conversation I overheard eight years ago between my son Sam and his best friend, Willie, aged six and seven, respectively: "Why don't you trade me Many Trails for Carl Yats . . . Yesits . . . Ya-strum-scrum." "That's not how you say it, dummy, it's Carl Yes . . . Yes . . . oh, I don't know." Sam and Willie had just discovered baseball cards. Many Trails was their decoding, with the help of first-grade English phonics, of the name Manny Trillo. The name they were quite rightly stumped on was Carl Yastrzemski. That was the first time I remembered seeing them put their incipient literacy to their own use, and I was of course thrilled.

Sam and Willie learned a lot about phonics that year by trying to decipher surnames on baseball cards, and a lot about cities, states, heights, weights, places of birth, stages of life. In the years that followed, I watched Sam apply his arithmetic skills to working out batting averages and subtracting retirement years from rookie years; I watched him develop senses of patterning and order by arranging and rearranging his cards for hours on end, and aesthetic judgment by comparing different photos, different series, layouts, and color schemes. American geography and history took shape in his mind through baseball cards. Much

This essay is reprinted by permission of the Modern Language Association of America from *Profession 91* (33–40). It was originally presented as the keynote address at MLA's Responsibilities for Literacy conference in September 1990 in Pittsburgh.

of his social life revolved around trading them, and he learned about exchange, fairness, trust, the importance of processes as opposed to results, what it means to get cheated, taken advantage of, even robbed. Baseball cards were the medium of his economic life too. Nowhere better to learn the power and arbitrariness of money, the absolute divorce between use value and exchange value, notions of long- and short-term investment, the possibility of personal values that are independent of market values.

Baseball cards meant baseball card shows, where there was much to be learned about adult worlds as well. And baseball cards opened the door to baseball books, shelves and shelves of encyclopedias, magazines, histories, biographies, novels, books of jokes, anecdotes, cartoons, even poems. Sam learned the history of American racism and the struggle against it through baseball; he saw the Depression and two world wars from behind home plate. He learned the meaning of commodified labor, what it means for one's body and talents to be owned and dispensed by another. He knows something about Japan, Taiwan, Cuba, and Central America and how men and boys do things there. Through the history and experience of baseball stadiums he thought about architecture, light, wind, topography, meteorology, the dynamics of public space. He learned the meaning of expertise, of knowing about something well enough that you can start a conversation with a stranger and feel sure of holding your own. Even with an adult—especially with an adult. Throughout his preadolescent years, baseball history was Sam's luminous point of contact with grown-ups, his lifeline to caring. And, of course, all this time he was also playing baseball, struggling his way through the stages of the local Little League system, lucky enough to be a pretty good player, loving the game and coming to know deeply his strengths and weaknesses.

Literacy began for Sam with the newly pronounceable names on the picture cards and brought him what has been easily the broadest, most varied, most enduring, and most integrated experience of his thirteen-year life. Like many parents, I was delighted to see schooling give Sam the tools with which to find and open all these doors. At the same time I found it unforgivable that schooling itself gave him nothing remotely as meaningful to do, let alone anything that would actually take him beyond the referential, masculinist ethos of baseball and its lore.

However, I was not invited here to speak as a parent, nor as an expert on literacy. I was asked to speak as an MLA member working in the elite academy. In that capacity my contribution is undoubtedly supposed to be abstract, irrelevant, and anchored outside the real world. I wouldn't dream of disappointing anyone. I propose immediately to head back several centuries to a text that has a few points in common with baseball cards and raises thoughts about what Tony Sarmiento, in his comments to the conference, called new visions of literacy. In 1908 a Peruvianist named Richard Pietschmann was exploring in the Danish Royal Archive in Copenhagen and came across a manuscript. It was dated in the city of Cuzco in Peru, in the year 1613, some forty years after the final fall of the Inca empire to the Spanish and signed with an unmistakably Andean indigenous name: Felipe Guaman Poma de Ayala. Written in a mixture of Quechua and ungrammatical, expressive Spanish, the manuscript was a letter addressed by an unknown but apparently literate Andean to King Philip III of Spain. What stunned Pietschmann was that the letter was twelve hundred pages long. There were almost eight hundred pages of written text and four hundred of captioned line drawings. It was titled *The First New Chronicle and Good Government*. No one knew (or knows) how the manuscript got to the library in Copenhagen or how long it had been there. No one, it appeared, had ever bothered to read it or figured out how. Quechua was not thought of as a written language in 1908, nor Andean culture as a literate culture.

Pietschmann prepared a paper on his find, which he presented in London in 1912, a year after the rediscovery of Machu Picchu by Hiram Bingham. Reception, by an international congress of Americanists, was apparently confused. It took twenty-five years for a facsimile edition of the work to appear in Paris. It was not till the late 1970s, as positivist reading habits gave way to interpretive studies and colonial elitisms to postcolonial pluralisms, that Western scholars found ways of reading Guaman Poma's *New Chronicle and Good Government* as the extraordinary intercultural tour de force that it was. The letter got there, only 350 years too late, a miracle and a terrible tragedy.

I propose to say a few more words about this erstwhile unreadable text, in order to lay out some thoughts about writing and literacy in what I like to call the *contact zones*. I use this term to refer to social spaces where cultures meet, clash, and grapple with each other, often in contexts of highly asymmetrical relations of power, such as colonialism, slavery, or their aftermaths as they are lived out in many parts of the world today. Eventually I will use the term to reconsider the models of community that many of us rely on in teaching and theorizing and that are under challenge today. But first a little more about Guaman Poma's giant letter to Philip III.

Insofar as anything is known about him at all, Guaman Poma exemplified the sociocultural complexities produced by conquest and empire. He was an indigenous Andean who claimed noble Inca descent and who had adopted (at least in some sense) Christianity. He may have worked in the Spanish colonial administration as an interpreter, scribe, or assistant to a Spanish tax collector—as a mediator, in short. He says he learned to write from his half brother, a mestizo whose Spanish father had given him access to religious education.

Guaman Poma's letter to the king is written in two languages (Spanish and Quechua) and two parts. The first is called the *Nueva corónica*, "New Chronicle." The title is important. The chronicle of course was the main writing apparatus through which the Spanish presented their American conquests to themselves. It constituted one of the main official discourses. In writing a "new chronicle," Guaman Poma took over the official Spanish genre for his own ends. Those ends were, roughly, to construct a new picture of the world, a picture of a Christian world with Andean rather than European peoples at the center of it—Cuzco, not Jerusalem. In the *New Chronicle* Guaman Poma begins by rewriting the Christian history of the world from Adam and Eve (Fig. 1), incorporating the Amerindians into it as offspring of one of the sons of Noah. He identifies five ages of Christian history that he links in parallel with the five ages of canonical Andean history—separate but equal trajectories that diverge with Noah and reintersect not with Columbus but with Saint Bartholomew, claimed to have preceded Columbus in the Americas. In a couple of hundred pages, Guaman Poma constructs a veritable encyclo-

FIGURE 1. *Adam and Eve.*

pedia of Inca and pre-Inca history, customs, laws, social forms, public offices, and dynastic leaders. The depictions resemble European manners and customs description, but also reproduce the meticulous detail with which knowledge in Inca society was stored on *quipus* and in the oral memories of elders.

Guaman Poma's *New Chronicle* is an instance of what I have proposed to call an *autoethnographic* text, by which I mean a text in which people undertake to describe themselves in ways that engage with representations others have made of them. Thus if ethnographic texts are those in which European metropolitan subjects represent to themselves their others (usually their conquered others), autoethnographic texts are representations that the so-defined others construct *in response to* or in dialogue with those texts. Autoethnographic texts are not, then, what are usually thought of as autochthonous forms of expression or self-representation (as the Andean *quipus* were). Rather they involve a selective collaboration with and appropriation of idioms of the metropolis or the conqueror. These are merged or infiltrated to varying degrees with indigenous idioms to create self-representations intended to intervene in metropolitan modes of understanding. Autoethnographic works are often addressed to both metropolitan audiences and the speaker's own community. Their reception is thus highly indeterminate. Such texts often constitute a marginalized group's point of entry into the dominant circuits of print culture. It is interesting to think, for example, of American slave autobiography in its autoethnographic dimensions, which in some respects distinguish it from Euramerican autobiographical tradition. The concept might help explain why some of the earliest published writing by Chicanas took the form of folkloric manners and customs sketches written in English and published in English-language newspapers or folklore magazines (see Treviño). Autoethnographic representation often involves concrete collaborations between people, as between literate ex-slaves and abolitionist intellectuals, or between Guaman Poma and the Inca elders who were his informants. Often, as in Guaman Poma, it involves more than one language. In recent decades autoethnography, critique, and resistance have reconnected with writing in a contemporary creation of the contact zone, the *testimonio*.

Guaman Poma's *New Chronicle* ends with a revisionist account of the Spanish conquest, which, he argues, should have been a peaceful encounter of equals with the potential for benefiting both, but for the mindless greed of the Spanish. He parodies Spanish history. Following contact with the Incas, he writes, "In all Castile, there was a great commotion. All day and at night in their dreams the Spaniards were saying, 'Yndias, yndias, oro, plata, oro, plata del Piru" ("Indies, Indies, gold, silver, gold, silver from Peru") (Fig. 2). The Spanish, he writes, brought nothing of value to share with the Andeans, nothing "but armor and guns con la codicia de oro, plata oro y plata, yndias, a las Yndias, Piru" ("with the lust for gold, silver, gold and silver, Indies, the Indies, Peru") (372). I quote these words as an example of a con-

FIGURE 2. *Conquista. Meeting of Spaniard and Inca. The Inca says in Quechua, "You eat this gold?" Spaniard replies in Spanish, "We eat this gold."*

quered subject using the conqueror's language to construct a parodic, oppositional representation of the conqueror's own speech. Guaman Poma mirrors back to the Spanish (in their language, which is alien to him) an image of themselves that they often suppress and will therefore surely recognize. Such are the dynamics of language, writing, and representation in contact zones.

The second half of the epistle continues the critique. It is titled *Buen gobierno y justicia,* "Good Government and Justice," and combines a description of colonial society in the Andean region with a passionate denunciation of Spanish exploitation and abuse. (These, at the time he was writing, were decimating the population of the Andes at a genocidal rate. In fact, the potential loss of the labor force became a main cause for reform of

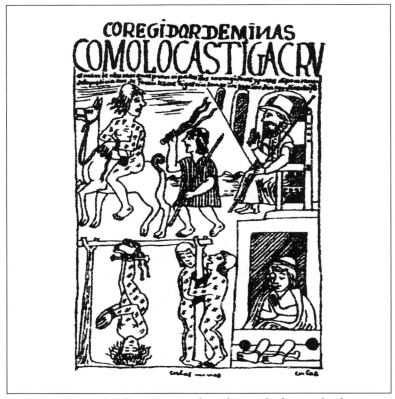

FIGURE 3. *Corregidor de minas. Catalog of Spanish abuses of indigenous labor force.*

the system.) Guaman Poma's most implacable hostility is invoked by the clergy, followed by the dreaded *corregidores,* or colonial overseers (Fig. 3). He also praises good works, Christian habits, and just men where he finds them, and offers at length his views as to what constitutes "good government and justice." The Indies, he argues, should be administered through a collaboration of Inca and Spanish elites. The epistle ends with an imaginary question-and-answer session in which, in a reversal of hierarchy, the king is depicted asking Guaman Poma questions about how to reform the empire—a dialogue imagined across the many lines that divide the Andean scribe from the imperial monarch, and in which the subordinated subject single-handedly gives himself authority in the colonizer's language and verbal repertoire. In a way, it worked—this extraordinary text did get written—but in a way it did not, for the letter never reached its addressee.

To grasp the import of Guaman Poma's project, one needs to keep in mind that the Incas had no system of writing. Their huge empire is said to be the only known instance of a full-blown bureaucratic state society built and administered without writing. Guaman Poma constructs his text by appropriating and adapting pieces of the representational repertoire of the invaders. He does not simply imitate or reproduce it; he selects and adapts it along Andean lines to express (bilingually, mind you) Andean interests and aspirations. Ethnographers have used the term *transculturation* to describe processes whereby members of subordinated or marginal groups select and invent from materials transmitted by a dominant or metropolitan culture. The term, originally coined by Cuban sociologist Fernando Ortiz in the 1940s, aimed to replace overly reductive concepts of acculturation and assimilation used to characterize culture under conquest. While subordinate peoples do not usually control what emanates from the dominant culture, they do determine to varying extents what gets absorbed into their own and what it gets used for. Transculturation, like autoethnography, is a phenomenon of the contact zone.

As scholars have realized only relatively recently, the transcultural character of Guaman Poma's text is intricately apparent in its visual as well as its written component. The genre of the four hundred line drawings is European—there seems to have been no tradition of representational drawing among the Incas—but in their execution they deploy specifically Andean systems of spatial symbolism that express Andean values and aspirations.[1]

In Figure 1, for instance, Adam is depicted on the left-hand side below the sun, while Eve is on the right-hand side below the moon, and slightly lower than Adam. The two are divided by the diagonal of Adam's digging stick. In Andean spatial symbolism, the diagonal descending from the sun marks the basic line of power and authority dividing upper from lower, male from female, dominant from subordinate. In Figure 2, the Inca appears in the same position as Adam, with the Spaniard opposite, and the two at the same height. In Figure 3, depicting Spanish abuses of power, the symbolic pattern is reversed. The Spaniard is in a high position indicating dominance, but on the "wrong" (right-hand) side. The diagonals of his lance and that of the servant doing the flogging mark out a line of illegitimate, though real, power. The Andean figures continue to occupy the left-hand side of the picture, but clearly as victims. Guaman Poma wrote that the Spanish conquest had produced "un mundo al reves," "a world in reverse."

In sum, Guaman Poma's text is truly a product of the contact zone. If one thinks of cultures, or literatures, as discrete, coherently structured, monolingual edifices, Guaman Poma's text, and indeed any autoethnographic work, appears anomalous or chaotic—as it apparently did to the European scholars Pietschmann spoke to in 1912. If one does not think of cultures this way, then Guaman Poma's text is simply heterogeneous, as the Andean region was itself and remains today. Such a text is heterogeneous on the reception end as well as the production end: it will read very differently to people in different positions in the contact zone. Because it deploys European and Andean systems of meaning making, the letter necessarily means differently to bilingual Spanish-Quechua speakers and to monolingual speakers in either language; the drawings mean differently to monocultural readers, Spanish or Andean, and to bicultural readers responding to the Andean symbolic structures embodied in European genres.

In the Andes in the early 1600s there existed a literate public with considerable intercultural competence and degrees of bilingualism. Unfortunately, such a community did not exist in the Spanish court with which Guaman Poma was trying to make contact. It is interesting to note that in the same year Guaman Poma sent off his letter, a text by another Peruvian was adopted in official circles in Spain as the canonical Christian mediation between the Spanish conquest and Inca history. It was another huge encyclopedic work, titled the *Royal Commentaries of the Incas,* written, tellingly, by a mestizo, Inca Garcilaso de la Vega. Like the mestizo half brother who taught Guaman Poma to read and write, Inca Garcilaso was the son of an Inca princess and a Spanish official, and had lived in Spain since he was seventeen. Though he too spoke Quechua, his book is written in eloquent, standard Spanish, without illustrations. While Guaman Poma's life's work sat somewhere unread, the *Royal Commentaries* was edited and reedited in Spain and the New World, a mediation that coded the Andean past and present in ways thought unthreatening to colonial hierarchy.[2] The textual hierarchy persists; the *Royal Commentaries* today remains a staple item on Ph.D. reading lists in Spanish, while the *New Chronicle and Good Government*, despite the ready availability of several fine editions, is not. However, though Guaman Poma's text did not reach its destination, the transcultural currents of expression it exemplifies continued to evolve in the Andes, as they still do, less in writing than in storytelling, ritual, song, dance-drama, painting and sculpture, dress, textile art, forms of governance, religious belief, and many other vernacular art forms. All express the effects of long-term contact and intractable, unequal conflict.

Autoethnography, transculturation, critique, collaboration, bilingualism, mediation, parody, denunciation, imaginary dialogue, vernacular expression—these are some of the literate arts of the contact zone. Miscomprehension, incomprehension, dead letters, unread masterpieces, absolute heterogeneity of meaning—these are some of the perils of writing in the contact zone. They all live among us today in the transnationalized metropolis of the United States and are becoming more widely visible, more pressing, and, like Guaman Poma's text, more decipherable to those who once would have ignored them in defense of a stable, centered sense of knowledge and reality.

Contact and Community

The idea of the contact zone is intended in part to contrast with ideas of community that underlie much of the thinking about language, communication, and culture that gets done in the academy. A couple of years ago, thinking about the linguistic theories I knew, I tried to make sense of a utopian quality that often seemed to characterize social analyses of language by the academy. Languages were seen as living in "speech communities," and these tended to be theorized as discrete, self-defined, coherent entities, held together by a homogeneous competence or grammar shared identically and equally among all the members. This abstract idea of the speech community seemed to reflect, among other things, the utopian way modern nations conceive of themselves as what Benedict Anderson calls "imagined communities."[3] In a book of that title, Anderson observes that with the possible exception of what he calls "primordial villages," human communities exist as *imagined* entities in which people "will never know most of their fellow-members, meet them or even hear of them, yet in the mind of each lives the image of their communion." "Communities are distinguished," he goes on to say, "not by their falsity/genuineness, but by *the style in which they are imagined*" (15; emphasis mine). Anderson proposes three features that characterize the style in which the modern nation is imagined. First, it is imagined as *limited,* by "finite, if elastic, boundaries"; second, it is imagined as *sovereign;* and, third, it is imagined as *fraternal,* "a deep, horizontal comradeship" for which millions of people are prepared "not so much to kill as willingly to die" (15). As the image suggests, the nation-community is embodied metonymically in the finite, sovereign, fraternal figure of the citizen-soldier.

Anderson argues that European bourgeoisies were distinguished by their ability to "achieve solidarity on an essentially imagined basis" (74) on a scale far greater than that of elites of other times and places. Writing and literacy play a central role in this argument. Anderson maintains, as have others, that the main instrument that made bourgeois nation-building projects possible was print capitalism. The commercial circulation of books in the various European vernaculars, he argues, was what first created the invisible networks that would eventually constitute the literate elites and those they ruled as nations. (Estimates are that 180 million books were put into circulation in Europe between the years 1500 and 1600 alone.)

Now obviously this style of imagining of modern nations, as Anderson describes it, is strongly utopian, embodying values like equality, fraternity, liberty, which the societies often profess but systematically fail to realize. The prototype of the modern nation as imagined community was, it seemed to me, mirrored in ways people thought about language and the speech community. Many commentators have pointed out how modern views of language as code and competence assume a unified and homogeneous social world in which language exists as a shared patrimony—as a device, precisely, for imagining community. An image of a universally shared literacy is also part of the picture. The prototypical manifestation of language is generally taken to be the speech of individual adult native speakers face-to-face (as in Saussure's famous diagram) in monolingual, even monodialectal situations—in short, the most homogeneous case linguistically and socially. The same goes for written communication. Now one could certainly imagine a theory that assumed different things—that argued, for instance, that the most revealing speech situation for understanding language was one involving a gathering of people each of whom spoke two languages and understood a third and held only one language in common with any of the others. It depends on what workings of language you want to see or want to see first, on what you choose to define as normative.

In keeping with autonomous, fraternal models of community, analyses of language use commonly assume that principles of cooperation and shared understanding are normally in effect. Descriptions of interactions between people in conversation, classrooms, medical and bureaucratic settings, readily take it for granted that the situation is governed by a single set of rules or norms shared by all participants. The analysis focuses then on how those rules produce or fail to produce an orderly, coherent exchange. Models involving games and moves are often used to describe interactions. Despite whatever conflicts or systematic social differences might be in play, it is assumed that all participants are engaged in the same game and that the game is the same for all players. Often it is. But of course it often is not, as, for example, when speakers are from different classes or cultures, or one party is exercising authority and another is submitting to it or questioning it. Last year one of my children moved to a new elementary school that had more open classrooms and more flexible curricula than the conventional school he started out in. A few days into the term, we asked him what it was like at the new school. "Well," he said, "they're a lot nicer, and they have a lot less rules. But know why they're nicer?" "Why?" I asked. "So you'll obey all the rules they don't have," he replied. This is a very coherent analysis with considerable elegance and explanatory power, but probably not the one his teacher would have given.

When linguistic (or literate) interaction is described in terms of orderliness, games, moves, or scripts, usually only legitimate moves are actually named as part of the system, where legitimacy is defined from the point of view of the party in authority--regardless of what other parties might see themselves as doing. Teacher-pupil language, for example, tends to be described almost entirely from the point of view of the teacher and teaching, not from the point of view of pupils and pupiling (the word doesn't even exist, though the thing certainly does). If a classroom is analyzed as a social world unified and homogenized with respect to the teacher, whatever students do other than what the teacher specifies is invisible or anomalous to the analysis. This can be true in practice as well. On several occasions my fourth grader, the one busy obeying all the rules they didn't have, was given writing assignments that took the form of answering a series of questions to build up a paragraph. These questions often asked him to identify with the interests of those in power over him—parents, teachers, doctors, public authorities. He invariably sought ways to resist or subvert these assignments. One assignment, for instance, called for imagining "a helpful invention." The students were asked to write single-sentence responses to the following questions:

> What kind of invention would help you?
>
> How would it help you?
>
> Why would you need it?
>
> What would it look like?
>
> Would other people be able to use it also?
>
> What would be an invention to help your teacher?
>
> What would be an invention to help your parents?

Manuel's reply read as follows:

> A grate adventchin
>
> Some inventchins are GRATE!!!!!!!!!!! My inventchin would be a shot that would put every thing you learn at school in your

brain. It would help me by letting me graduate right now!! I would need it because it would let me play with my friends, go on vacachin and, do fun a lot more. It would look like a regular shot. Ather peaple would use to. This inventchin would help my teacher parents get away from a lot of work. I think a shot like this would be GRATE!

Despite the spelling, the assignment received the usual star to indicate the task had been fulfilled in an acceptable way. No recognition was available, however, of the humor, the attempt to be critical or contestatory, to parody the structures of authority. On that score, Manuel's luck was only slightly better than Guaman Poma's. What is the place of unsolicited oppositional discourse, parody, resistance, critique in the imagined classroom community? Are teachers supposed to feel that their teaching has been most successful when they have eliminated such things and unified the social world, probably in their own image? Who wins when we do that? Who loses?

Such questions may be hypothetical, because in the United States in the 1990s, many teachers find themselves less and less able to do that even if they want to. The composition of the national collectivity is changing and so are the styles, as Anderson put it, in which it is being imagined. In the 1980s in many nation-states, imagined national syntheses that had retained hegemonic force began to dissolve. Internal social groups with histories and lifeways different from the official ones began insisting on those histories and lifeways *as part of their citizenship,* as the very mode of their membership in the national collectivity. In their dialogues with dominant institutions, many groups began asserting a rhetoric of belonging that made demands beyond those of representation and basic rights granted from above. In universities we started to hear, "I don't just want you to let me be here, I want to belong here; this institution should belong to me as much as it does to anyone else." Institutions have responded with, among other things, rhetorics of diversity and multiculturalism whose import at this moment is up for grabs across the ideological spectrum.

These shifts are being lived out by everyone working in education today, and everyone is challenged by them in one way or another. Those of us committed to educational democracy are particularly challenged as that notion finds itself besieged on the public agenda. Many of those who govern us display, openly, their interest in a quiescent, ignorant, manipulable electorate. Even as an ideal, the concept of an enlightened citizenry seems to have disappeared from the national imagination. A couple of years ago the university where I work went through an intense and wrenching debate over a narrowly defined Western-culture requirement that had been instituted there in 1980. It kept boiling down to a debate over the ideas of national patrimony, cultural citizenship, and imagined community. In the end, the requirement was transformed into a much more broadly defined course called Cultures, Ideas, Values.[4] In the context of the change, a new course was designed that centered on the Americas and the multiple cultural histories (including European ones) that have intersected here. As you can imagine, the course attracted a very diverse student body. The classroom functioned not like a homogeneous community or a horizontal alliance but like a contact zone. Every single text we read stood in specific historical relationships to the students in the class, but the range and variety of historical relationships in play were enormous. Everybody had a stake in nearly everything we read, but the range and kind of stakes varied widely.

It was the most exciting teaching we had ever done, and also the hardest. We were struck, for example, at how anomalous the formal lecture became in a contact zone (who can forget Atahuallpa throwing down the Bible because it would not speak to him?). The lecturer's traditional (imagined) task—unifying the world in the class's eyes by means of a monologue that rings equally coherent, revealing, and true for all, forging an ad hoc community, homogeneous with respect to one's own words—this task became not only impossible but anomalous and unimaginable. Instead, one had to work in the knowledge that whatever one said was going to be systematically received in radically heterogeneous ways that we were neither able nor entitled to prescribe.

The very nature of the course put ideas and identities on the line. All the students in the class had the experience, for example, of hearing their culture discussed and objectified in ways that horrified them; all the students saw their roots traced back to legacies of both glory and shame; all the students experienced face-to-face the ignorance and incomprehension, and occasionally the hostility, of others. In the absence of community values and the hope of synthesis, it was easy to forget the positives; the fact, for instance, that kinds of marginalization once taken for granted were gone. Virtually every student was having the experience of seeing the world described with him or her in it. Along with rage, incomprehension, and pain there were exhilarating moments of wonder and revelation, mutual understanding, and new wisdom—the joys of the contact zone. The sufferings and revelations were, at different moments to be sure, experienced by every student. No one was excluded, and no one was safe.

The fact that no one was safe made all of us involved in the course appreciate the importance of what we came to call "safe houses." We used the term to refer to social and intellectual spaces where groups can constitute themselves as horizontal, homogeneous, sovereign communities with high degrees of trust, shared understandings, temporary protection from legacies of oppression. This is why, as we realized, multicultural curricula should not seek to replace ethnic or women's studies, for example. Where there are legacies of subordination, groups need places for healing and mutual recognition, safe houses in which to construct shared understandings, knowledges, claims on the world that they can then bring into the contact zone.

Meanwhile, our job in the Americas course remains to figure out how to make that crossroads the best site for learning that it can be. We are looking for the pedagogical arts of the contact zone. These will include, we are sure, exercises in storytelling and in identifying with the ideas, interests, histories, and attitudes of others; experiments in transculturation and collaborative work and in the arts of critique, parody, and comparison (including unseemly comparisons between elite and vernacular cultural forms); the redemption of the oral; ways for people to engage with suppressed aspects of history (including their own histories); ways to move *into and out of* rhetorics of authenticity; ground rules for communication across lines of difference and hierarchy that go beyond politeness but maintain mutual respect; a systematic approach to the all-important concept of *cultural mediation*. These arts were in play in every room at the extraordinary

Pittsburgh conference on literacy. I learned a lot about them there, and I am thankful.

Notes

1. For an introduction in English to these and other aspects of Guaman Poma's work, see Rolena Adorno. Adorno and Mercedes Lopez-Baralt pioneered the study of Andean symbolic systems in Guaman Poma.

2. It is far from clear that the *Royal Commentaries* was as benign as the Spanish seemed to assume. The book certainly played a role in maintaining the identity and aspirations of indigenous elites in the Andes. In the mid-eighteenth century, a new edition of the *Royal Commentaries* was suppressed by Spanish authorities because its preface included a prophecy by Sir Walter Raleigh that the English would invade Peru and restore the Inca monarchy.

3. The discussion of community here is summarized from my essay "Linguistic Utopias."

4. For information about this program and the contents of courses taught in it, write Program in Cultures, Ideas, Values (CIV), Stanford Univ., Stanford, CA 94305.

Works Cited

Adorno, Rolena. *Guaman Poma de Ayala: Writing and Resistance in Colonial Peru*. Austin: U of Texas P, 1986.

Anderson, Benedict. *Imagined Communities: Reflections on the Origins and Spread of Nationalism*. London: Verso, 1984.

Garcilaso de la Vega, El Inca. *Royal Commentaries of the Incas*. 1613. Austin: U of Texas P, 1966.

Guaman Poma de Ayala, Felipe. *El primer nueva corónica y buen gobierno*. Manuscript. Ed. John Murra and Rolena Adorno. Mexico: Siglo XXI, 1980.

Pratt, Mary Louise. "Linguistic Utopias." *The Linguistics of Writing*. Ed. Nigel Fabb et al. Manchester: Manchester UP, 1987. 48–66.

Treviño, Gloria. "Cultural Ambivalence in Early Chicano Prose Fiction." Diss. Stanford U, 1985.

I

SPACES

First Contact: Composition Students' Close Encounters with College Culture

PAUL JUDE BEAUVAIS
Salem State College

When Mary Louise Pratt suggested that classrooms can serve as "contact zones"—that is, as "social spaces where cultures meet, clash, and grapple with each other, often in contexts of highly asymmetrical relations of power" (34)—she also noted that "the idea of the contact zone is intended in part to contrast with the ideas of community that underlie much of the thinking about language, communication, and culture that gets done in the academy" (37). Pratt's essay attempts to correct some facile concepts of community that have become common in our academic discourse. In fact, the essay invites a conclusion that Pratt never states explicitly: *any* sense of community in today's multiversities must be forged by sometimes fractious conflict in the contact zones where cultures collide. However, Richard E. Miller has argued that Pratt's own examples of contact zones are "curiously benign" in that Pratt "offers no examples of how her students negotiated [their] struggles in writing or of how their teachers participated in and responded to their struggles" (391). Miller's own essay provides a striking example of struggle in a composition class, and in this essay I will provide several more examples. In doing so, I will demonstrate that the first-year composition class can be a particularly important contact zone in

A slightly different version of this essay appeared in *The Journal of Teaching Writing* 15.1 (1996): 25–49. Reprinted by permission.

that it can serve as an arena for exploring the pedagogical value of several types of *first* contacts that new students experience in the other contact zones of the university.[1]

While several scholars have offered promising proposals for utilizing the classroom contact zone to explore power and difference, I have not seen a study of how the classroom might be used to explore what may be the most pressing concern facing first-year college students: their adjustment to life on a college campus.[2] In their first semester on campus, students experience numerous "first contacts." One type of first contact is that between the students and the university itself, an institution that first-year students see personified in its representatives: the administrators, faculty, and staff members whom they encounter. Another type of first contact is that of students with other students who come from diverse—and disparate—sociocultural backgrounds. Within the contact zone of the composition classroom, students can be given opportunities to think, talk, and write critically about their initial experiences in college. To create these opportunities, I have developed a sequence of reading and writing assignments that focus on college life. For first-year students in the composition classroom, these assignments can serve the general function that Pratt attributes to texts produced in contact zones: the assignments can "constitute a marginalized group's point of entry into the dominant circuits of print culture" (35).

In designing a course with a thematic focus on college life, I was inspired in part by David Bartholomae's now-classic essay "Inventing the University." However, while Bartholomae has suggested that each new student must invent the university for himself or herself, he is primarily concerned with the ways in which students discover the writing conventions and habits of thought characteristic of the various disciplines that constitute the university. Certainly I share Bartholomae's concern—and my own course attempts to acquaint students with some of the discourse conventions of the academy—but I am intrigued by a dimension of the university that Bartholomae does not explore: the multifaceted lives that students lead outside of the classroom but within the living space that the university provides. To paraphrase Bartholomae, I believe that every generation of students must invent college life, and they must do so within a network of constraints. Some of these constraints are imposed by the students' own assumptions, values, and abilities, while others are imposed by the university life that other students have shaped and by the imperatives that the institution itself imposes. To invent college life, students must discover the potential as well as the limits of their agency within the university. They must identify the arenas in which their participation is required or encouraged, those in which it is grudgingly tolerated, and those in which it is unwelcome. They must also invent or discover modes of discourse that are acceptable to their various audiences in the university yet also suitable for their own particular ends. Thus, for some students the invention of college life requires a process that Pratt (borrowing from Fernando Ortiz) terms "transculturation"—that is, a process "whereby members of subordinated or marginal groups select and invent from materials transmitted by a dominant or metropolitan culture" (36). And as they negotiate the constraints imposed by multiple audiences in a hierarchical institution, students may discover the truth of Pratt's warning about writing in a contact zone: they may discover that the reception of their texts will be "highly indeterminate" (35).

In assembling the reading and writing assignments for College Writing, I settled on three general areas which, as it happened, correspond to the three temporal modes: past, present, and future. I see each of these modes as corresponding to a different identity that I would like my students to assume: the historian, the ethnographer, and the rhetor. I'll offer a very brief explanation of the assignments in each of these modes, and I'll follow each explanation with an analysis of one student paper that illustrates how students discover the social power—and the limits on the power—of their discourse.

Remembering the Past: The Student as Historian

One of my goals is that students become familiar with the history of life at American universities in general and at their own university in particular. To pursue this goal, students complete summary/reaction and comparison/contrast assignments on two readings. The first of these readings is an excerpt from Helen Lefkowitz Horowitz's *Campus Life*, a study of student culture in American universities since the eighteenth century. From the Horowitz reading, students learn that the struggle to balance newfound social freedom and academic responsibility is at least as old as the American university. Most of my students are surprised when they read Horowitz's account of an eighteenth-century educational system in which students "were completely dependent upon their faculty not only for their system of education but also for their living arrangements"—a system in which students "had no legitimate recourse other than withdrawal . . . if they found their instructor vindictive or their food rotten" (26). Even more surprising for students is Horowitz's account of campus disturbances in the early 1800s, an era when Yale students bombed a dormitory and North Carolina students horsewhipped the university president and stoned two faculty members. However, my students recognize in their own university the remnants of the eighteenth-century student cultures that Horowitz describes, and most students are quick to recognize themselves and their classmates as the descendants of the pleasure-loving "College Men," the career-minded "Outsiders," and the social-activist "Rebels."[3] The more recent antecedents of these cultures become familiar to them when they read an excerpt from Richard Kern's *Findlay College: The First Hundred Years*, a history of the institution that they attend.[4] This excerpt describes two protests on campus in the 1960s. The first protest was a demonstration against the college's no-alcohol policy: Kern describes how several hundred students occupied the student union and drank beer to protest the policy. The second demonstration was arranged by Findlay's Black Student Union, which occupied the cafeteria and burned copies of the college newspaper after it published a racist letter. Kern's work introduces students to a history of activism at their campus—an activism that is barely evident today but nevertheless is familiar in light of recent events at Pennsylvania, Rutgers, and other campuses. It also introduces two types of conflicts that occur within the contact zones of the university: conflicts between students and the university administration, and conflicts within the student body.

After students read and respond to these essays, they conduct their own interviews of students who attended college at least ten years ago. They use these interviews to assemble profiles of the interview subjects' college experiences. (See Appendix A for a detailed description of this assignment.) In doing so, students polish their skills in handling the mechanics of quotation and paraphrase (a requirement for all sections of College Writing at the University of Findlay), while exploring further the nature of college life for previous generations of students.

Many of my students interview family members, so their profiles provide evidence of the disparate educational backgrounds of their families: a student editing group may consider a profile of an Ivy League graduate, a graduate of a state college, and a trade-school student. Other students interview members of the Findlay faculty, and their interviews reveal how the representatives of the institution fared in their own first contacts with higher education. What they discover is sometimes disturbing, and how they handle this assignment reveals some limits in the authority of student writers.

As an example of the dilemmas that students encounter in preparing their profiles, I offer the case of Penny, a student who interviewed her advisor, Dr. M.[5] In discussing her experiences as a first-year student in the late 1970s, Dr. M talked at length about the difficulties of moving from a small farming community to a major metropolitan university. In the course of the interview, Dr. M mentioned that she roomed with two other women in her first semester at college and that she and the other White occupant of the room experienced numerous conflicts with their one African American roommate. Noting that the African American roommate had different study and social habits, Dr. M then chuckled and asserted that she and her White roommate "drove [the African American roommate] out of the room" by midsemester.

As I listened to Penny's recorded interview and read her transcription of it, I jotted a note saying "sounds despicable to me" in the margin next to Dr. M's comments. When Penny prepared a profile of her advisor, she did mention Dr. M's conflict with a roommate; however, she did not specify the race of the roommate who was driven out of the room. I asked Penny why she had not done so. She replied that she felt uncomfortable about including the incident in a profile that she would have to show to her advisor and to other students, and she added that she thought the incident could create the wrong impression. In fairness to Penny and to Dr. M, I should add that Penny's reservations could be justified: since she didn't ask follow-up questions about her advisor's roommate conflicts, she couldn't provide details concerning the specific conflicts that Dr. M experienced and the specific actions she took.

In looking back at Penny's interview and profile, I see several issues that merit attention. First, of course, is her advisor's seeming inability to negotiate amicably her first contact with an African American student. What I find particularly troublesome, though, is not the prospect of that failure but rather Dr. M's lighthearted discussion of it nearly two decades later. Perhaps Dr. M's inability to recall her African American roommate's name is a natural result of the passage of time, but it's also possible to see in this lapse of memory a reduction of the roommate to a racial identity. Concerning Penny's handling of the material, I would note that her assignment provided her with an opportunity to accomplish what Pratt identifies as one important function of contact-zone writing: the opportunity to "mirror back" to the audience "an image of themselves that they often suppress and will therefore surely recognize" (35). However, instead of mirroring back Dr. M's unsuccessful first contact with difference and her subsequent attempt to ameliorate that experience, Penny chose to erase the racial dimension of Dr. M's experience. Penny's rationale for doing so may seem suspect (if understandable): she is reticent to cast an unfavorable light on her mentor, a person whom she admires.[6] However, Penny's response may also be governed at least in part by the asymmetrical power relations holding between her and Dr. M. On the one hand, Penny recognizes that she has the power to tarnish Dr. M's reputation. On the other hand, Dr. M occupies a position of power over Penny. As a representative of the university, Dr. M signs Penny's registration forms and will write letters of recommendation when Penny applies to graduate school (an event that already figures in Penny's plans). Thus, Penny's reluctance to include the sensitive material could signal her recognition of her own vulnerability: as Penny imagines the reception of her text, she can anticipate undesirable consequences. Still, I think it worth noting that Penny's reluctance to discuss Dr. M's offensive behavior is itself an acknowledgment that she recognizes the insensitivity (at the very least) of Dr. M's actions and comments. Instead of seeing her advisor's attitudes as a validation of those attitudes, Penny chooses to see the attitudes as an aberration.

I'm not certain whether Penny could recognize that Dr. M's "aberrant" behavior is all too familiar in the university; however, I do know that other students have been quick to recognize the racial element in dormitory conflicts today. In class discussions that occurred while students were working on the interview assignment, students were quick to offer recent examples of racial conflicts among students at Findlay. One student reported an incident in which the American roommates of a Chinese student had piled garbage on her bed, and another student reported that a Hispanic student found a note that said "Go back to Iran where you belong" taped to his door. Indeed, the discussion of college life in the past leads naturally to a discussion of more recent events, many of which concern the tensions that students experience in their living environments.

Exploring the Present: The Student as Ethnographer

Another goal of College Writing is to acquaint students with some basic research conventions. To this end I have them read excerpts from Michael Moffatt's *Coming of Age in New Jersey*, a participant-observer study by an anthropologist who lived in a Rutgers dormitory for a year. Early in his study of college life in the 1980s, Moffatt identifies "three different zones of relative autonomy and control in college" (35). He notes that between the freedom that students experience in their dorm rooms and the relative lack of freedom that they experience in the classroom, there exists "an intermediate zone" into which students walk whenever they leave the privacy of their rooms (35–36). Moffatt's study provides abundant information about students' lives in this intermediate zone, offering extensive insights concerning the conflicts and compromises that are inescapable aspects of campus life. In the course of his study Moffatt also offers extensive reports of students' attitudes about race, sex, and politics.

After reading Moffatt my students produce their own "autoethnographies"—Pratt's term for "texts in which people undertake to describe themselves in ways that engage with representations others have made of them" (35). First the students write comparison/contrast reading reports in which they compare their own lives as dorm students or commuters at Findlay to those of the Rutgers students; however, this unit also requires a more substantial paper—a participant-observer research project on some aspect of life at the Findlay campus. (See Appendix B for a detailed description of this assignment.) The best student research papers usually result from close observation of the minutiae of college life: students have studied seating arrangements in the cafeteria, the allocation of living space within shared dorm rooms, and the range of behaviors appropriate in dorm lounges. They also have compared graffiti in men and women's restrooms and counted derogatory racial comments in dorm conversations. Through this research students learn some basic conventions of research methodology as well as writing conventions, and they also acquire some sense of the disparate values competing for priority as students on campus negotiate not only the university's regulations but also the tacit assumptions governing their interactions with other students.

The study of racial slurs, conducted by a student I'll call Joe, proved particularly controversial. Based on a combination of direct observation and survey research, Joe reported that on average a Findlay student hears 10.2 racial slurs directed towards African Americans during each week of the academic year, 1.5 directed toward Asians, and 1 directed toward Whites. Almost all of these racial slurs are offered at gatherings within private rooms (and, since such gatherings at Findlay tend to be single-race congregations, White students would use and hear racial slurs directed toward African Americans and Asians but not toward Whites). Joe concluded that "students of the nineties may be a bit more hypocritical than Moffatt's subjects," revealing a larger gap between their publicly professed egalitarianism and their private intolerance.

Unlike Penny, Joe seized an opportunity to "mirror back" behavior that his audience would have preferred not to scrutinize. In doing so he risked a hostile reception for his work, and he also risked polarizing the class along racial lines. Joe's report was disturbing for students of all races: like Pratt's own students, they all had the experience of "hearing their culture discussed and objectified in ways that horrified them" (39). However, Joe's research proved especially disturbing to some African American students: his statistics suggested legitimate ground for mistrust among some who might otherwise have remained ignorant of the extent of prejudice on campus.

To address the threat that Joe's report posed, students adopted two strategies. The first of these was a retreat to silence: by not responding to Joe's report, the students were able to hasten the conclusion of an uncomfortable episode. This was the strategy adopted by the other members of Joe's four-person editing group. However, when I used Joe's report as a reading assignment for several other sections of College Writing, the students in those sections adopted a different strategy: to minimize the threat that Joe's report posed, they identified flaws in his methodology. One White student noted that a minuscule minority of intolerant White students would account for the majority of the slurs reported. An African American student noted that African Americans and Asians are underrepresented in most research conducted on campus and that their own attitudes were probably not reflected accurately in Joe's study. Another African American student observed that at least some of the reported epithets were directed by one African American student toward another and that Joe's study was insensitive to how the signification of "nigger" differs in such cases.

In attacking the flaws in Joe's research, the students identified a weakness that is typical of most ethnographic studies that my first-year students have conducted: most of these students have not yet mastered the processes of conducting social-science research or the conventions for reporting that research. Thus, their work is an approximation of the discourse that the academy authorizes, and even first-year students can recognize it as such. However, if Joe's autoethnography is an approximation, it is also an appropriation. Joe was able to use (however imperfectly) an academic mode to frame an oppositional discourse: one that implicitly indicted both his fellow students (for their duplicity) and the administration (for its complicity) in creating conditions that encourage intolerance. Since Joe's study contained an implicit critique of his peers, their hostile reception of his study was predictable; however, I find it significant that their responses revealed their own emerging understanding of the researcher's responsibilities.

Also significant was the students' ability to refine Joe's critique. In considering the complaints that students of one race lodged against those of another, the students were able to distinguish those that are rooted in genuine intolerance from those rooted in the intrinsic difficulties of dorm life. As one student observed, another student's complaint about "loud rap music" might really have been two complaints, one revealing a personal preference and/or a cultural bias against a particular genre of music and the other indicating a grievance over a violation of university quiet-hour policies. The discussion also revealed some ways in which perception is limited by position: while Joe noted that several male White students voiced their opposition to interracial dating, male African American students often point out that the university's recruiting practices have created a campus where African American men significantly outnumber African American women—a fact that White students often do not consider.

Furthermore, students reached a near-consensus on several points. While Joe noted that students "are strongly divided as to the role of the university in 'interfering' vs. 'ameliorating' flare-ups," almost all students agreed that the university exerts too much control over their lives and that it exercises its power in an arbitrary manner. Indeed, the students' images of the administration resemble those that the colonized might draw of a colonizing power: they see the administration as governing by fiat without the consent of the governed. Thus, students agree that it is in their own best interest to resolve conflicts on their own. They do not want to give the university an excuse for exerting further control over their actions in the dormitory.

Shaping the Future: The Student as Rhetor

As the end of the term nears, my students prepare proposals for changes in the policies or procedures of the university. (See Appendix C for a detailed description of this assignment.) In requiring this assignment I am asking my students to imagine a better future for the university, a different future that would result if their proposal were implemented. Since the students write the proposal in a form appropriate for the college newspaper—and thus for an audience that includes faculty, staff, and administrators as well as students—I am asking them to negotiate the competing expectations of multiple audiences who sometimes possess antithetical interests.

The range of topics addressed in this assignment will be familiar to most teachers. Students routinely offer complaints about the college cafeteria, the dormitory visitation and noise policies, and the lack of parking spaces. While these proposals address concerns that most students share, I receive some proposals each semester that express concerns of specific factions within the class: a proposal to include Spanish programs and contemporary African American music on the campus radio station, one to match international students with American roommates, and another to make campus cultural programs more accessible to commuters.

To make the proposal assignment something more than an academic exercise, I encourage students to submit their proposals to administrators or campus organizations that could implement the proposals. When students have done so, their experiences have confirmed Pratt's observation that the reception of a contact-zone text is indeterminate. On some occasions the students are successful. For example, one student was given a summer job to implement the peer tutoring system that he had proposed, and other students have achieved more modest successes. However, students usually find that their most ambitious proposals are undermined by their position in the university. While administrators usually are generous in making themselves available to discuss past experiences and current policies with students who are conducting research, the same administrators are much less willing to consider the actual proposals brought by students. Thus, students often discover that the university's normal process of decision making provides few opportunities for student-initiated change.

Consider the experience of Jean. Dissatisfied with the university's single rate for all dorm residents, Jean offered a proposal that would have based dorm rates on the square footage allocated to each student. At present, students pay $1,100.00 per semester for a shared room regardless of the size of that room and the number of roommates with whom they must share the space. Jean's proposal would produce the same total revenue as the existing policy. However, under Jean's plan each student would pay $13.00 for each square foot of living space, a change that would create a six-level fee schedule that ranges from $810.00 to $1,250.00 per semester.

Well-reasoned and immaculately drafted, Jean's proposal seemed to merit serious consideration. Her research demonstrated that the disparities in accommodations on our campus are sufficiently large to constitute a substantial injustice, and her proposal identified a feasible solution to the problem. However, when Jean submitted the proposal to an administrator who earlier had provided some of her data, he immediately dismissed it as "too complicated." His reaction disturbed Jean: while she was prepared for failure, she did expect that her proposal would receive serious consideration. In fact, the perfunctory dismissal suggests that Jean was willing to give more thought to a significant campus-life issue than was the administrator. In light of the administrator's response, Jean might well question the value of rational argument as a tool for social change.

Jean's experience teaches a hard lesson: her agency as a rhetor is not solely a product of her rhetorical skills but also a product of the subject position that she occupies within the university, a position that undermines the authority of her discourse. Thus Jean's experience suggests a corollary to Pratt's observation that, for marginalized groups, texts produced in contact zones provide a point of entry into the dominant circuits of print culture. Instead, the reception of such texts may provide the marginalized writer one more index of her subordinate status.

Despite their limited success in converting their plans into policies, students remain willing to devote considerable time and energy to preparing proposals that would improve the quality of their campus life. I have seen students spend hours accumulating data. They have compared textbook prices on their own campus with those at other universities, contrasted meal plans at Findlay with those of other private colleges, contacted contractors to determine the cost of building recreational facilities, and counted parking spaces available in lots at various times. They have also proven themselves to be respectful but merciless critics of each other's work. Each proposal for open visitation in the dorms is met by questions concerning security, and each request for better recreational facilities is countered by questions concerning funding. Perhaps the appeal of the proposal assignment in particular (but also of the other assignments for the course) results from the opportunity to have their ideas taken seriously by a peer audience, even when the ideas are dismissed by other elements of the university.

Community and Democracy

I am tempted to conclude that the students in my first-year composition classes discover that their mutual concerns are at least as abundant as the issues that divide them and that these mutual concerns could provide a basis for a true sense of community. This conclusion would be in keeping with my desire to assist students in making connections and resolving conflicts. The danger, of course, is that such a conclusion may well be illusory, a mere product of my desire. As Joseph Harris has noted, "community" is "a concept both seductive and powerful, one that offers us a view of shared purpose and effort and that makes a claim on us that is hard to resist" (13). Because the concept of "community" is so seductive, I could easily succumb to an illusion that Pratt identifies: the illusion that my classroom practices can unify the social world, constructing it in my own image (39). Since I recognize this tendency in my own work, I will offer a more modest claim here, one that does not "rehabilitate" a contact zone by converting it into a community.

I will suggest, then, that when I as a teacher promote forms of academic writing for my classes, I position myself as an "other" for my students: I stand as a representative of an institutional hierarchy that constrains their options for expression. In adopting this position I influence my students by pulling their texts toward the conventions of the academy, even though I recognize that those conventions are being contested within the academy. However, the students are pulled as well by their own stake in the topics about which they write and by the responses that they receive from their classmates. This combination of forces, I believe, creates the necessary conditions for the transculturation of the students' discourse. When I strive to help students discover the identities of historian, ethnographer, and rhetor, I am trying to promote what Pratt terms "a selective collaboration with and appropriation of idioms of the metropolis or the conqueror" (35). In introducing academic modes of discourse, I recognize that the students will need to adapt those modes to suit the particular demands of their own positions within the university.

Near the conclusion of her essay, Pratt notes that "those of us committed to educational democracy are particularly challenged as that notion finds itself besieged on the public agenda. Many of those who govern us display, openly, their interest in a quiescent, ignorant, manipulable electorate" (39). I would add that more than a few university administrators are interested in a quiescent, manipulable student body. All too often this goal is attainable. In a discussion of the intellectual identities available to college students, Jim Merod has noted that undergraduates are "often confused by the attempt to sort through requirements, choices of majors, and the means of writing essays that will satisfy various professorial tastes and assignments" (127). Since these students' first contacts with the university sometimes resemble those of explorers encountering an alien culture, the representatives of the university may be tempted to treat these students as the uninitiated upon whom knowledge must be bestowed.

However, Merod suggests that the university bears a greater responsibility:

> Students are not merely the necessary audience (or clientele) for the propagation of knowledge and the continuation of intellectual traditions. They provide immediate access to the future. The purpose of intellectual work is not just to advance theoretical

understanding and to enrich intellectual practices but to widen and deepen the social relevance of knowledge—to put ideas into more useful contact with democratic principles, to make all institutions within the Western sphere of influence more democratic .... (127–28)

Thus, Merod suggests, an intellectual identity is most likely to have relevance for students if it enables them to participate in a democratic society. I would add that an intellectual identity is most likely to have *immediate* relevance to students if it enables them to participate *immediately* in the shaping of the institution where they conduct their own studies.

Under the actual circumstances that students encounter, this goal is not always attainable. However, if the students are not always able to reinvent the institutional structures of college life, they are at least able to draw the blueprints for a campus that would better reflect their own visions. Moreover, they are able to assess and alter some of the tacit assumptions that govern their behavior in realms where the power of the university barely reaches. This last point is particularly important: I would argue that Moffatt's "intermediate zone" of "relative autonomy"—the zone of social interaction on campus but outside of the classroom—is the contact zone in which first-year students are best able to experience their own power as well as their responsibilities. It is there, I believe, that they can participate immediately in the project that both Merod and Pratt advocate: the project of democratizing Western institutions. If another contact zone—the first-year composition class—can assist students in this project while providing a point of entry into the discourse of the academy, then it can serve a function that is empowering as well as reproductive.

Notes

1. For those readers well versed in social anthropology, the title "First Contact" will be familiar. I have borrowed it from an ethnological film by anthropologists Bob Connolly and Robin Anderson. (See also Connolly and Anderson's book of the same title.) Released in 1982, Connolly and Anderson's film explores a 1930 encounter between an

Australian gold prospecting expedition and the Ganiga tribespeople in New Guinea. That encounter, the first contact between Ganigas and westerners, was captured on film by Michael Leahy, who had brought along a Leica camera to document the expedition's exploits. The first contact between the Australians and the Ganigas was marked by both conflict and cooperation, by mutual misunderstanding and groping efforts at cross-cultural communication. Some of the most striking moments in Connolly and Anderson's film detail the anthropologists' trip in 1980 to Papua, New Guinea, where they showed the 1930s photographs to the surviving Ganiga participants. As we watch the Ganigas looking at their younger selves in the old photographs, we see the extent to which Ganiga culture was changed by the modernization that followed its first contact with Western forces. However—and perhaps more significant—the photographs also provide an occasion for the Ganigas to remember the fears and hopes, the enrichment as well as the exploitation, that they experienced in their dealings with the prospectors.

2. For example, Patricia Bizzell has suggested the need for "studying how various writers in various genres have grappled with the pervasive presence of difference in American life and developed virtues out of necessity" (168). Bizzell adds, "I would include analysis of student writing, for its employment of contact zone rhetorical strategies, and I would include 'texts' of all kinds, as required by the contact zones under study—posters, songs, films, videos, and so forth" (168). While Bizzell does not make college culture the focus of her course, she emphasizes issues of difference akin to those that I am considering.

3. Horowitz argues that in the 1970s the culture of career-seeking "New Outsiders" prevailed over those of the hedonistic "College Men" and the socially conscious "Rebels." However, my own students argue that all three cultures are evident on the campuses of the 1990s.

4. My references to "Findlay students" serve as reminders that publication schedules often lag behind other events in our lives. Several years after I submitted "First Contact" to the editor of *Professing in the Contact Zone*, I moved from the University of Findlay to Salem State College. However, I still teach a first-year composition course that is similar to the one described in this essay. I no longer use the Kern reading, but I have found other texts to replace it. And my students at Salem State face many of the same challenges as my students at Findlay, so most of the present-tense verbs in my essay still seem appropriate to me.

5. I have changed the names of all students, professors, and administrators mentioned in this essay. The students have given permission for me to cite their works.

6. In truth, I too am reluctant to cast aspersions on the professor in question: I have seen too much of Dr. M's caring, sensitive treatment of students to believe that the incident of two decades ago would be repeated today. Nevertheless, her chuckle still haunts me.

Works Cited

Bartholomae, David. "Inventing the University." *When a Writer Can't Write: Studies in Writer's Block and Other Composing-Process Problems.* Ed. Mike Rose. New York: Guilford, 1985. 134–65.

Bizzell, Patricia. "'Contact Zones' and English Studies." *College English* 56.2 (1994): 163–69.

Connolly, Bob, and Robin Anderson. *First Contact.* New York: Viking, 1987.

First Contact. Dir. Bob Connolly and Robin Anderson. Arundel Productions, 1982.

Harris, Joseph. "The Idea of Community in the Study of Writing." *College Composition and Communication* 40.1 (1989): 11–22.

Horowitz, Helen Lefkowitz. *Campus Life: Undergraduate Cultures from the End of the Eighteenth Century to the Present.* Chicago: U of Chicago P, 1987.

Kern, Richard. *Findlay College: The First Hundred Years.* Nappanee, IN: Evangel, 1984.

Merod, Jim. *The Political Responsibility of the Critic.* Ithaca: Cornell UP, 1987.

Miller, Richard E. "Fault Lines in the Contact Zone." *College English* 56.4 (1994): 389–408.

Moffatt, Michael. *Coming of Age in New Jersey: College and American Culture.* New Brunswick: Rutgers UP, 1989.

Pratt, Mary Louise. "Arts of the Contact Zone." *Profession 91.* New York: MLA, 1991. 33–40. (Originally presented as the keynote address at MLA's Responsibilities for Literacy conference in September 1990 in Pittsburgh.)

Appendix A: Interview/Profile Assignment Guidelines

This interview/profile assignment provides an opportunity for you to converse with a person who can offer you insights concerning what college was like ten (or more) years ago. Your assignment is to interview a person who attended college at least ten years ago and to inquire concerning what the person remembers about his or her college years. In doing so you may learn how college has—or has not—changed.

Components of the Assignment

The assignment includes five requirements:

1. Submitting a name for my approval. After you have chosen a person to interview, please prepare a file card containing the person's name, a description of where and when the person attended college, and a brief explanation of why you have selected him or her. Submit the card to me for approval before you interview the person.

2. Transcribing the interview. After you have conducted the interview, please type a verbatim transcript of the questions and answers. You will use this transcript as you prepare a profile of your interview subject.

3. Preparing a draft of the profile. After you have attempted to convert the interview into a profile, you will bring a draft of the profile to an in-class group session to obtain feedback on your work-in-progress.

4. Meeting with me to discuss your draft. After you have obtained feedback from other class members, I will meet individually with each of you to discuss your profile.

5. Writing a polished profile. The final product of this assignment should be a coherent, interesting profile (1,000–2,000 words) of the person you have interviewed. This profile should focus on the person's undergraduate college education and should convey his or her experiences and insights.

Selecting a Person to Interview

You may interview anyone who attended college as an undergraduate at least ten years ago. I would recommend (but will not require) that you interview someone who is pursuing a career that you would like to pursue yourself.

Arranging the Interview

Make an appointment. Don't expect to walk in and conduct the interview immediately.

Make your purpose clear. Your subject should understand that you are conducting the interview as part of a college assignment.

Obtain permission to tape the interview. If the subject is unwilling to be taped, find someone else to interview.

Preparing for the Interview

Do some background research before the interview. When you make the appointment, ask the subject for a resume. Read the resume carefully before conducting the interview; it can suggest productive questions.

Prepare questions. Plan two or three lines of thoughtful questioning; these prepared questions will provide you with a sense of security at the interview. Some of your questions may focus on your subject's family background, personal life, and professional career; however, most of the questions should focus on the subject's college memories. These questions should address not only the academic but also the social aspects of the subject's college years, and they should invite the subject to consider those academic and social experiences in light of life after college. What were the most memorable events of the subject's college years? What was a typical day like? What sort of living arrangements did the person have? What courses did the person take? How much time did the person spend studying? In what activities did she or he participate? What aspects of college life were most enjoyable? What aspects were irritating? How well did the person's education prepare him or her for a career? What aspects of the subject's education were most useful? What aspects were lacking? These are just a few of the questions you could ask.

Check your equipment before the interview. Be sure that your tape recorder works and that the batteries are fresh. If you are planning to take photographs, consider what equipment will be appropriate for the lighting conditions at the interview setting.

During the Interview

Be on time for the interview appointment.

If a line of prepared questions proves unproductive, shift to a new line. The interview itself should inspire some questions.

Be attentive. Pay attention to what your subject is saying, but also make note of details such as the subject's mannerisms, tone of voice, and appearance. Observe the setting itself and note items of interest that reveal something about the subject's personality.

After the Interview

As soon as you leave the interview, write down as many details as you can remember—they will add life to your profile, but many details will slip from your memory if you don't record them immediately.

Allow at least three hours for typing the transcript. Although the transcript will prove invaluable when you are writing the profile, the transcription of the interview can be much more time consuming than you might imagine.

Select the best material you have available, and rework this material into a profile of your subject. This profile will differ from the interview transcript in that it will be a coherent essay that uses your own words and insights to present a clear portrait of your subject's views on his or her own education. You may quote from your subject extensively, but you must frame any quotations within your own essay structure.

Deadlines

Please observe the following deadlines:

Th 9/8   Submit a file card with the name of your interview subject, a description of where and when the person attended college, and an explanation of why you have selected the person as your interview subject.

Th 9/15   Bring the tape of the interview and two copies of an interview transcript to class. Submit the tape and one copy of the transcript in a manila folder.

T   9/20   Bring two copies of a profile draft to class. Read one copy to a peer response group, and submit the other copy in a manila folder.

Th 9/22   Meet with me for an individual conference about your paper.

T   9/27   Submit two copies of a polished profile in a manila folder.

Appendix B: Research Assignment Guidelines

Throughout Chapter 2 of *Coming of Age in New Jersey*, Michael Moffatt reports on participant-observer research that he conducted at Rutgers University in the late 1970s and mid 1980s. Based on this research Moffatt is able to offer some generalizations concerning college life; however, those generalizations may not describe college life for students at other campuses in other time periods.

Your assignment is to conduct research to determine whether Moffatt's findings on a particular college-life topic are applicable to a particular population of Findlay students in the present day. Your research methods should include personal observation and direct questioning of a representative group or subgroup of Findlay students. Through your research you should determine whether Moffatt's generalizations are applicable to this group of students.

The section headings within Moffatt's chapter indicate some of the topics that he explores: "Work and Play," "Autonomy," "Private Pleasures and the Extracurriculum," "Individualism, the Real World, and the Friendly Self," "Boys and Girls Together," "Youth Culture and College Culture," and "Coming of Age." Within these sections, he discusses sex and romance, cross-sex friendships, clothing styles, alcohol consumption, fraternities, hazing, race relations, extracurricular activities, and numerous other topics. Moffatt's comments on these topics should suggest possibilities for your own research.

Please be sure to *narrow your topic*. You cannot do justice to the entire range of topics that Moffatt considers in his 45-page chapter, nor should you attempt to do so. The best projects will select a fairly narrow topic, identify Moffatt's findings concerning the topic, and then report on research that establishes whether Moffatt's findings are applicable to Findlay students today.

Components of the Assignment

Your report should contain the standard elements of a formal research project. The following items are essential:

1. An *abstract* that provides an overview of the contents of your report.

2. An *introduction* that orients the reader to the purpose of your research, explains the conditions under which you conducted it, and offers a "thesis" that reveals the most important insight(s) that you were able to draw about the class from your research.

3. A *review of previous research* that summarizes and analyzes Moffatt's findings concerning one aspect of college life (and could also report observations from Horowitz and Kern).

4. A precise *statement of the research question(s)* that your own study is attempting to answer (i.e., questions concerning whether some of Moffatt's generalizations would accurately describe a particular group of Findlay students today).

5. A detailed *description of the research design*, including information about the subjects you studied and the methods you used.

6. A *results* section that explains your findings in detail by reporting your answers to the research questions, providing some examples of observed behavior to support your answers, and offering selected quotations that illustrate students' attitudes concerning the topic you are studying.

7. An *analysis* section that considers what the results mean (i.e., an analysis of why Moffatt's findings do or do not apply to your research subjects and an explanation of what conclusions we can draw about the students you studied).

8. A *works cited* page that includes a bibliographic entry for Moffatt's book as well as entries for any optional sources that you use.

Some Procedural Advice

As you conduct your research, you may find the following suggestions helpful:

1. In selecting a group of students to study, you should try to find about six to ten students who are representative of a particular group (e.g., the first-year class, the football team, African American male students, etc.). This population may be narrower than the population that Moffatt studied—you can try to determine whether his generalizations remain valid for a small subgroup rather than a large group.

   If you want to try to generalize about a very large group (e.g., the entire male or female undergraduate population) then you will need more research subjects. (For a large-group study, you can follow Moffatt's model: the residents of a single dorm floor should constitute an adequate sample; however, you should obtain enough information about your subjects to determine whether the population differs significantly from the larger student body.) Try to select subjects who you will be able to observe in settings where you may obtain answers to your research questions.

2. Select a topic that can be studied through direct observation: I want you to be able to observe the behavior of your subjects instead of having to rely solely on their own accounts of their beliefs or behavior. (For example, if you're studying "friendliness," you will need to observe students to determine the actual ways that they demonstrate whether they are friendly.)

   In addition to personal observation, you should solicit responses directly: you can interview your subjects individually, administer written questionnaires, conduct group-discussion sessions, or use other techniques designed to obtain responses germane to your topic.

3. Keep a notebook, and make entries in it concerning your observations. If you do not make regular entries, you won't have a record of the behavior that you observe or the comments that you hear.

   In keeping your notebook, you may want to set up your observations by using variations on the reporter questions: What happens? Who is involved? Where does it take place? When does it take place? How does it happen? Why does it happen? Also, you should copy down verbatim any important comments that your research subjects offer, either in conversations that you observe or in response to your questions.

4. When you prepare your final report, you should be selective in using the material you have available. Try to identify examples and quotations that represent typical views and behavior, but also try to provide some sense of the diversity of attitudes or behaviors that you observed.

IMPORTANT: You *must* protect the confidentiality of your research. Please (1) change the names of all the participants when you prepare drafts of your report to show to the class and me, (2) use fictitious names for dormitories, fraternity houses, or other settings in which you are doing your observations, and (3) do not show your materials to any students outside of this classroom.

Additional Instructions

In addition to the basic guidelines given above, you should be aware of the following instructions:

1. You should submit *two* copies of your report in a manila folder, along with the notebook that you kept throughout the observation period and any other written documents you assembled. (I will keep one copy of your report and return the other copy, the notebook, and any other materials to you after I read them.)

2. Your report should be between 1,800 and 3,000 words long.

3. Your report should be typed and double-spaced.

4. It should follow the grammar, punctuation, and spelling conventions of standard American English.

5. It should follow the conventions for informal documentation of all quotations and paraphrases of the participants.

6. It should follow the conventions for formal MLA or APA documentation of any quotations and paraphrases from written sources.

Grading Criteria

In grading your report I will consider the following criteria:

1. The content of your report and notebook (i.e., how well you've succeeded in summarizing Moffatt's findings on a topic, formulat-

ing your own research question(s) to test whether Moffatt's findings hold true at Findlay today, explaining your methods, reporting your results, explaining what the results mean, and keeping detailed field notes).

2. The form of your report (how well you've succeeded in making the phrasing, organization, documentation, and mechanics of your report clear and appropriate).

Help Available

I would be delighted to meet with you to discuss this assignment. I also would be delighted to offer advice concerning research topics and designs. Please don't hesitate to contact me if you need help on any aspect of this assignment.

Appendix C: Persuasive Proposal Assignment

To complete this assignment you must prepare an essay (1,200 to 2,400 words in length) that recommends a particular policy or practice for the University of Findlay. Your essay may either (1) propose an entirely new policy or practice that would improve the university or (2) propose a substantial change to improve an existing policy or practice. The audience for your report is the readership of *The Pulse*: the students, faculty, staff, and administration of the university. If you prepare the essay well, the majority of that audience should find your proposal clear and convincing.

Proposal Topics

A "policy" proposal would recommend a rule to which the university could adhere (e.g., a rule prohibiting first-year students from participating in intercollegiate athletics). A "practice" proposal would recommend a particular procedure that the university could use (e.g., a new practice of calculating grades on a letter scale with pluses and minuses). (The distinction between the two types of proposals is somewhat arbitrary—most policies require some procedures, while most practices require some rules.)

Your proposed policy or practice may concern any aspect of Findlay's operations—academic, administrative, social, or other. The proposal must affect a substantial segment (but not necessarily all) of the university's population. While your proposal may advocate either (1) an *entirely new* policy or practice or (2) a *substantial change* to improve an existing policy or practice, you should *not* simply *defend* an existing policy or practice.

Preparing the Report

You should present your proposal in a formal essay modeled on the opinion columns that appear in newspapers and magazines (e.g., the "My Turn" essays in *Newsweek* and the "Point of View" essays in *The Chronicle of Higher Education*). These essays usually employ one of the following organizing patterns:

1. A thesis-and-support organizing pattern. In this pattern the introduction offers a thesis statement and the rest of the essay supports the thesis.

2. A problem-and-solution organizing pattern. In this pattern the essay begins with a description of a problem and then proposes a solution to the problem.

Other organizing schemes also are possible. Regardless of how you organize your proposal, you will probably need to (1) describe the current policy or practice (if one exists), (2) analyze the merits and shortcomings of the existing policy or practice, (3) offer an alternative to the existing policy or practice, (4) consider the costs (both financial and human) of the proposed alternative, (5) explain any disadvantages of the proposed policy or practice, and (6) explain why the benefits of the proposed alternative outweigh the costs and disadvantages.

I am asking you to write a proposal rather than a research paper; however, you may need to conduct some research in order to understand a policy or practice. Likely sources of information include the university catalog, other university documents (such as dorm regulations), and interviews (with students, faculty, administrators, or staff).

Additional Instructions

In addition to following the guidelines given above, you should be aware of the following instructions:

1. Your essay should be typed and double-spaced.

2. It should follow the grammar, punctuation, and spelling conventions of standard American English.

3. If you use research materials, then you should follow the principles that we have discussed for fair usage. You do not have to include formal MLA documentation, but you should use informal in-text citations to identify quotations and paraphrases.

4. You should bring two copies of a rough draft to class on Thursday, November 17. (You'll give one copy to me, and you'll read the other copy to your peer review group.)

5. You should submit *two* copies of your essay in a manila folder on Tuesday, November 22. (I will keep one copy and return the other to you after I read it.)

Grading Criteria

In grading your summary I will consider two criteria:

1. The quality of your content—that is, of the research and reasoning that your report exhibits.

2. The quality of your presentation—that is, of the skill with which you present your ideas in your report.

Multiculturalism, Contact Zones, and the Organization of English Studies

PATRICIA BIZZELL
College of the Holy Cross

Our Ptolemaic system of literary categories goes creaking and groaning onward, in spite of the widely acknowledged need to overhaul it in response to multiculturalism. This is not to say that there have not been attempts to revise course design in light of new materials and methods. See, for example, *Writing and Reading Differently* (Atkins and Johnson, 1985), *Gender in the Classroom* (Gabriel and Smithson, 1990), and *Cultural Studies in the English Classroom* (Berlin and Vivion, 1992), which address the pedagogical consequences of deconstruction, feminist literary theory, and cultural studies, respectively, while also incorporating more diverse literatures. But these attempts to foster innovation in the individual classroom still leave the basic structure of English studies intact.

In Kristin Ross's description of the multicultural world literature and cultural studies program at the University of California at Santa Cruz, she comments indirectly on this problem when she identifies as one stumbling block to the Santa Cruz program the faculty's unwillingness "to depart from their specialized fields" (668). They fended off demands to diversify their course material with such plaints as "'But I don't have a Ph.D. in South African literature'" (668). Ross gives good reasons for forging ahead

An earlier version of this essay appeared as "'Contact Zones' and English Studies" in *College English* 56.2 (1994): 163–69. Used with permission.

in spite of such plaints, but she doesn't say much about the underlying structure of English studies that still makes us think our scholarship must be organized along national or chronological lines, even though these are inimical to the process of integrating new materials and methods because devised to serve and protect the old ones.

The persistence of the old basic structure can be seen even in an impressive new collection published by the Modern Language Association with the avowed intention of fostering innovation: Stephen Greenblatt and Giles Gunn's *Redrawing the Boundaries: The Transformation of English and American Literary Studies* (1992). Even here, boundaries are not redrawn in fundamentally new ways. Rather, the old, familiar structure of English studies is visible, for instance in chapter divisions that carve literary studies into chronological periods, such as "Seventeenth-Century Studies" (British literature) and "American Literary Studies to the Civil War." Ten such chapters are followed by eleven more, most with the word "Criticism" in the title, implying that here we turn from primary to secondary texts. Yet it is here that we find the most attention to literature by women, gay people, and people of color: separate chapters are devoted, for example, to "Feminist Criticism" and "African American Criticism." Thus other traditional boundaries appear to be reasserted rather than redrawn. Moreover, the field of composition studies appears to remain behind even more impenetrable traditional boundaries. Not only is "Composition Studies" given a separate chapter (in the second set of eleven), but there must be an additional, separate chapter just to explain why composition studies is included in this book at all ("Composition and Literature").

I think we need a radically new system to organize English studies, and I propose that we develop it in response to the materials with which we are now working. Instead of finagling the new literatures and pedagogical and critical approaches into our old categories, we should try to find comprehensive new forms that seem to spring from and respond to the new materials. Instead of asking ourselves, for example, "How can I fit Frederick Douglass into my American Renaissance course?" we need to ask, "How should I reconceive my study of literature and composition now that I regard Douglass as an important writer?"

It could be argued that we don't need any new system of categories, that what we should do is simply to knock down the old system and then let everyone do what he or she pleases. This appears to be the approach taken by another recent attempt to chart new courses, MLA's 1987 English Coalition Conference. Peter Elbow, in his account of this conference, *What Is English?* (1990), tells us there was a "remarkable consensus" at the conference on "the central business of English studies" (17), and it was as follows:

> *Using language* actively in a diversity of ways and settings—that is, not only in the classroom as exercises for teachers but in a range of social settings with various audiences where the language makes a difference.

> *Reflecting on language use.* Turning back and self-consciously reflecting on how one has been using language—examining these processes of talking, listening, writing, and reading.

> Trying to ensure that this using and reflecting goes on in *conditions of both nourishment and challenge,* that is, conditions where teachers care about students themselves and what they actively learn—not just about skills or scores or grades (18; emphasis in original).

The tone here, of course, is quite different from that of *Redrawing the Boundaries*—the focus is clearly on pedagogy rather than on the body of scholarly knowledge. I applaud this focus on pedagogy, and I admire the principles laid down above. But I can't help noticing that they appear to have very little to do specifically with the discipline of English studies. To me, they sound like the kind of principles I urge on faculty from all disciplines in my school's writing-across-the-curriculum program. There isn't a course at my school where these principles couldn't be put advantageously into practice. How, then, do they define "the central business of English studies"?

What these principles leave out, as Elbow himself notes, is what people read and write *about* in literary studies. He acknowledges that "you can't make meaning unless you are writing or reading about *something*; . . . practices are always practices *of a* content" (19; emphasis in original). Yet the topic of literary content appeared to be taboo at the conference. As Elbow tells it:

> The question of literature was left strikingly moot. Not only was there no consensus, there was a striking avoidance of the issue. It's not that it didn't come up; the question of literature arose recurrently. . . . Yet every time we somehow slid away from the issue into something else. (96, 97)

This sounds to me like repression, not freedom, but I sympathize with the conference members. Small wonder they could not find a way to talk about literature, with the old system of organizing it discredited for lack of inclusiveness and no new system yet accepted. But I am concerned that this kind of avoidance leaves graduate and undergraduate curricula dangerously lacking in guidance—dangerously vulnerable to "cultural literacy" pundits who would shove into the breach the only system still known, namely the old, bad traditional one. Indeed, this threat appeared at the conference itself, and Elbow, although an advocate of composition pedagogics in which each writer is to do pretty much as he or she pleases, was sufficiently troubled by it that he proposes his own list of literary contents for English studies in an appendix.

But exactly how are we to develop a new system of organization from the new materials of study, supposing we agree that this is needed? To do so would seem to require that we make generalizations about the new material—about what, say, Asian American literatures might require to be studied adequately—that would be extremely difficult, if not downright presumptuous, to make. I think we need an approach to the diverse world literatures written in English we are now studying that focuses not on their essential nature, whatever that may be, but rather on how they might, not "fit" together exactly, but come into productive dialogue with one another.

I suggest that we address this problem by employing Mary Louise Pratt's concept of the "contact zone":

> I use this term to refer to social spaces where cultures meet, clash, and grapple with each other, often in contexts of highly asymmetrical relations of power, such as colonialism, slavery, or their

aftermaths as they are lived out in many parts of the world today. (34)

This concept can aid us both because it emphasizes the conditions of difficulty and struggle under which literatures from different cultures come together (thus forestalling the disrespectful
glossing over of differences), and because it gives us a conceptual
base for bringing these literatures together, namely, when they
occur in or are brought to the same site of struggle or "contact
zone."

A "contact zone" is defined primarily in terms of historical
circumstances. It is circumscribed in time and space, but with
elastic boundaries. Focusing on a contact zone as a way of organizing literary study would mean attempting to include all material relevant to the struggles going on there. Pratt's main example
of a "contact zone" here is Peru in the late sixteenth and early
seventeenth centuries, where she wants to study the interaction
among texts by Native Americans (newly discovered by twentieth-century scholars) and the canonical Spanish accounts. I submit that the United States is another such contact zone, or, more
precisely, a congeries of overlapping contact zones, considered
from the first massive immigration of Europeans in the seventeenth
century up to the present day. "Multiculturalism" in English studies is a name for our recognition of this condition of living on
contested cultural ground, and our desire to represent something
of this complexity in our study of literature and literacy.

If we understand that we are teaching in, and about, contact
zones, Pratt suggests that we must stop imagining our job to be
transmitting a unitary literature and literacy. Under this old model:

> The prototypical manifestation of language is generally taken to
> be the speech of individual adult native speakers face-to-face (as
> in Saussure's famous diagram) in monolingual, even monodialectal
> situations—in short, the most homogeneous case linguistically
> and socially. The same goes for written communication. (38)

Now, Pratt suggests that we need a new model:

> a theory that assumed different things—that argued, for instance,
> that the most revealing speech situation for understanding lan-

guage was one involving a gathering of people each of whom spoke two languages and understood a third and held only one language in common with any of the others (38).

This model treats difference as an asset, not a liability.

Given American diversity, our classrooms are getting to be more like Pratt's new model than like the old one. If we respond by "teaching the contact zone," we can foster classrooms where, as in Pratt's experience:

> All the students in the class . . . [heard] their culture discussed and objectified in ways that horrified them; all the students saw their roots traced back to legacies of both glory and shame. . . . [But] kinds of marginalization once taken for granted were gone. Virtually every student was having the experience of seeing the world described with him or her in it. (39)

Acknowledging its difficulties, I am suggesting that we need a new system of organization in English studies to make this kind of teaching—and scholarship—not only possible, but normative.

In short, I am suggesting that we organize English studies not in terms of literary or chronological periods, nor essentialized racial or gender categories, but rather in terms of historically defined contact zones, moments when different groups within the society contend for the power to interpret what is going on. As suggested above, the chronological, geographical, and generic parameters of studying any contact zone are defined on the basis of including as much material as possible that is relevant to the issue being contested. Time periods can be short or long, literatures of different groups, languages, or continents can be considered together, all genres are admitted, and so on.

For example, the New England region from about 1600 to about 1800 might be defined as a contact zone in which different groups of Europeans and Native Americans were struggling for the power to say what had happened in their relations with each other. Thus canonical Puritan histories, autobiographies, and captivity narratives would be studied in connection with historical commentaries and memoirs by non-Puritan Europeans (traditionally treated as "minor"), European transcriptions of Native American speeches (problematic but invaluable), and letters, histories, and spiritual autobiographies written by Native Americans in English (unknown in the academy until very recently). The object would not be to represent what the lives of the diverse European immigrant and Native American groups were really like. Rather, the attempt would be to show how each group represented itself imaginatively in relation to the others. We would, in effect, be reading all the texts as brought to the contact zone, for the purpose of communicating across cultural boundaries.

There are several advantages to this approach. First, it provides a rationale for integrating English studies multiculturally. No longer would we be trying to squeeze new material into inappropriate old categories, where its importance could not be adequately appreciated. We would be working with categories that treated multiculturalism as a defining feature, that assumed the richest literary treasures could be found in situations in which different histories, lifeways, and languages are trying to communicate and to deal with the unequal power distribution among them. We would no longer need to ask prejudicial questions, such as whether Frederick Douglass was as "good" on some putative absolute scale of expository value as Henry Thoreau. Rather, we would look at the rhetorical effectiveness of each writer in dealing with the matter in hand—for example, the need to promote civil disobedience in the contact zone created by White and Black efforts to define and motivate action in response to slavery in the antebellum United States.

Second, this approach fully integrates composition and rhetoric into literary studies. Studying texts as they respond to contact zone conditions is studying them rhetorically, studying them as efforts of rhetoric. The historical context provides a way to focus the rhetorical analysis. Moreover, professional and student writing can also be seen as contending in contact zones and experimenting with the textual arts of the contact zone that rhetorical analysis emphasizes. Thus boundaries between "content" (literature) and its traditional inferior, pedagogy (composition), are usefully blurred, as are the distinctions between "high" literature and other kinds of writing, including student writing. Donald McQuade makes a persuasive argument for blurring these boundaries in "Composition and Literature."

At the end of her essay, Pratt calls for the development of what she calls "the pedagogical arts of the contact zone":

> exercises in storytelling and in identifying with the ideas, interests, histories, and attitudes of others; experiments in transculturation and collaborative work and in the arts of critique, parody, and comparison (including unseemly comparisons between elite and vernacular cultural forms); the redemption of the oral; ways for people to engage with suppressed aspects of history (including their own histories); ways to move *into and out of* rhetorics of authenticity; ground rules for communication across lines of difference and hierarchy that go beyond politeness but maintain mutual respect; a systematic approach to the all-important concept of *cultural mediation.* (40; emphasis in original)

David Bartholomae has recently suggested that we imagine these "arts" translated into exercises in an English class. Imagine, for example, a class in which literature is analyzed for the ways it moves among rhetorics of authenticity, students experiment with attending to suppressed aspects of their own history as part of establishing their writerly personae, and scholarly writing is both shared and opened for parody. Pratt calls this work "cultural mediation"; my phrase for it is "negotiating difference"—studying how various writers in various genres have grappled with the pervasive presence of difference in American life, and developed virtues out of necessity. I would include analysis of student writing, for its employment of contact zone rhetorical strategies; and I would include "texts" of all kinds, as required by the contact zones under study—posters, songs, films, videos, and so on.

Reorganizing literary studies along these lines would mean redesigning courses. For example, at Holy Cross we offer first-year students a choice of either a composition course (a course in the personal essay), or a course that introduces them to literary study by teaching the close reading of works grouped according to genre. Under the new paradigm, there would be no need for two separate courses. The abilities needed both to enter literary studies and to refine one's own writing would be the skills of analyzing and imitating rhetorical arts of the contact zone. Students would learn to critique strategies of negotiating difference in the writing of others and to practice them in their own. So we could offer just one course, writing intensive but including some reading and analysis of literature (broadly defined).

It would also mean reorganizing graduate study and professional scholarly work in ways I hardly dare to suggest. I suppose that one would no longer become a specialist in American literature, a "Shakespeare man," or a "compositionist." Rather, people's areas of focus would be determined by the kinds of rhetorical problems in which they were interested.

My main object is to get people to work on the project. I have no coherent alternative program to present. But I believe that if we reorganize literary studies in this way, we will be giving a dynamic new direction to our profession. We will be creating disciplinary parameters within which boundaries really can be redrawn, to come to terms with the demands of multiculturalism. This new paradigm will stimulate scholarship and give vitally needed guidance to graduate and undergraduate curricula. It might also lead us, in the multicultural literary archives, to stories of hope that can lend us all spiritual sustenance as we renew efforts to make the United States a multicultural democracy. If we are not given to complete the task, neither are we allowed to desist from it.

Works Cited

Atkins, G. Douglas, and Michael L. Johnson, eds. *Writing and Reading Differently: Deconstruction and the Teaching of Composition and Literature*. Lawrence: U of Kansas P, 1985.

Bartholomae, David. "The Tidy House: Basic Writing in the American Curriculum." *Journal of Basic Writing* 12 (Spring 1993): 4–21.

Berlin, James A., and Michael J. Vivion, eds. *Cultural Studies in the English Classroom*. Portsmouth, NH: Heinemann, 1992.

Elbow, Peter. *What Is English?* New York: MLA, 1990.

Gabriel, Susan L., and Isaiah Smithson, eds. *Gender in the Classroom: Power and Pedagogy*. Urbana: U of Illinois P, 1990.

Greenblatt, Stephen, and Giles B. Gunn, eds. *Redrawing the Boundaries: The Transformation of English and American Literary Studies*. New York: MLA, 1992.

McQuade, Donald. "Composition and Literature." Greenblatt and Gunn 482–519.

Pratt, Mary Louise. "Arts of the Contact Zone." *Profession 91*. New York: MLA, 1991, 33–40. (Originally presented as the keynote address at MLA's Responsibilities for Literacy conference in September 1990 in Pittsburgh.)

Ross, Kristin. "The World Literature and Cultural Studies Program." *Critical Inquiry* 19 (Summer 1993): 666–76.

Contact Zones: Composition's Content in the University

KATHERINE K. GOTTSCHALK
Cornell University

For almost twenty years I have been immersed in one of the nation's most unusual first-year writing programs, one that I must constantly explain, and defend, both to outsiders and to myself. This article came into being when I realized that Mary Louise Pratt's "contact zone" theory helps me to elucidate how Cornell's First-Year Writing Seminars operate, clarifying as the theory does some of the benefits of our atypical approach to "composition's content," especially in avoiding problems of composition programs which find themselves in the position of subjugated service units. Using the perspective of contact zone theory, I will argue that it is unwise to seek just one appropriate subject matter or one discipline for all teachers and students in a writing program's composition classes, just as it is unwise for writing programs (or centralized writing-across-the-curriculum programs) to try to dictate the proper content or method for writing in other disciplines. Such approaches are based on a myth of homogeneity, of "imagined community," whereas (often chaotic) heterogeneity is actually the norm. Recognition that heterogeneity is at work can mean drawing on the heterogeneous nature of language and returning the ownership, and teaching, of language to the disciplines; recognizing heterogeneity can mean recognizing the diverse natures and needs of both students and instructors, rather than trying to homogenize their experiences, and, in turn, it can mean welcoming innovation and variation in our choices and plans for courses.

Using Contact Zone Theory to View Composition Programs

Mary Louise Pratt uses the term *contact zones* "to refer to social spaces where cultures meet, clash, and grapple with each other, often in contexts of highly asymmetrical relations of power, such as colonialism, slavery, or their aftermaths as they are lived out in many parts of the world today" ("Arts" 34). The asymmetrical relations of power may show themselves in many matters, including the crucial one of who controls the language, whose language is heard. Where those with power in a situation believe that their voice is the only legitimate one, that "the situation is governed by a single set of rules or norms shared by all participants" ("Arts" 38), the result is often a mistaken view (from the top) of the contact zone and its language as homogenous, where in fact it is not.[1] Pratt derides this notion of the "imagined community," the assumption of "a unified and homogeneous social world in which language exists as a shared patrimony" ("Linguistic" 50), of a world in which "it is assumed that all participants are engaged in the same game and that the game is the same for all players" ("Linguistic" 51). Always active will be resisters such as (in Pratt's example) Felipe Guaman Poma de Ayala, the Andean who, in 1613, in an intercultural text of his own creating, tried to rewrite and make heard the story of Andean culture and the Spanish conquest ("Arts" 34–37; *Imperial Eyes*, ch. 1). With such insights of contact zone theory, Pratt proposes, we can "reconsider the models of community that many of us rely on in teaching and theorizing" ("Arts" 34); we can look for sites of asymmetrical relations and clashing interactions, such as classrooms or writing programs as a whole, and seek to make better use of the diverse cultural capital brought by participants to these contact zones—thus recognizing heterogeneity, rather than imagining homogeneity, and helping all voices to communicate and be heard, and drawing on their perspectives.

Composition programs are likely to provide sites in which competing and colonializing voices will converge, given that many arenas view writing as an outlying territory over which they claim ownership; writing courses and programs must "serve" those arenas, exporting a product to them. For the purposes of this exploration, I am considering composition programs and classes as contact zone communities in which cultures "meet, clash, and grapple," cultures that may include those of the administrators of the writing program, the staff members who teach the courses, the students who take them, the faculty in the many departments who later teach the students, the administrators of the university at large, and various parties in the world outside the university. We can with all justice describe first-year composition courses and their students, instructors, and even writing program administrators as frequently victimized by uncritical colonization from "above," positioned as they are on the feeble end of highly asymmetrical relations of power.

It is therefore almost horrifyingly easy to use the language of contact zone theory to provide a parodic (and too familiar) sketch of composition programs that are treated as subjugated services. Geographically isolated or marginalized, the composition offices are placed by administrative powers in the poorest accommodations (not infrequently in basements). Members of an underdeveloped nation, staff (often adjuncts—not even citizens) are paid at substandard rates designed to suit the needs of the colonizing nations who can't afford to treat them better, and who won't locate the classes in their own countries, using their own citizens to teach them. The content of composition courses becomes subject to the dictates of other departments' administrators, who think they know what is best for composition classes, teachers, and their students (they may want to specify the books to be read or have outsiders decide whether students have passed the course). Language belongs to the industrialized nations; composition courses are the country where students prepare for entry into civilized territory. Composition teachers, however, are not expected to leave, although it is assumed that they would like to escape. Everyone is unhappy: faculty and administration believe that the writing program doesn't teach service skills well enough as an export product, students are angry at having to spend time in this "Third World" of study, and composition administrators and staff struggle constantly to gain some power (funding, classrooms, staff), to teach courses in the ways they believe to be best, to do their work well in the context of the university, and on their own terms.[2]

An odd (if familiar) twist, however, is that writing programs, writing teachers, compositionists, even while struggling with their own oppression, have a tendency to fall prey to the very colonizing tendencies that they condemn, with results equally displeasing and open to parodic description through contact zone language. At the same time that we instructors of writing are often extremely careful to provide our own students with contact zones in our classrooms that are enabling ones, in which all voices are heard, in other areas (given the chance) we'd like to be colonizers ourselves. The composition nation, we teachers and administrators notice, has a wonderful export product, and maybe we could take over the university with it, if we could just wrest away the power from those other departments and administrators that currently keep us poor and subservient. We begin at home, if we are administrators, by wanting to tell each of our composition teachers what to teach. We want to choose for students the subjects that will most benefit them as topics for their writing. We want to tell other departments just what their students ought to know about writing. Fairly often we also have some pretty good ideas about how faculty in those departments ought to straighten out their own writing. We do not take into account the necessary, normal resistance of those who suspect that their territory is being occupied, that someone is trying to replace their voices, their stories, their language, with a new language. We are surprised when we are met with rebellion or subversion. What, students and instructors and faculty ask, about *my* particular interests? *My* areas of expertise?

But contact zone theory does far more than make available parodic overviews of composition programs in language that is already too familiar. It also provides insights into how they might be restructured so that such parodies will not come so readily to mind. Pratt tells us that a contact zone perspective "emphasizes how subjects are constituted in and by their relations to each other. It treats the relations among colonizers and colonized . . . not in terms of separateness or apartheid, but in terms of copresence, interaction, interlocking understandings and practices"

(*Imperial Eyes* 7). The cultures that converge around and in the composition classroom and affect its content, in other words, can be viewed not as separate, segregated, but as already immersed in "copresence, interaction." The question is how to make use of our understanding of this convergence. How do we use increased understanding of interactions to break the powerful hold of a homogenous view of the nature of writing or of texts most appropriate for teaching, whether held by a university's board of trustees or the faculty of the chemistry department or the writing program director? How can we situate composition and its content more favorably and usefully in the university, disturbing or eliminating the debilitating asymmetrical relations described above which exist in far too many writing programs and courses?

If, as experience suggests, writing programs and courses often become colonized and subjugated in the university's hierarchy, one solution is to do away, when possible, with the sites in which subjugation can take place. The teaching of writing need not be placed entirely in a separate colony; it can also be distributed into the various states which claim ownership of writing. Cornell's current approach to the teaching of writing, in recognition of some of the problems described above, began in 1966 when the university decided to disperse the teaching of first-year writing seminars throughout many spaces, into many disciplines, rather than enclosing it within a specific "composition course" with one content, taught by one department.[3] In this (still continuing) plan, students select the subjects they want to study in order to learn to write; instructors (including graduate students, lecturers, and faculty) in many disciplines (about thirty, from Africana Studies to Medieval Studies to the Writing Workshop) teach writing in subjects in which they are expert. Each semester, about 170 of these seminars are offered by around 170 teachers to some 3000 students, who enroll from six of Cornell's seven colleges, from Agriculture to Arts. Students may choose from around 100 topics each semester. Almost all of Cornell's first-year students are required to take two of these writing seminars.[4]

From an outside view, the considerable diversity of the program's offerings and its lack of a consistent content have sometimes seemed to provide opportunities primarily for clashes and chaos, rather than a welcome means with which to give students and instructors alike greater freedoms within the often control-ling and even repressive structures of a university.[5] When I began as director of first-year writing seminars, I was aware of the strengths but more acutely aware of the weaknesses of the ap-proach. Questions confronted me: Isn't there one "best" content or theory of content that can guide all teachers? Who should teach writing courses? Can and should nonexperts teach? Should all students learn a consistent body of information? What can all instructors learn about language to share with their students? What guidelines should all instructors follow; how much consis-tency do students need? As I worked on these questions over the years, reading articles and books and attending conferences, I often wondered why I flinched when someone seemed to proffer me the one "right answer" as to what the "best" theory of composition's content might be, and why I am cautious about dictating subject matter or methods to instructors. Why do I, as a writing program administrator and teacher (like, I suspect, many other teachers and administrators) so often resist admirable pro-posals, whether from social constructionists, expressivists, or whomever, even when I am in sympathy with their positions? The contact zone lens helped me explain my own resistance, and hence that of students, faculty, and administrators; it helped me realize why redistributing the teaching of writing was a solution to some of the problems of subjugated writing programs. I real-ized that resistance is natural when, as members of clashing cul-tures, we feel that someone is trying to take over "our" territory or is not recognizing our voice, or when we feel our own rights or dignity to be threatened by others, especially others with power over us, who do not see or recognize our difference. It is there-fore wise to find the least hegemonic approach possible to the teaching of writing; it is wise to find or create spaces which all can occupy much more symmetrically and much more by choice than is often the case. And, of course, it is assuredly wise to rec-ognize and take advantage of clashes between differing cultures, values, and disciplines, rather than pretending that they do not exist.

When viewed from the contact lens perspective, then, a wide distribution of responsibility for the teaching of writing, and of the areas in which it is studied, makes sense, given the heterogeneous nature of writing and how it is learned, and the heterogeneity of instructors, students, and administrators.

The Foundation: Ownership of Language in the Disciplines

Moving the teaching of writing out of the exclusive domain of the English department or of a writing program might seem a chaotic approach to teaching writing until one considers the social grounding of writing and of the genres in which it is practiced and best learned. "All approaches to writing instruction are at bottom social," says David Russell: "Growth in writing means that students . . . move toward acquiring the genres, the habits of discourse, the voices of social groups involved in organized activities *while* students more and more fully participate in (either directly or vicariously) the activities of those groups and eventually contribute to and transform them—not *before* they participate in them" ("Vygotsky" 185, 186). Russell compares teaming to write with teaming to play a game—one does not learn to "throw balls": one learns to play ping-pong, or jacks ("Activity Theory" 57). In line with Russell's argument, Aviva Freedman goes so far as to argue that students will normally learn far more about writing in disciplinary classes than in their composition classes. Freedman points out that school genres of writing are complex, sophisticated, rhetorical transactions. As she reports, her "research revealed that through being immersed in the extraordinarily rich discursive contexts provided in disciplinary classrooms . . . students began to be able to ventriloquate the social language, to respond dialogically to the appropriate cues from this context" (134–35). In composition classes she found less support and guidance for the production of writing in terms of "collaborative engagement, between novices and experts, in authentic, meaningful tasks," genre-producing tasks, than she found in the disciplinary class (135). Discouragingly, she concludes that

"The composition class seems bare and sparse by contrast [with the disciplinary teacher's class]" (135).

Russell and Freedman each approach the question of the proper situation and content of writing courses from the perspective of genre theory, but their point that learning to write occurs best within social groups or actual disciplinary contexts is applicable for use within contact zone theory, which itself draws on the interaction of social groups.[6] A disciplinary class can form a contact zone for rich, productive rhetorical transactions, such as the "literate arts" that Pratt describes as being practiced by subjects who must try to assume and manipulate a language not their own—"autoethnography, transculturation, critique, collaboration, bilingualism, mediation, parody, denunciation, imaginary dialogue, vernacular expression" ("Arts" 37). A teacher versed in contact zone theory can recognize and draw on the rhetorical arts that are bound to appear when students find themselves in the strange lands of new disciplines, confronted with modes of writing that they do not understand and that they may wish to resist, at the same time that they must, as subjects/students, learn the discourse.

What better place, then, to work on language and negotiation than in a writing class placed in a discipline? In fact, some of the literary arts of the subjugated that Pratt describes resemble the moves that David Bartholomae, arguing for critical engagement of students with texts, recommends using to encourage students to grapple meaningfully with a subject as they write about it in languages not their own. They should, he says, rework their texts, "perhaps breaking or experimenting with the narrative structure . . . , perhaps writing alternative openings or endings, perhaps writing alternative scenes of confrontation, perhaps adding text that does not fit . . . , perhaps adding different voices or points of view" (28). These are moves that will lead to less "legitimate" rather than more "legitimate" voices, to more chaotic texts; they are moves that are necessary before students learn to play the game—if they choose to do so. And, interestingly, when Bartholomae gives this advice, he has been explaining how he uses Pratt's "Arts of the Contact Zone" essay to "help make the point that writers need to understand the degree to which their writing is not their own" and to help make it more so (26). Students, as learners, move slowly into new languages, the languages of disciplines, or new subject matters, even when they are willing subjects. In the classroom, the play of power is ever present, and language—writing—is the means by which student and teacher negotiate the territory, more or less successfully, depending on how linguistically aware both students and teachers are—or how much the teacher can enable students to move from the position of "colonized" to equal participant, a move that both Bartholomae and Pratt urge. To provide excellent contact zones for growth in writing, then, in the most typical organized activities in which writing occurs and in which students choose to participate, a writing program can draw on the university's many disciplines, locating the teaching of writing in classrooms with teachers well versed in the subjects students must learn and learn to write about.

Instructors of Writing in the Disciplines

Shifting the site of writing instruction into the disciplines proves beneficial not just because of the nature of how writing is learned but also for the sake of instructors themselves, as well as relations between instructors and administrators: many of the tense interactions involved with the composition course simply disappear. With writing situated squarely as part of the responsibility handled by faculty in the disciplines, a writing program administrator's work with instructors can become more a matter of collaboration, rather than of (for instance) policing for adherence to dictated course subjects and methodologies. The operations of power are less in evidence—in fact are less extensive—because instructors may be responsible for their own subjects and their own application of methods in fields in which they are expert practitioners. Of course the writing program must provide instructors with preparatory orientation for teaching writing, in what, admittedly, seems to be an (unavoidable?) colonizing move, and it should provide continued opportunities for instructors to collaborate with each other in the exercise of their academic freedom. On the whole, as Sharon Crowley has argued so forcibly, academic freedom shouldn't exist for the benefit only of the already empowered (167–68): lack of freedom is what often leads to bad teaching and to rebellion of the disempowered.

In fact, the worst work I see often comes from TAs who must follow someone else's plan. When they have a chance to design their own writing courses, many produce excellent plans. This should not surprise anyone. Do most teachers prefer opportunities to cultivate and benefit from their own strengths and skills, or to have to conform to someone else's preferences and talents? Where do we put our greater efforts? Administrators of writing programs may not like every course they see, or every method chosen—I don't—but we do not have to pretend to have the right answer for every teacher, student, subject, goal, situation. Instructors can also find their own good answers. At Cornell, with training and encouragement faculty and graduate students in disciplines far afield from English produce some of the most innovative, effective writing seminar designs. Awards and fellowships have been awarded in anthropology, the biological sciences, and music. Fields such as government and history produce some of the most concerned teachers of writing, concerned, through the study of language, for students as citizens of their disciplines and of the world.

Indeed, with the dispersal of the teaching of writing into the disciplines, one major potential benefit is that instructors in those disciplines may be less apt to consider the teaching of writing to be a matter solely of grammar—they are more likely to experience the much richer contact zone negotiations with language for themselves; and they are therefore less likely to place the responsibility for teaching and assigning writing elsewhere—such as exclusively on faculty in a writing program. Increased understanding of writing pedagogy, including how to make use of the contact zone nature of the writing classroom itself, can be gained from the preparation that teachers go through and from ongoing and frequent experience with students and their texts, which may not be the case with such intensity elsewhere. Faculty who think of writing as a matter of correctness and "skills" are often those who do not teach writing and who have not had to consider how to integrate writing into their courses in ways that help students both learn and learn to write. The more that responsibility for the teaching of writing is integrated throughout the university, the more the institution's and our students' ideas about the nature of writing may grow.

Students of Writing and Choice in the Disciplines

In the end, of course, it is students who may benefit most if we can break up the subordinated and isolated situation of composition programs. I've already argued the benefits of instruction in writing that occurs within particular disciplines, and it is clear that students benefit from any improvements in their instructors. But it is time to look directly at students as participants in contact zones and examine how the dispersal of the teaching of writing into many disciplines, many locales, can offer benefits.

No one needs to be reminded that not all students are the same—many theories about composition's content are based on concern for diversity, on the need to design courses that recognize and work from each student's cultural capital: see, for example, Patricia Bizzell, who proposes organizing writing classes around historical contact zone moments. And yet writing programs often try to put students into the same course, as though one course can fit several thousand students. Students thus become the voiceless, unreasoning patients, receptacles who should gratefully receive the information and advice that the doctor provides, as in one of Pratt's examples of hegemony at work ("Linguistic"). Students are too often viewed as subjects without a language, without countries they already inhabit.

But writing programs provide an excellent opportunity to allow students to participate actively in selecting which part of the writing terrain they choose to inhabit. Given a program that offers a variety of courses, such as Cornell's, will students be interested in a course that teaches them to be "effective communicators in a multicultural democracy, the United States" (Bizzell 8), or in another that "offers guided practice in reading and writing the discourses of the academy and the professions" (Lindemann 312)? Do they eagerly seek a course in a totally alien subject that will probably place them in an active contact zone (e.g., the white male student who chooses to enroll in "Emerging from the Melting Pot: Self-Reconception by Women of Color"—

one of the Cornell seminars)? Or do they seek what Pratt refers to as a "safe house" ("Arts" 40), a site in which they hope and seek to retreat from the stress of the many sites with competing or clashing values and voices in their lives and relax in "horizontal homogeneous, sovereign communities with high degrees of trust, shared understandings, temporary protection from legacies of oppression" (e.g., a homesick Chinese woman who selects as her writing seminar "Half the Sky: Women in Modern China")? Some students, buried in the study of as-yet alien subjects, select "The Personal Essay," in which the primary texts read and studied are their own. This writing may provide just the kind of release and self-knowledge that they need. Some students indeed agree with James Moffett that "the main issues in writing, after all, concern the composing of the inner life" (260). They know they'll do plenty of more objective writing elsewhere.

I talk with many students as they make such choices, and I am encouraged to find that they most often choose wisely, for their own particular needs. Even when a student's choice is based on what I would call a "bad" reason ("I want a course that doesn't have much reading"), the reason matters to the student, and may, when considered in terms of the student's particular "situatedness," have merit. Only in the imagined unified and homogenous community can we know definitively in what games students are already involved and confidently dictate appropriate new games for them. Our students play many games, have diverse needs. Of course, once students move into a new subject, they are indeed in new and unfamiliar territories with rules controlled by others. But surely students may learn to play new games more readily when they have some choice, have a vested interest in them. Pratt gives a telling example of a similar situation when she vividly describes her son's skillful moves to resist or subvert the teacher-dictated language games in his grade school that "often asked him to identify with the interests of those in power over him" ("Arts" 38) at the same time that he was excelling at linguistic (and other) arts in the game he had chosen for himself, baseball.

More important than the benefits of choice for students are the "understandings and practices," as Pratt puts it, that can result from critical immersion in disciplinary writing opportunities (such as baseball). While giving students the freedom to choose their own seminar topics initially places them in an empowered position, they will still find themselves confronted to a greater or lesser degree in their seminars with writing situations in which they must try to learn languages not their own, in which they are both subjects and subjected in a territory in which others have more power, more knowledge. Writing experiences embedded in disciplines can help students understand that writing situations will vary during their college years and after. Contact zones exist everywhere. And students do, after all, transfer learning experiences in writing: "human beings can consciously apply experience from one set of activities (discipline or community) to another set of activities (discipline or community)" (Russell 189). It seems especially appropriate, then, that at Cornell almost all students must take two writing seminars, virtually guaranteeing them of two very different experiences. During one semester, a student may analyze modern photography; during the next, she or he may study women's stories. There is plenty of encouragement for the student to learn how writing is situated in different arenas and how to negotiate those terrains and all their complexities.

Administrative Concerns for Control

Not surprisingly, it is hard, whether as an English department or as a writing program, to release control over writing. We find ourselves afraid of what might happen if we aren't running the country and organizing the inhabitants. Just as instructors may fear and avoid small group discussions in a classroom because of their loss of control when conversation and learning become self-directed, the administration of a university or writing program (or the state's legislature) may find it hard to believe that dispersing control and responsibility will work, even though failing to do so means facing the difficulties of resistance and subversion and losing the riches provided through heterogeneity. Three fears are particularly common.

One not unreasonable concern is that the instructors of disciplinary writing seminars will not actually teach writing. Will a TA in astronomy truly teach writing, not just astro? This can indeed be a problem if an instructor does not know, and will not learn, how to look first through the lens of writing to envision her subject and her students. At heart, such instructors are often (through fear or thoughtlessness) dictators who find that increased student involvement through writing breaks up the preferred one-way flow of information from instructor to student: they do not recognize, and do not want to recognize, the tensions of the contact zone of their classes even when those tensions are present. Theirs is the imagined homogenous community in which the teacher seeks "to unify and harmonize" his world. It is easier not to notice the potentially rebellious subjects. As Pratt points out, the "essentializing discursive power is impervious until those who are seen are also listened to" (*Imperial Eyes* 153). But little can be done to prevent this kind of failure to listen, or failure to teach writing; such failures cannot be prevented even by trying to control the subject being taught. In an effort at such control, Erika Lindemann and others have argued that literature itself, the normal topic for composition classes in English departments, is too distracting or disruptive a subject for composition courses. But the danger can inhere even in a course called the "Practice of Prose," which I have taught. Somehow one finds something else to teach, something other than writing. Indeed, this type of "bad" teaching—not teaching what we are supposed to be teaching—is scarcely unique to composition courses. There will be some bad teachers no matter what we do—and we have to remember that the judgment "bad" comes from the outside; the view of those in the classroom in regard to what is happening may be very different. Accepting heterogeneity means accepting it in all respects.

Another common fear is that inexperienced teachers and graduate students, and even faculty, from "nonwriting" fields are incapable of designing appropriate writing seminars, even when willing to do so. Writing programs that use untenured part-timers or adjuncts fear giving responsibility to them. One suspects, however, that such fear is sometimes actually the self-protective scorn of those in the writing nation for ignorant, unwashed outsiders or immigrants, scorn rooted in an essentializing view (similar to the way in which instructors sometimes view students, as from above). To admit that writing can be taught successfully elsewhere is to give up power over the writing territory, to fling open the borders. Admittedly, anxiety about inexperienced instructors is justified if the instructors concerned don't write well, haven't ever given much thought to language or writing, and don't want to do so now. In such cases, they shouldn't teach writing, and yes, some selectivity about who teaches is needed. Furthermore, institutions should not hire adjuncts at the last minute so that they have no time to prepare to teach. If they do or must make such hires, their fears are justified, and they probably need to control both content and methods.

But many graduate students and adjuncts can write, do think, and can be given time to prepare and to receive training. As I've argued earlier, the disenfranchised flourish with some enfranchisement. Allowing a wider range of instructors to develop their own syllabi increases the opportunities to find out what they have to offer—in Pratt's terms, to listen as well as to look, to take advantage of copresence, to improve interaction and to develop interlocking understandings and practices. Students encounter a richer array of writing experiences in their writing seminars; instructors may have opportunities to learn from each other and from their students in interdisciplinary encounters. Encouraging instructors from "nonwriting" disciplines to explore writing within the fields they love may lead them to discover the pleasures of actually knowing students through their writing, to experience the pain of discovering, again through that writing, that they hadn't taught what they thought they had, and perhaps even to decide to use more writing in their other courses because they've tried it in the writing seminar and discovered its importance. Better by far to make writing the responsibility of many fields, benefiting from the wide array of writing experiences offered, and suffer through the occasional weakly designed course (which is occasionally taught, in any case, by instructors at any rank, in any department) than to let departments say, "That's not my job. We've placed the teaching of writing in *your* territory. *You* teach students the 'skills.'"

There is a third, especially inflammatory fear about distributing responsibility for the content and teaching of composition across the curriculum: How do we verify what the courses are teaching? Don't we have to have some consistent rules to ensure we know what's going on? Shouldn't every composition section emphasize, for example, documentation, or argument, or audience? In this area, the urge for uniformity, for a homogenous approach dictated from a superior perspective, can be particularly strong. Indeed, the evaluation form for Cornell's First-Year Writing Seminar includes questions about issues that we rather fervently hope the seminars will have addressed: use of evidence, awareness of audience, and so on. So we "encourage" a degree of consistency. But not even professional compositionists agree about what elements of writing ought to appear in every composition course, and the effort to agree even on common general goals can prove a daunting task.[7] At Cornell those who work with instructors therefore try to help them learn about the possibilities and the bases on which they might make their choices and then encourage them to work out plans that fit within the context of their disciplines, their experiences, their students' needs—all of which will, of course, continue to vary even for each instructor. In other words, we try to draw on contact zone theory, and we hope instructors will do so as well: Here are the players—how can we all cooperate and interact through the development of writing in the study of a subject? How do the tensions play out? The result is not consistency—students can't expect to learn exactly the same things about writing in every seminar—but isn't that the point? Isn't it an impossibility to hope that one composition course can prepare a student for writing in every situation? This is not to say, as has been obvious, that the situation can be ideal for those who prepare instructors in a large, diverse program such as Cornell's. Such work will necessarily and regularly involve trying to find a balance between providing and avoiding regulation. It will include ironic situations such as determining to what extent, and how, to try to regulate teachers who use (for example) their own authority in ways that obscure differences and create myths of homogeneity. Nevertheless, when those who control writing programs act out of fear of problems such as those described above and opt to teach writing through a highly regulated program, I believe that they will encounter the greater difficulties of trying to rule too large and diverse a colony as if language were homogenous, as if instructors and students were homogenous. Cornell has opted for a minimalist approach to regulation, providing roughly unifying standards to help ensure that all participants act as if they are citizens of the same country, if not of the same states. Our guidelines ask for continued and intensive attention to language and for limits on the amount of reading so that there is time and space for student writing. The guidelines direct all instructors of seminars to assign at least six new essays in a semester, work through at least three major rewrites, and assign no more than seventy-five pages of reading at the very most in a week. The preparation that instructors receive encourages them to discover their own ways to integrate the teaching of writing into the study of the subject, with many carefully thought out and sequenced preparatory and formal writing assignments. While we assuredly hear of what I consider to be "failures" (but which may be successes to those involved), we also receive ample evidence that the guidelines are followed, perhaps because they help provide the interaction that writing classes require. In any case, we know that embracing heterogeneity means (as one of my colleagues puts it) "embracing the real variation and fray of language use in the disciplines."

Conclusion

I began this essay by using the language of contact zone theory to provide a parodic overview of subjugated, "service" composition programs. Given that the close examination of language is at the heart of contact zone theory, I would like to conclude by looking at the word *composition* itself through a contact zone lens. Doing so can provide a final, refreshing point of view concerning the subject and site of the composition class. *Composition* is a word I have used fairly frequently in this essay, as it is the common term used at many colleges and universities. At Cornell, however, we do not speak of "composition" or "composition courses." Why? What is wrong with our using the term? How is the term *composition* itself implicated in contact zone interactions?

We avoid using the term *composition* because to use it defines writing as situated and controlled in a composition classroom. As I have shown, writing is taught at Cornell by faculty and graduate students in many disciplines; they teach writing through their disciplines. They are not "composition" teachers and do not think of themselves as such. Were the writing program administration to ask faculty or graduate students to think of themselves as composition instructors, we would, with such control over the language, also seem to be trying to control what they taught and how they taught it. We would not win: it was thanks to the subversion and ironies of instructors who taught against the term that "Freshman Writing" seminars finally became "First-Year Writing" seminars. A recent article in *College Composition and Communication* opens up the definition and control of space through language still further, asking, "What would happen if we reconceived ourselves as 'writing experts' working in the public realm instead of 'composition teachers' working within the university? Or if we identified ourselves as the field of 'rhetoric and writing'? ... Is our continued self-identity as *composition* teachers helping ensure our continued subordinate status?" (Porter et al. 632). Insistence on the word *composition* may indeed contribute to "continued subordinate status." The world may little know or care what is done in the often marginalized world of "composition," although it depends on that world to provide needed labor. But the world knows it must claim "writing" as its own. Thus the nature of interaction among the participants changes.

Mary Louise Pratt's concept of contact zones has been eagerly embraced by teachers of first-year writing courses in terms of individual designs for the content of a course and in terms of the interactions among students and the interactions of instructors with their students. As the administrator of first-year writing seminars in a large writing program, I have found it illuminating to apply contact zone theory to the larger design of writing programs; doing so suggests why it can be effective to work toward release of control over composition's content, moving instead toward more dispersal of power, with both the content and the teachers of composition spread throughout the disciplines rather than housed solely in writing departments[8] or English departments. To situate the teaching of writing thus can benefit students, instructors, and administrators; it can help the university as a whole to understand and claim the teaching and learning of writing as its own.

Notes

1. See Pratt's "Linguistic Utopias" for examples of the ease with which the language of the patriarchy is assumed to represent the only perspective, the only voice and authority.

2. See Keith Hjortshoj's "The Marginality of the Left-Hand Castes: A Parable for Writing Teachers" for an excellent discussion from another viewpoint about why writing is marginalized. Hjortshoj writes from the point of view of one who is a publishing anthropologist as well as director of an upper-level "writing in the majors" program.

3. For a historical overview of the development of Cornell's First-Year Writing Seminars, see my "Putting—and Keeping—the Cornell Writing Program in Its Place: Writing in the Disciplines."

4. For a full overview, see the Web site for the John S. Knight Institute for Writing in the Disciplines: http://www.arts.cornell.edu/knight_institute/index.html.

5. The "outside view," however, is less often one of alarm or disbelief than was once the case. In September 2000, the strength of the program was recognized by the Time/Princeton Review college guide when it designated Cornell the private research university "College of the Year" on the basis of its writing-in-the-disciplines approach.

6. One might view the production of genre itself, as it is currently being discussed by Russell and others, as the result of shifting contact zone pressures: the colonized and the colonizers must produce texts; these seemingly conform in genre to the legitimized voice of the most powerful but are constantly modified or subverted according to the needs and pressures of the colonized co-users/co-opters of the genre through what Pratt describes as the "processes of appropriation, penetration or co-optation of one group's language by another" ("Linguistic" 61).

7. For instance, it took two years for one group of expert faculty from various institutions to draft an "Outcomes Statement," modified from much feedback at conference sessions and workshops. See "The WPA Outcomes Statement for First-Year Composition" in WPA, *Writing Program Administration* 23.1–2 (Fall/Winter 1999): 59–70.

8. Composition classes offered by writing programs often have their own subject matters. With Patricia Bizzell, however, I believe that "the writing process" is not usually an adequate subject. (See her "Theories of Content.")

Works Cited

Bartholomae, David. "What Is Composition and (If You Know What That Is) Why Do We Teach It?" *Composition in the Twenty-First Century: Crisis and Change.* Ed. Lynn Z. Bloom, Donald A. Daiker, and Edward M. White. Carbondale: Southern Illinois UP, 1996. 11–28.

Bizzell, Patricia. "Theories of Content." Conference on College Composition and Communication Convention. Nashville. 17–19 Mar. 1994.

Crowley, Sharon. "A Personal Essay on Freshman English." *Pre/Text* 12.3–4 (1991): 156–76.

Freedman, Aviva. "The What, Where, When, Why, and How of Classroom Genres." *Reconceiving Writing, Rethinking Writing Instruction.* Ed. Joseph Petraglia. Mahwah, NJ: Erlbaum, 1995. 121–44.

Gottschalk, Katherine. "Putting—and Keeping—the Cornell Writing Program in Its Place: Writing in the Disciplines." *Language and Learning Across the Disciplines* 2.1 (1997): 22–45.

Hjortshoj, Keith. "The Marginality of the Left-Hand Castes (A Parable for Writing Teachers)." *College Composition and Communication* 46.4 (1995): 491–505.

John S. Knight Institute for Writing in the Disciplines. Apr. 2001. Cornell University. 3 Aug. 2001 <http://www.arts.cornell.edu/knight_institute/index.html>.

Lindemann, Erika. "Freshman Composition: No Place for Literature." *College English* 55.3 (1993): 311–16.

Moffett, James. Response to "Spiritual Sites of Composing." *College Composition and Communication* 45.2 (1994): 258–63.

Porter, James E., Patricia Sullivan, Stuart Blythe, Jeffrey T. Grabill, and Libby Miles. "Institutional Critique: A Rhetorical Methodology for Change." *College Composition and Communication* 51.4 (2000): 610–42.

Pratt, Mary Louise. "Arts of the Contact Zone." *Profession 91.* New York: MLA, 1991. 33–40. (Originally presented as the keynote address at MLA's Responsibilities for Literacy conference in September 1990 in Pittsburgh.)

———. *Imperial Eyes: Studies in Travel Writing and Transculturation.* New York: Routledge, 1992.

———. "Linguistic Utopias." *The Linguistics of Writing: Arguments between Language and Literature.* Ed. Nigel Fabb, Derek Attridge, Alan Durant, and Colin McCabe. Manchester: Manchester UP, 1987. 7–26.

Russell, David. "Activity Theory and Its Implications for Writing Instruction." *Reconceiving Writing, Rethinking Writing Instruction.* Ed. Joseph Petraglia. Mahwah, NJ: Erlbaum, 1995. 51–78.

———. "Vygotsky, Dewey, and Externalism: Beyond the Student/Discipline Dichotomy." *Journal of Advanced Composition* 13 (Winter 1993):173–97.

Frontiers of the Contact Zone

THOMAS PHILION
Roosevelt University, Chicago

frontier n **1** *a : an international border* **b** *: the area along a frontier* **2** *: a region just beyond or at the edge of a settled area* **3** *: an undeveloped area or field for discovery or research*

THE AMERICAN HERITAGE DICTIONARY
(SECOND COLLEGE EDITION)

If there is one idea that has become eminently clear at this point in the emerging professional conversation about contact zones, it is that English Studies is itself a contact zone, or a social space in which "cultures meet, clash, and grapple with each other, often in contexts of highly asymmetrical relations of power" (Pratt 34). Evidence in support of this claim can be found in most, if not all, of the essays that make up this collection. In "Multiculturalism, Contact Zones, and the Organization of English Studies," for example, Patricia Bizzell juxtaposes her "teaching the conflicts" and "writing-centered" approach to English Studies with more mainstream and literature-based proposals for curricular and pedagogical reform. Correspondingly, in his essay "Fault Lines in the Contact Zone," Richard Miller highlights conflicting perspectives within the field of composition studies with regard to student writing that falls outside the boundaries of the expected. Additional evidence can be found in various reports published in professional journals about battles over unions, adjunct teaching, tenure, and critical pedagogy. English Studies—like other social spaces, such as the United States Congress, international airspace off of China, and the Internet—is a site of intense power struggles and vigorous discussions about the proper allocation of time, resources, energy, and ideological commitments.

If the field of English Studies is, as I am suggesting, a contact zone, then one "frontier" within this social space is the area of secondary English teacher education. Although recent demographic changes in schools and universities have produced significant increases in secondary English teacher education majors, and therefore in the number of professors in college English departments who teach courses that address issues in secondary literacy teaching, the field as a whole is still largely ignored and/or overlooked by the powers that be. Patricia Bizzell, for example, in her essay here, does not take into account the special needs of English education majors and professors in arguing for her proposed curricular and pedagogical changes. Correspondingly, mainstream conferences and journals in English Studies rarely call attention to issues in secondary English teacher education, nor to the role of secondary English education in college English departments. English teacher education courses represent an "international" border through which a substantial cohort of undergraduate and graduate English majors pass every year (and will increasingly pass over the next several years), but very few English professors beyond the ones directly involved in teacher preparation seem to know of their existence, nor of their connection to the larger endeavor of English Studies.

What does the landscape of secondary English teacher education look like? What issues and problems do students and professors face in this frontier? How might a knowledge of these issues and problems contribute to the emerging professional conversation about contact zones? How might it contribute to conceptions of teaching and learning in college English courses? In the remainder of this essay, I will develop some provisional answers to these questions. Rather than write comprehensively, I will focus upon one particular subfrontier of secondary English teacher education: the seminar in student teaching. To be exact, I will use Pratt's notion of contact zones to describe and analyze this frontier and to offer an account of student teaching that represents some of the issues and problems that beginning teachers and university English professors face in the linked sub-frontier of a high school English classroom. Through this description and analysis, I will make the case that sociocultural conflict and negotiation are recurring features of secondary English teacher education, and that storytelling is one creative means that beginning teachers and university professors can use to respond productively to this sometimes troubling dimension. Having foregrounded and reflected upon these notions, I will revisit Mary Louise Pratt's notion of contact zones, and especially her assumptions about K–12 teaching. In addition, I will present some implications for the teaching of English in colleges and universities. I will contend that college English professors and secondary English teacher educators together have a mutual responsibility to listen to and learn from one another, and to prepare undergraduate and graduate English majors to successfully negotiate the sociocultural conflicts and struggles that inevitably take place within the frontier of secondary English teacher education.

The Seminar in Student Teaching

Within the frontier of secondary English teacher education, there is perhaps no more significant course on the teaching of literacy than the seminar in student teaching. In student teaching, undergraduate and graduate English majors who are preparing to teach full-time in middle school and high school English classrooms get their first substantial opportunity to teach—to enact the various assumptions and practices related to literacy instruction that they have developed over the duration of their teacher training and their careers in schools and literacy classrooms. Undergraduate and graduate English majors immerse themselves in the cultures of secondary schools and literacy classrooms, and they experiment with different and sometimes innovative methods of teaching. Through this process, they develop broader perspectives on teaching and learning, and on the nature of their own learning experiences prior to student teaching.

In most colleges and universities, the seminar in student teaching is a semester-long course designed to support beginning teachers as they make the transition to full-time teaching. Undergraduate and graduate English majors teach three to five classes, and then they return to the university once a week to discuss their successes in teaching, and to explore various issues and questions. Typically, students who enroll in this course do not take any other courses, and there is little required reading; instead, students talk and write about their teaching experiences, and sometimes develop materials such as videos and portfolios that represent their teaching and learning over the duration of the student teaching seminar. Evaluation in this course usually consists of rating scales that address various qualities of teacher competency, as well as formative (descriptive and nonjudgmental) feedback on journal writing and classroom teaching. University professors and instructors observe student teachers roughly four to six times a semester, complete observation reports and/or rating scales, and assign grades, often in collaboration with mentor teachers in the schools, and sometimes even with the beginning teachers themselves. Although student teaching seminars traditionally have been housed in colleges of education, they are more and more frequently—as in the example that I will discuss here—housed in college English departments or jointly assigned to colleges of education and English departments.

Pratt's notion of contact zones provides a useful conceptual lens through which to read the nature of this challenging and sometimes life-transforming course. While the issues and problems that beginning teachers discuss in student teaching seminars are pedagogical and discipline-based, they also are sociocultural in nature. Typically, as beginning teachers move from their college or university to a given school and classroom, they confront the different—albeit often overlapping—norms and expectations of adolescents, mentor teachers in the schools, and university supervisors and professors. They become aware of the particular social and organizational qualities of schools and literacy classrooms, and the codes of language and behavior that are privileged, fostered, overlooked, and sometimes challenged within these contexts. Furthermore, as beginning teachers interact with adolescents, mentor teachers, and university supervisors, they become aware of the wide variety of ethnic and sociocultural backgrounds that exist in schools and literacy classrooms, as well as the complex ways in which these backgrounds inform, influence, promote, undermine, and disrupt teaching and learning. Like students in service learning courses, undergraduate and graduate English majors in student teaching seminars have to negotiate the complexities of sociocultural norms and expectations that shape everyday life in spheres beyond that of the university, and they are encouraged to reflect critically upon the relationship between these sociocultural norms and expectations and others that they have become familiar with as a result of their experiences in college English courses and other learning environments.

College English professors who teach seminars in student teaching face sociocultural challenges similar to those experienced by beginning teachers: within the context of their weekly meetings and biweekly or monthly visits to schools, professors must support beginning teachers and help them to assimilate the sociocultural norms and expectations that prevail in schools and literacy classrooms. On the other hand, they need to foster in beginning teachers a healthy skepticism with regard to these norms and expectations, such that critical teaching and learning might occur. In contrast to other university courses, in which professors are clearly positioned as the instructional authority, the student teaching seminar requires university professors to share and negotiate instructional authority, and in many ways to accept a marginal status in relation to their students. In student teaching, the customs and practices of everyday life in schools and literacy classrooms carry much more weight with beginning English teachers than do the ideas and practices of university professors. University professors need to speak and act creatively in order to capture the attention of their mentees and thus be able to intervene critically in their professional development.

A Storytelling Approach to Student Teacher Evaluation

The account of student teaching that I will present and analyze in the next section of this essay is one example of a creative practice in which I routinely engage for the purpose of negotiating the frontier of student teaching. Instead of using assessment rubrics and rating scales to evaluate student teachers, I write descriptive narratives, or "thick descriptions," of the teaching practices that I observe during classroom visitations (see my essay "A Storytelling Approach").

My rationale for this storytelling approach to student teacher evaluation is both intuitive and theoretical. On the one hand, I myself have learned how to negotiate sociocultural conflicts by reading stories, and I know that most beginning English teachers, at one time or another, have had the same experience. On the other hand, I am opposed to the rating scales typically employed by supervisors of student teachers. Rating scales provide student teachers with decontextualized and summative feedback on their teaching; like grades, they draw attention to the assumptions and authority of university professors (or abstract criteria of evaluation), and they provide little, if any, guidance as to how to revise and improve one's work. In rejecting this approach, and in enacting my "storytelling" method, I am adhering to the notion commonplace in composition studies that formative evaluation—again, descriptive and nonjudgmental feedback—can provide learners with insights about how to improve their work that are much more powerful than grades or other summative commentary (see Knoblauch and Brannon; Atwell; Elbow). I am also embracing the notion that written storytelling has the potential to inspire significant and long-lasting changes in the perspectives of people who pay careful attention to it (Chambers; Coles).

My storytelling approach to student teacher evaluation also is informed by Mary Louise Pratt's notion of contact zones. In "Arts of the Contact Zone," Pratt explains how traditional studies of classroom linguistic interaction tend to emphasize almost entirely the point of view of teachers and teaching, with very little consideration of the point of view of pupils and what she calls "pupiling" (38). Student teacher rating scales function similarly (for example, several typical rating scale components are "classroom management," "organization," and "clarity of expression"). However, in teacher education courses prior to student teaching, beginning teachers are repeatedly advised to listen closely to their students. "Your students will teach you all you need to know" is a common refrain. In enacting a storytelling approach to student teacher evaluation, I am trying to negotiate the disjuncture between these competing points of view. If the knowledge necessary to improve teaching lies in no small part in students and what they say and do in English classrooms—as both Pratt and many teacher educators suggest—then it seems to me that university professors who supervise student teachers should write accounts of student teaching that highlight students' perspectives and discourse. By providing student teachers with detailed and highly descriptive accounts of classroom teaching, university teachers can provide beginning teachers with rich resources that invite beginning teachers to rethink their pedagogical assumptions and practices, and to fashion new ones that produce more engaged and challenging classroom learning.

Provocative Words: "Are you proud to be an American?"

Over the last several years, I have written many detailed accounts of student teaching.[1] Of all of the narratives I have written, the most compelling is the one I wrote after my third visit to Jai Loong's classroom during the first semester of the 1992–93 school year.[2] In this account of student teaching, many of the sociocultural issues and problems that undergraduate and graduate English majors face in student teaching in urban settings are easily readable, not only for myself, but also for Jai and other readers. In this section, I will describe and analyze the first part of this narrative. I will contend that university supervisors and beginning English teachers need to be attentive to the sociocultural conflicts that are manifested here, and especially to the ways in which these conflicts get negotiated in secondary schools and classrooms. I also will highlight the type of constraints that secondary English teacher educators face in attempting to inspire the beginning teachers whom they supervise to examine critically the sociocultural conflicts that occur in their classrooms.

Prior to my third visit to Jai's classroom, he had warned me that the class I was about to observe was an especially difficult one to teach. Situated at the end of the day, this class had not responded enthusiastically to Jai's teaching. In fact, Jai informed me that the students were downright uncooperative. Even though Jai had a lot to offer his students—he was a graduate student with an M.A. in English from a major research university, and, like several of his students, he was Korean American and lived in the diverse cultural milieu in which his school was located (the school served several thousand students with great linguistic diversity)—he had not yet created an engaging social space for teaching and learning. Part of the problem, Jai told me, was that most of his students were not proficient with the English language. In addition, his mentor teacher—a veteran African American teacher—had a reputation for running a tight ship in terms of classroom management and discipline. Jai felt constrained by her instructional methods, and was ill at ease trying to replicate her authoritative persona with his students.

This is the first part of the narrative that I wrote after my observation of Jai's lesson. In this initial section, Jai organizes his students to collaboratively brainstorm a response to the question "Are you proud to be an American?"

> "Good afternoon."
>
> Jai begins his eighth-period English class, in Room 113 of Hamilton High School, by asking his students if they remember their homework assignment from the night before. He doesn't get much response, but he tells his students that they can do their present assignment without having finished their homework. He looks disappointed. His sixteen students, needless to say, don't celebrate.
>
> Jai explains his assignment: "Are you proud to be an American?" he asks. "Find a partner and decide among yourselves what makes you proud of America, or what makes you feel ashamed of America."
>
> From the back row I hear: "Are we going to turn this in? How much do you want us to write?" I sit in the back row, in one corner, and have ready access to these voices.
>
> Jai emphasizes that he will allot five minutes for the completion of this assignment. I'm pleased since I have urged him to think about how he can better anticipate questions and direct his students before they break into groups.
>
> Students break into pairs and begin to talk. I overhear one student to my right talking about problems in America—gangs, drugs, etc. . . . Another student sitting in front of me says that he is not an American. He is a new arrival in this country. His partner explains that he can still respond to the question, if he responds as if he were an American, and so this recent immigrant talks about how he has difficulty with the language and the

different culture of America (I believe that this student is from Eastern Europe). I look around and notice the ethnic diversity of this classroom: two or three Asian students sit in front, some Indian or Pakistani students sit to my right side, two Latino or Hispanic youths sit on the other side of the room, and one African American student sits in the back row on the opposite side from me. All in all, there are sixteen students in scattered rows of desks.

"OK, let me hear from each of the groups."

Jai writes on the board "Are" and "Are not" and solicits responses to his question "Are you proud to be an American?" He explains that he has noticed that most students have written down more responses that fall under "Are not" proud, and so he begins with reasons to be proud. Various students call out their reasons for being proud—"freedom," "rights," "Constitution," "government." Jai asks, "Can you expand?" and receives a list of three or four rights guaranteed under the United States Constitution. I notice that an African American male in the back of the room makes jokes about the problems of America.

Jai moves to reasons for not being proud of America. "Crime," "drugs," "economy," "racism," "AIDS" and others are called out. A litany of social problems. The African American student in the back row suggests "fags" to one of his partners. "That will really get him," he says. A few moments later, a student, recently arrived from Eastern Europe, and just to the left of me, says "fags" just loud enough for Jai to hear. Jai appears stunned and ignores the response, though he obviously is disturbed. I remember that before Thanksgiving Jai had told a story in our seminar about a class discussion in which he had tried to defend the rights of gay and lesbian persons in a larger discussion about civil rights. These boys know how to get under Jai's skin.

I begin to think of strategies to help Jai deal with this rambunctious bunch. I write in my notepad that a circle could help Jai keep everyone in sight and force students to respond directly to him and to one another. I also write that Jai might more clearly emphasize the use of hands, and that if he was a more commanding presence in the classroom he would not have to deal with some of this noise. Excluding offending students from the class and being authoritative about acceptable language in his classroom would be other options. None of these solutions, of course, addresses in a more critical way the issues of prejudice and social relations.

Here, I represent what I perceive as a very complex and provocative contact zone, or a social space characterized by cultural diversity and power negotiation. At the center of this social space stands Jai, a beginning teacher still finding his feet as a literacy educator, but one who possesses a good deal of authority to direct the nature of classroom learning. In the rows and desks surrounding Jai are students who are variously engaged with the lesson that he has set in motion. Last but not least, I myself am situated on the periphery of this social space—a white assistant professor feverishly scribbling notes about everything I see and hear, and thus a symbol of the power and influence of the university, and of the instructional ideas and practices that Jai has become an advocate of through his teacher education courses.[3] The conflicts that Jai faces here are multiple, complex, and grounded in issues of language, identity, and culture. On the one hand, Jai is enacting the stance of a pedagogue committed to collaborative learning; like the educators he has read in English teacher education courses (e.g., Newkirk, 1990), Jai is asking his students to create, rather than receive, knowledge. On the other hand, several of Jai's students are clearly unprepared, or unwilling, to engage in this sort of teaching and learning. The conflict here can be read as strictly pedagogical in nature—as a problem that many teachers face when they attempt to switch from teacher-directed to student-directed teaching and learning.

The difficulty that Jai's teaching provokes, however, can and ought to be read in ways other than the strictly pedagogical. Jai is separated from his students by more than simply his methods of teaching and his status as a teacher; he also is a highly successful learner and fluent speaker of English—something that cannot be said of the majority of his students. Consequently, Jai struggles to think of ways to invite his students to elaborate upon their ideas, and to develop more meaningful responses to his questions. In addition, as the closing scene in this narrative excerpt indicates, Jai has a different political perspective and relationship to authority than do his students; in classes prior to this one, Jai has argued in favor of gay rights—a notion that some students find ridiculous. Jai's willingness to reveal his political commitments—and his unwillingness to impose his authority upon his students—creates the context for the unsolicited oppositional discourse ("fags") that students articulate at the very end of his lesson. Perhaps because Jai is aware of my presence, and the way in which an articulation of anger or censure would undermine the student-centered teaching that he is attempting to enact (as well as his own convictions about the nature of student-teacher relationships), he does not respond proactively to his students' unsolicited oppositional discourse. Instead, he carries on with his lesson, embarrassed, but not defeated.

My own position in this classroom is equally complicated and conflicted. Like Jai, I am distanced—even more so—from students as a result of my ethnic and cultural background (middle class, rural, and Western European), my education, and my lack of familiarity with these particular students. Like Jai, I am unable to voice any immediately useful response to the unsolicited oppositional discourse that occurs at the end of this passage. However, the one advantage that I do have is that it is not my role to intervene; instead, my role is to read and write, and to reflect critically upon Jai's teaching. In my notes, I list ways of responding to the unsolicited oppositional discourse that I have observed: ways that range from reorganizing the classroom to kicking kids out of class. I encourage Jai to consider these options, but I also remind him that none of these options—including the one that he actually enacted in class—really addresses the underlying sociocultural tensions embedded in the oppositional discourse that both of us heard.

While I am comfortable with the advice that I give to Jai in the narrative excerpt above, what I now find most interesting about this paragraph is the way in which it reveals the constraints that I face as a writer and a university professor in this particular secondary school setting. Although I give Jai some good ideas for responding to the unsolicited oppositional discourse that he faces, I avoid a more complicated response that might alienate Jai's mentor teacher—for example, a response like that which Richard Miller shapes. Unlike Miller, I do not, at least in this instance, feel comfortable articulating a stance that says, essentially, make oppositional discourse a subject of study. Given the age of high school students, and what Jai has told me about his mentor teacher, I know that such a stance—a more developed enactment of Jai's prior conversation about gay rights—would not be welcomed by Jai's mentor teacher, nor by the administration at her school. Consequently, I merely indicate that the options that I describe for dealing with Jai's students' unsolicited oppositional discourse—options that I know Jai's mentor teacher and her administrators will find, at least in part, reasonable—are ineffective responses to the larger problems of intolerance and social stereotyping. In this respect, then, my silence with regard to the underlying instructional issues that Jai's students' oppositional language occasions reveals my complicity with the larger social and political structures that shape secondary teaching, a complicity that—at least in this passage, at this time—troubles me, and leads me to wonder about the nature of my own commitment to student-centered learning.

More Difficult Words: *Letters from an American Farmer*

The point I am making here is that within the frontier of secondary English teacher education, college English professors are constrained to articulate and instantiate ideas circulating within English Studies more generally speaking. Within the contact zone of student teaching, for example, college English professors must acknowledge the authority of prevailing power structures in secondary schools and literacy classrooms, just as their students must accommodate and make room for prevailing norms and expectations. Indeed, the external systematic constraints that secondary English educators must negotiate are more numerous and significant than those faced by any other group of college English teachers, and they clearly distinguish the work of secondary English education from other types of work prevalent in college English departments. However, there always exists a potential for creative manipulation. Through creative storytelling—through narrative writing such as that which I am representing here—secondary English teacher educators can temporarily surmount the systematic constraints that they face and, in so doing, invite beginning English teachers to think critically about their teaching.

   In the paragraphs below, I present the remainder of my account of Jai's teaching. In this subsequent excerpt, I represent Jai leading a discussion of a selection from a canonical work in American literature: J. Hector St. Jean de Crèvecoeur's *Letters from an American Farmer.* Here is the remainder of the narrative that I wrote about Jai's teaching.

"OK, turn to page 86."

Students open up their books to the essay *Letters from an American Farmer.* The textbook appears to be a fairly dated anthology. The essay Jai's students are looking at was written by J. Hector St. Jean de Crèvecoeur, a European who visited and temporarily settled in America prior to the Revolution. He believes that America is a great experiment in freedom and opportunity. As Jai tells his students, "he loves America." Jai explains that this immigrant arrived from France and was, in contrast to the views just shared, proud to be an American.

Jai told me before class that he wanted to help his second language students learn to read better. "I'm going to point you to particular sections," he now says. Jai directs his students to a single sentence in the middle of the essay, reads it aloud, and then explains what the author is saying. "He is trying to explain why it is such a good thing to live in America. He is saying that Americans have come from Europe and are starting new lives." The class is silent. The young African American in the back row puts his head down on his desk.

"I know that most of you are from other countries—do you feel that you are hanging onto old ideas, old prejudices?" Jai asks. An Asian male in the front of the room responds to Jai. He says that he has had to change his point of view, and that America offers a freer form of government. The African American male in the back begins to spit rap sounds with his head down on the desk.

Jai continues to draw on the experiences of some of his students. He asks several students whom he knows are new arrivals in this country if they have had to change their thinking as a result of living in America.

Suddenly, the African American student in the back row interrupts. "I don't understand," he says loudly. Jai listens and asks this student, Kevin, to explain. "I just don't get it," he says. "Help me out," Jai says. Kevin explains that the whole issue of being an "American" doesn't make sense to him. "I mean, there is no one American, so how can he talk about what an American is? I mean, there is no one religion."

Jai agrees and focuses Kevin's attention and that of the class on a new passage—one that refers specifically to the "melting pot" concept of America. Jai explains the point of this passage, that a unique American culture is forged out of diversity, and asks, "What is American culture?" A conversation ensues about various kinds of food and the lack of an "American" food aside from hamburgers and pizza.

I think to myself—well, if there is no one culture, then do we form a "new race" as Crèvecoeur suggests? Jai gets to this question by focusing on a new passage, one in which the author claims that new immigrants need to leave behind their old cultures. Another short conversation ensues: "So you don't think people should leave behind their culture?" Jai says. The class is unanimous that they should not. "I'm not sure I believe this either," says Jai. Jai moves to another section, and reads a sentence, but again he is interrupted.

"So when this author talks about Americans, he means people from Europe," says Kevin.

"Yes," says Jai.

"Well then he's excluding African Americans. This story is bullshit—the whole book is bullshit. We need some new books in here."

The class and I wait for Jai's response. "So how would you rewrite this sentence?" Jai asks. Kevin replies that he would have it include the experiences of African Americans—he would explain that while this "new" America was being fashioned, "we" (White Europeans) were enslaving blacks, selling them false promises, and denying them freedom.

"That would be a good story," Jai replies. "But consider the fact that this story, the way it is written here, lets us see how some White people thought at this time. I think the way it is written here is more valuable because it's real—Europeans didn't even think of including African Americans in the human race. So we get an idea of what their prejudices were without having them explicitly stated." Kevin nods his head—I don't think he buys it.

An Asian girl in the front row responds. "What about this part when he says individuals from all nations form a new man?"

"I think he is talking about Europeans," Jai replies. Jai reads from another section where the author explicitly says that Europeans are the ones forming this "new race."

"I think it is good for you to have a strong opinion, Kevin" says Jai. Jai explains further how the author is so infatuated with the freedoms he experiences that he loses sight of the limits of those freedoms. I'm reminded of how the rhetoric of "newness" is very American, a language that Bill Clinton used effectively in campaigning for the presidency.

The class is almost over. Jai places homework on the board and attempts to analyze another passage. His students don't respond—they are now distracted. After the excitement of Jai's exchange with Kevin, more mundane analysis is beside the point.

Like the prior excerpt, this one indicates the degree to which sociocultural conflicts inform and circumscribe teaching and learning in secondary schools and literacy classrooms. Within the context of this passage, Jai is again grappling with the oppositional language and behavior of his students, and in particular, his student Kevin.

While this oppositional language and discourse can be read as a function of Jai's willingness to engage his students in open-ended discussion about literary texts, or perhaps of Kevin's apparent inability to abide by school rules, it also can be read as a function of the sociocultural diversity embedded in this classroom. Every person in this classroom—myself and Jai included—has strong opinions to share with regard to Crèvecoeur's writing, and these strong opinions are in no insignificant way shaped by larger social and cultural forces (Kevin, for example, articulates a stance informed by his knowledge of African American history, other students take stances shaped significantly by immigrant experiences, and Jai and I articulate notions developed substantially through our graduate English education experiences).

What distinguishes this passage from the earlier one, however, is the degree to which Jai is able to enact a productive response to the oppositional language and behavior that he hears within this particular classroom contact zone. Using the excerpt from *Letters from an American Farmer* as a starting point, Jai explores with his students the difference between their perspectives on America and that recorded by Crèvecoeur. While Jai appeared confused and surprised by his students' oppositional perspectives at the beginning of his lesson, in this instance he seems prepared for them, and even indicates his own identification with their oppositional perspectives ("I'm not sure I believe this either"). Although his response to Kevin's oppositional discourse is argumentative, and therefore not really reciprocal in nature, Jai overlooks his illicit language. In addition, Jai's question in response to Kevin's contention that the textbook is bullshit serves the purpose of uncovering in a more complex way the basis of Kevin's oppositional perspective. Even though Jai does not endorse the particulars of Kevin's response to his hastily prepared question ("So how would you rewrite this sentence?"), Jai is respectful of his overarching stance in relationship to Crèvecoeur's text and defends it in conversation with another student ("I think he is talking about Europeans"). In other words, even though Jai articulates an essentially defensive response to Kevin's unsolicited oppositional discourse, he does use Kevin's oppositional discourse to his pedagogical advantage—to acquire insight into a hidden perspective, and to make a point about the nature of reading and literary study that is perhaps not appreciated by his students, but important nonetheless.

In this subsequent narrative, I also articulate what I perceive as a more productive response to adolescent oppositional discourse. Again, my role is not to respond directly to Kevin's argument—I am present in this classroom to advise and think critically. Consequently, in a brief analytical commentary following the above excerpt, I shared with Jai some of my ideas related to his lesson, and especially his interaction with Kevin. I explain that if Jai is serious about addressing the social issues that Kevin raises, then he will need to bring diverse texts into his class, and create conditions where students can explore issues such as "What does it mean to be an American?" and "Can we live together without a shared understanding of what it means to be an American?" in more focused and careful ways. My closing paragraph urges Jai to move in this direction, to radically alter the nature of the curriculum that he offers to his students.

> Jai just might find that placing something like *Letters from an American Farmer* within a larger context of an exploration of issues of race and class and gender will encourage students to get interested in texts and so to read better. If his students know why they are reading—in order to explore how people think differently about this idea of America—then they just might get interested and find it easier to read. Malcolm X's view is different from that of the author of *Letters,* which is different from that of other new arrivals to this country. Getting high school students to talk to one another about their different perspectives, and about the different experiences that people have in America, and about the difficulty of creating unity among these diverse individuals, seems to me to be an important and valuable goal for any English teacher to have.

Here, in contrast to my prior response to oppositional discourse, I do not share ideas that are meant merely to help Jai integrate himself more successfully into the prevailing culture of his school. Instead, I piggyback upon Kevin's argument, and point out the pedagogical value inherent in making Kevin's oppositional discourse a subject of intense scrutiny and study. Like Patricia Bizzell and Mary Louise Pratt, I argue for an approach to teaching that celebrates diversity and takes seriously the relationship between authoritative and marginal or oppositional perspectives. The rationale for undertaking this approach, I indirectly suggest, flows from the story that I have just told. This is not an argument that is merely theoretical in nature—it is embedded in Jai's classroom experiences, and in the words and actions of his students, and therefore ought to be considered carefully.

Contact Zone Theory and K–12 Literacy Pedagogy

When I first read Mary Louise Pratt's "Arts of the Contact Zone," I was immediately intrigued by it. Addressing a diverse audience of K–16 literacy educators, business and union leaders, and community activists, Pratt uses her experiences as a parent and literary scholar to advocate a more inclusive, more diverse approach to literacy education. At the heart of her essay is the idea of contact zones, a notion that she shows can be applied equally well to the study of literature and to elementary and college teaching. Through reference to her son, and his experiences in school, Pratt makes the point that teachers ought to pay attention to kids more carefully than they usually do; her son, she argues, ought to have had opportunities to read and write about his intrinsic interests, and to develop other interests just as compelling. Through her reference to a text produced by Felipe Guaman Poma de Ayala, Pratt shows that there can be a great deal of value in oppositional discourse—in language that seeks to creatively negotiate the clashes and social divides separating one or more social groups. Not wanting to remain theoretical, Pratt discusses her own classroom teaching, and the changes in curriculum and instruction that she made in collaboration with several of her colleagues at

Stanford. Pratt highlights the usefulness of college curricula that examine diverse cultural and ideological positions and experiences, and of instruction that allows students to engage in their own creative position-taking, empathizing with others, reacting angrily, returning to safe houses, and creating their own informed insights into contemporary and historical social issues and conflicts.

I have used Pratt's ideas to understand and support my own approach to teaching, and to conceptualize the nature of the experiences that I have had in student teaching seminars and other teacher education courses. However, from time to time, I also have questioned Pratt's ideas, sometimes in light of my reading of other critics engaged with her work, and sometimes in light of my own experiences in working at the frontier of secondary English teacher education. In this section, I will share some of the questions that I have raised as a result of my experiences, in the hope that these ideas may illuminate dimensions of Pratt's work that have not yet been appreciated.

One important question has to do with Pratt's representation of K–12 teachers. One of the more interesting arguments that Pratt makes in her essay, albeit indirectly, is that K–12 teachers (and to a lesser extent college teachers) do not give enough time and attention to unsolicited oppositional discourse. Through her presentation of Guaman Poma's narrative and her account of the poor reception that this narrative received from the King of Spain, Pratt makes the argument that teachers often behave like kings in relation to their oppositional subjects: they ignore or overlook oppositional discourse, and do everything within their power to contain it.

While I myself am drawn to this argument, I find that in my own work with beginning English teachers—college English majors—I more often than not find that teachers attend reasonably well to the oppositional discourses of their students. Perhaps because their own authority is so tenuous, perhaps because they are usually close in age to teenagers, and therefore sensitive to their needs and interests, beginning English teachers—in my experience—do not fit the representation (or, some would say, stereotype) that Pratt advances in her essay. Even though beginning English teachers may not always respond critically to oppositional discourse, they do take it seriously, and often delight in highlighting its emergence, especially when it takes forms that do not overtly challenge or disrupt prevailing norms and expectations. My own sense is that, in general, critics from within what Pratt terms "the elite academy" need to be careful that in writing about K–12 education they do not reinforce largely stereotypical representations of teachers as unfeeling despots oblivious to or unwilling to consider the intrinsic needs and interests of their students.

My second question is related to the first: In my experience, there are often some very good reasons why K–12 teachers (and even kings) do not pay attention to unsolicited oppositional discourse. Perhaps because Pratt is distanced from the frontier of K–12 education, she does not acknowledge the multiple and significant constraints that teachers face in responding creatively and thoughtfully to unsolicited oppositionality. Lack of time, too many responsibilities, a fear of what will follow from acknowledging adolescent oppositionality, a need to focus on pedagogical goals and methods deemed important by authoritative adult communities—these are all obstacles that make it difficult for teachers, beginning and experienced alike, to respond critically to oppositionality.

A third question has to do with the nature of power and authority in K–12 classrooms and in literacy classrooms more generally. While I think Pratt is right to focus on the ways in which teachers control and manipulate learning to their own advantage, and often in opposition to their students' needs and interests, I also think that she overlooks the capacity of students to exert power and authority in the classroom, and to steal authority from teachers. What my experiences in supervising student teachers tell me is that teachers are often located on the weaker side of a power relationship in relation to their students; in various ways, in an infinite number of contexts, students manipulate the circumstances of their learning such that their own needs and interests are made the focus of attention. Indeed, this is exactly what I read Jai's students as doing in the narrative that I have presented here. Power in classrooms, I want to suggest, is shared and negotiated—especially in classrooms led by student teachers. Depending on how that negotiation takes place and develops, teachers may well find themselves routinely on the weaker side of a power relationship.

One final implication of the critical reflection that I have engaged in here is that storytelling may well be a powerful means by which teachers can renegotiate power relationships with their students and creatively mediate the obstacles and challenges they face in classrooms where sociocultural conflicts manifest themselves in problematic ways. In other words, I believe that storytelling can function as a means of personal empowerment—as a creative art of the contact zone—that can enable teachers to develop more dialogic, democratic, and critical teaching environments. In the narrative that I have presented here, Jai is most successful when he engages in something like dialogue with his students; in my own role as a supervisor of beginning teachers, I am most successful, I believe, when I tell stories to beginning teachers that help them better appreciate the multiple perspectives that shape and potentially inform classroom teaching. Through storytelling—a type of writing and speaking that does not impose ideas upon readers, but that instead explores multiple perspectives—both teachers and students can find ways of making room for perspectives other than their own, while at the same time drawing attention to their own intrinsic needs and interests.

College English and the Frontier of Secondary English Education

Throughout this essay, I have endeavored to show how contact zone theory can be applied to the context of secondary English education, and how the lessons learned from this application can illuminate hidden features of context zone theory. In this section, I wish to suggest additional implications for the teaching of college English.

One important implication is that an awareness of everyday life in the frontier of secondary English education can be of immense use to college English teachers. In teaching the composition and literature courses that precede student teaching, college

English professors discuss texts and engage their students in reading and writing activities that teach them useful ways of thinking critically about language, their own ideas, and the world. What college English courses do less well is introduce students to the sorts of conflicts and obstacles that they can expect to face once they take their critical reading and writing abilities out into the broader world. Because college English courses are typically insulated from the material and social constraints of the "real world," they do an inadequate job, in general, of advising English majors about what to do with their critical reading and writing abilities once they move into other social spaces.

Clearly, an enhanced awareness of the issues and problems that college English majors face in student teaching—just one of the many frontiers that college English majors move into as they make the transition from college or university—can help college English teachers to think about how to improve upon their classroom teaching. By becoming more aware of life in the frontier of secondary English education, college English professors can develop strategies for preparing their students to make the transition that inevitably will occur toward the end of their college careers. Approaches to the teaching of English such as those advanced by Patricia Bizzell in this volume, for example, would be even more powerful if they took into account the needs and interests of secondary English education students. In advocating a "contact zones" approach to the teaching of English, Bizzell and other teachers who advocate this approach might point out some of the limitations inherent in trying to enact this approach in contemporary secondary schools and classrooms—the primary limitation being the lack of textbooks and other useful resources. Rather than ignoring this systematic constraint, college English teachers would do well to incorporate it into their pedagogy, and to discuss how and why a contact zone approach to English Studies might be creatively modified and adapted to connect with the context of middle school and high school teaching.

What I am arguing for here is not "career preparation," as some would call it, but the value of an enhanced awareness of what lies beyond college English courses, of the frontiers that college English majors will pass through after they leave their college English courses. With this awareness in mind, college

English teachers might offer their students examples of how to negotiate the sociocultural conflicts that inevitably occur when critical readers enter contexts beyond "the elite academy." In doing so, they will provide college English majors with more reasons to enact the critical reading and writing strategies that they advocate, and more effective ways of doing so over the entirety of their lives. They also will provide more support for the development of creative and effective teachers—something that only a collaborative effort between teacher educators and liberal arts professors can truly foster.

Notes

1. All of the accounts that I have written, including the one that I cite here, were written in my capacity as a supervisor of student teachers in a college English department. At the time that I wrote these narratives, I was assistant professor of English and assistant director of a secondary English teacher education program. Although I have since moved from this position, I continue to work closely with college English teachers and to teach courses in which college English majors enroll.

2. All student teacher and adolescent names used in this essay are pseudonyms.

3. Although I am a representative of the university, and, in particular, of ideas and practices that Jai explored in his teacher education courses (and thus of those in power, from whom Jai hopes to receive high grades), I never actually taught Jai prior to this student teaching seminar. However, I knew about some of Jai's experiences in teacher education courses as a result of classroom observations that I conducted prior to this seminar.

Works Cited

Atwell, Nancie. *In the Middle: New Understandings about Writing, Reading, and Learning*. Portsmouth, NH: Heinemann, 1998.

Chambers, Ross. *Room for Maneuver: Reading (the) Oppositional (in) Narrative*. Chicago: U of Chicago P, 1991.

Coles, Robert. *The Call of Stories: Teaching and the Moral Imagination.* Boston: Houghton, 1989.

Elbow, Peter. *Writing with Power: Techniques for Mastering the Writing Process.* New York: Oxford UP, 1998.

Knoblauch, C. H., and Lil Brannon. *Rhetorical Traditions and the Teaching of Writing.* Upper Montclair, NJ: Boynton/Cook, 1984.

Newkirk, Thomas, ed. *To Compose: Teaching Writing in High School and College.* Portsmouth, NJ: Heinemann, 1990.

Philion, Thomas. "A Storytelling Approach to Beginning Teacher Evaluation." *Great Beginnings: Reflections and Advice for New English Language Arts Teachers and the People Who Mentor Them.* Ed. Ira Hayes. Urbana, IL: NCTE, 1998. 144–50.

Pratt, Mary Louise. "Arts of the Contact Zone." *Profession 91.* New York: MLA, 1991. 33–40. (Originally presented as the keynote address at MLA's Responsibilities for Literacy conference in September 1990 in Pittsburgh.)

Safe Houses and Sacrifices: Filling the Rooms with Precious Riches

DAPHNE KEY
Peru State College

By wisdom a house is built, and by understanding it is established; by knowledge the rooms are filled with all precious and pleasant riches.
PROVERBS 24.3–4 (NEW REVISED STANDARD VERSION)

In "Arts of the Contact Zone," Mary Louise Pratt defined con tact zones as "social spaces where cultures meet, clash, and grapple with each other, often in contexts of highly asymmetrical relations of power" (34). The *clashing* and *grappling* instantly suggested to me the prospect of one victor emerging in battle, and I have learned from my own classroom experiences in North Carolina, Florida, Hawaii, Alabama, Northern Virginia, and Nebraska that racial, cultural, and ideological differences can create a battlefield scenario. However, my students have taught me that clashing and grappling must be reconceived and redefined as respectful power redistribution in our heterogeneous classrooms and communities. The power redistribution can allow all participants to emerge victorious. All can leave with self-respect and broader understanding of topics discussed and debated—those critical characteristics often destroyed in many confrontations. It is in contact zones that these characteristics can be formed and developed; however, they are developed only when those in power are willing to sacrifice enough to let others grow.

As Pratt concluded her now oft-cited essay, she recognized that in order for all participants to grow, contact zones must become—or provide for—the creation of "safe houses," which she defined as "social and intellectual spaces where groups can constitute themselves as horizontal, homogeneous, sovereign communities with high degrees of trust, shared understandings, temporary protection from legacies of oppression" (40). Several years ago in a community literacy project, seven African American women in rural Alabama shared their wisdom with me—a White, middle-class English teacher—and showed me how safe houses can be built and filled with understanding, knowledge, and respect. But I had to sacrifice my power and arrogance; that is, I had to sacrifice my need to unify "the social world, probably in . . . [my] own image" (39). By doing so, I lost nothing; rather, I gained some much needed wisdom and sensitivity.

After ten years of teaching English, grades four through college, I found myself in Montgomery, Alabama, and I took a sabbatical, of sorts, and began working at the Family Guidance Center, a nonprofit organization focusing on family counseling, parenting, and child care issues. I was given the opportunity of my life, I now realize, to explore reading and writing in the real world, to encourage literacy use without grades. As part of a grant, I implemented a reading and writing enhancement project as part of a training program for child care providers in Montgomery and nearby counties. In order to express their knowledge about child care issues, the participants of this project constructed a "safe house" in which to read, write, talk, and perform. As a result of fostering understanding and creating knowledge from life experiences, the rooms were indeed "filled with all precious and pleasant riches."

As I attempt to describe this project and the construction of our "safe house," I realize that I may sound nostalgic, that I may be accused of expressing my own experience in less than intellectually rigorous terms; however, I will take my chances that my thoughts may make their way into a safe house of pedagogical discussion. The experiences about which I write changed me, the way I teach, and the way I view the world; consequently, "so must my language change" (Bridwell-Bowles 350). The child care providers in Alabama taught me how theory must be shaped and exercised in the real world, and, frankly, facilitating this project was the most exhilarating and rewarding "teaching" job I have ever had. I came to learn firsthand that those of us who promote academic literacy have much to learn from those who use literacy in everyday lives far removed from the often privileged and isolated world of academic life.

Prior to moving to Alabama, I taught in Hawaii, where I was a "haole," a "pushy" White missionary, of sorts, proclaiming the good news of *The Little, Brown Handbook*. My diverse students there gently but firmly showed me that I wielded power in writing classes—subtle power that dictated topic, interpretation, and "correctness," a power which could "silence and discredit" (Spellmeyer 269). My university students in Hawaii and the adults in Alabama forced me to face and analyze not only my power but also the power of the linguistic and cultural conventions which I had been attempting, with good intentions, to transmit.

As in Hawaii, years of hurt, fear, and oppression in Alabama have influenced the interplay of perceptions of marginalized groups and the dominant culture (Ogbu). Like so many other places in America, one's skin color, clothes, socioeconomic status, and language combine to create one's definition of self in Alabama, historically marked by years of racial strife, particularly. However, one's definition of self also can be re-created by examining one's experiences, one's stories of life. When I was contemplating how to begin this literacy project with adults who were trying to grow professionally, I was reading Paulo Freire. His words and beliefs awakened me, and, although I didn't know exactly how I would begin the project, I knew that I would start with the child care providers' own stories and experiences. I would start with the participants' knowledge of children and respect it. I believed that respect and trust had to bind me and the child care providers together—as human beings—before any stories, which might reveal racial, economic, and historical issues affecting the well-being of the children in their care, could be shared. I had to refrain from the posture of teaching *them* what *I* thought *they* needed to know about literacy and children's issues. The agency's executive director trusted me to follow my instincts, and we proceeded to enter a contact zone.

To announce the project, I stood in front of about eighty exhausted child care providers—mostly African American and White women—who had been keeping children since six in the morning. They had come to a night meeting to organize those in the child care profession in the Montgomery area. Although some were college educated and held managerial positions, many of these providers had minimal formal education and made minimum wage. All day long, they fed hungry children, changed diapers, wiped runny noses and tears. All day long, they nurtured and loved the children in their care until late in the evening. In many ways, they were surrogate parents, for they spent their days with these children. Also, they served as important first teachers of language to the children in their care. I saw that their love of children and the work they performed were our common bonds, crisscrossing all racial, educational, and socioeconomic differences.

Looking at their tired faces, I wondered if I could really convince these providers to commit to a series of workshops relating to emergent literacy issues. I knew that many would be hesitant about coming to workshops focused on what they might perceive as just reading and writing skills. I also sensed that some might be intimidated by the prospect of attending a workshop in which they themselves *might* have to speak, to read, to write—in essence, to reveal themselves through their own language usage in front of their professional peers and an English teacher, who by virtue of the combination of occupational title, race, dress, and language usage might have the power to intimidate. This combination of factors can create a powerful perception of "*correct*" people (Key 31) in the minds of some who have come to believe that they are "*in the lowest category of society*" (30) or "too old to fix" (35), and I wondered if some members of the group I was addressing might feel this way.

Looking at my audience, I instinctively told a story of growing up in the rural South, an important regional and cultural connection to these people whom I had never met. In front of them, I held up a quilt I had made, and I talked about the story of each square. I told of my grandmother and her daughters quilting around a frame on winter days, telling stories with me at their feet listening. I spoke of wearing dresses and petticoats made from feedsacks, the feedsack fabric then recycled into quilts. Some women shut their eyes and nodded in quiet understanding. I then asked if they had stories to tell to children and if they would like to make a quilt. I saw smiles on tired faces, and some women cautiously ventured to the workshop series which I entitled The Joy of Telling Stories to Children.

Seven African American women came to the first workshop. Quietly dignified, they came in twos and threes, and, sitting around a table, they waited for me to tell them what they were going to learn. I wanted them to be proud of their language and to share that pride and enthusiasm with the children in their care. I wanted them to experience the importance of telling stories, listening to others, writing stories, and reading aloud to children. But I asked them to tell me about themselves and their work.

First, each woman talked of the love she felt for "her children." Each talked of the importance of education. Then I asked them about their English classes in school and how they felt about teaching language skills. Eye-rolling, knowing smirks—one or two people recalled a pleasant memory, but the most positive memory focused on the pride one participant still felt that her own mother had taught her to read and to write. This recollection of life in Selma, Alabama, in the first half of the twentieth century, would become her first story later recounted at literacy events throughout the state.

One woman, however, recalled being corrected in speech and writing by English teachers; then they all nodded in silent agreement. At this juncture, we discussed how this speech correction affects people. Someone breathed a sigh of relief; someone else laughed, and someone confessed that she had been scared to come to this workshop because she might not speak or read or write "*appropriately.*" The minute this fear was honestly stated or "named," a tension or formality dissipated (Fine 120). One woman admitted later on television that she had planned to sit in her car and wait for her friend, that she had no intention of participating. After thirty minutes, however, her friend, who loved quilt making, enticed her to get out of the car and come into the first workshop.

During the first meetings, we told stories of our own childhoods while we drew on quilt squares. As we drew and talked, I discussed Nancie Atwell's explanation of Donald Graves's concept of artistic rehearsal, that of drawing "a picture in order to plan . . . [one's] writing" (Atwell 8). Next we decided that I would tape-record the story that each person most wanted to share with children—the story each person believed might positively affect the children in her care. I asked each person to assess the needs of the children whom she taught and to recall a story from her past to which the children might relate. Then I would transcribe the stories as told.

At the next session, when I returned story drafts, silence fell. The women read, smiled—delighted in seeing their stories captured in print. The participants read their drafts to each other, and *re-vision* occurred naturally. The participants debated words, phrases, order, transition, and style. They tried to define their styles and to maintain their voices, for their stories were part of them. They discussed the audience for their stories—children (at least, initially)—and, in so doing, discussed themes, vocabulary, and alliteration. They made decisions regarding dialect and Standard English. One participant expressed surprise that I had preserved dialect during the transcription process: "Why, Daphne, you wrote it like I talk." I asked her how she felt about her "talk," and she laughed, and said that she liked the way it looked and sounded and that it would stay in the story. In later workshops, some participants who had told their stories in dialect chose to change dialect to Standard English; the choice was theirs. With one story, I had, during transcription, rearranged some story elements, in a reflex action, as I had done in countless student essays. And after some hesitation, a not-so-delighted author called me to the corner of the room and said matter-of-factly that she would write her story and organize it for textual production herself. I assured her the story was hers, and she quickly claimed ownership and responsibility. The author would not allow the appropriation of her text. She felt confident in writing it herself, and she felt safe in telling me that it was her story. I was the typist, not the self-appointed editor. I was learning that I did not need to remake everyone in "my image" and that in a true "safe house" the participants would not allow it.

The women had seen an opportunity to share their thoughts, and they knew that they must resist becoming writers in my "image," writers of "correct" thoughts. Starting our workshop with their ideas on childrearing, instead of mine or those in a text-book, had cracked a door in education-as-usual, one they refused to let slam shut.

At the next session, the not-so-delighted author entered the workroom lugging video equipment. Laughing, she said that she had decided to read her story on camera, so I could "understand" the order and words she had chosen. She told me she wanted me to "*see*" how she told stories. She instructed me to operate the camera. Indeed, when I saw her read her text, I understood her story—as she told it. At that point, I had to wrestle with my own need to shackle her paragraphs. As Pratt suggested, I was struggling with a desire to create a homogeneous, unified group who reflected my image of the world by tidying their stories so that they might ring "equally coherent, . . . and true for all . . ." (39). Living by Freire's words was going to be a constant personal battle, a constant reassessment of my own motives, my own shackles.

After that day, I videotaped all stories being read at now-weekly meetings. The women analyzed aspects of their storytelling: their delivery, expression, voice, gestures. Some women still wanted to tape-record their stories for transcription, but most now brought their own handwritten stories to share. Purses opened at the beginning of our sessions to reveal carefully folded, treasured stories, now unfolded to be read and shared in what was becoming a safe house, akin to what Anne Ruggles Gere described as a community of writers outside the academy in a world "constructed by desire, by the aspirations and imaginations of its participants" (80)—not by the single imagination of its facilitator.

As more stories surfaced, inhibitions and fears blocked some stories. Suzanne Britt states in "The First Person" that, frequently, "I-messages . . . [are] hardest for women. Women . . . [have been] raised to give in to you" (222). In our first encounter with pro-noun insecurity, I realized that Cora Davis[1] wanted to tell a story from her childhood in which she had witnessed African Americans being hosed by Whites in Mississippi. She was having trouble writing the story because of my presence in the group. Although I was sacrificing power in linguistic and pedagogical decisions, I was still a "you" to whom she had "been raised to give in." In her first drafts, White people were "they," and she and her family, the victims of this physical violence, were other people—they were "you." After I asked her many questions about the incident, she finally told the story and "named" (see Fine; Shuman) the individual participants by racial identity and personal name. We found that one's ability to use "I" is a critical signal about one's belief in one's right to tell a story, in one's perception of self in relation to others. Also, "I" became a critical factor to be examined, for I—Daphne—literally represented "you," as defined by Britt. However, I allowed myself to be named concretely and safely; I did not shut down because I was uncomfortable. Finally, the author wrote and read a powerful story which closed with her dream of racial harmony and mutual respect for all people; my job was to videotape it, not to tell it.

That particular day we not only dealt with pronouns and communication blocks, we also spent the first of many hours discussing racial problems, children of interracial marriages, and ways to deal with these issues in day care centers. That day we learned about the effects of racism on children from a woman who knew firsthand what those effects were; I could not have transmitted that knowledge to her from a textbook or from my life experience, nor did she need for me to do so. We learned from the participant's life, from her pain, and she received respect from the group for her wisdom, her hope, and her perseverance. We "clashed and grappled" that day, and "no one was excluded, and no one was safe" (Pratt 39). But as we painfully and tearfully listened, the walls of the safe house were being made stronger around us. Difference and power, masked and marked by pronouns, gave way to respect—respect for having lived and for persevering with dignity.

That day the safe house was strengthened not only by respect but also by hope, a renewed sense of hope to which our literacy celebrations would give witness. As a community of writers with many different stories to tell, the women decided to hold an old-fashioned storytelling event and share with families and friends their stories of pain and beauty, of living. The women met the day before the first literacy celebration and arranged the room in which the event was to be held. I stood back. Each participant invited guests, and, on a hot, June Sunday afternoon in Montgomery, more than one hundred persons from all walks of life—African Americans and Whites, males and females, adults and children, college professors and child care providers—attended a "Celebration of Reading and Writing," an event which highlighted the talents and work of the first group of participants. At this event the child care providers received corsages, certificates, and copies of children's stories which they had authored and which had now been illustrated by area junior high school students and local artists. Following the presentations, the participants decided to call the children from the audience to sit at their feet and listen to their stories; the group's now-finished quilt served as a backdrop.

One participant delighted us all when she described her uncle with whom she used to spend the summers. She said that her uncle didn't read books to her and her cousins; rather, on quiet summer evenings, *he read his mind to them.* She described an adult who was important to her: "He . . . was very tall, so pretty to me. He was so beautiful—like a cloud with long silver hair. He spoke with a *soft* voice, a very soft, sweet voice, and his stories would put us to sleep" (Bennett). Jeanetta Brooks told of growing up in rural Alabama with little money. As her life story unfolded, we all learned that she valued education and that her parents had instilled in her a sense of pride, a desire to read and write. With no money for "fancy pencils and paper," her mother had taught her children to write by using a cardboard box for a chalkboard and cooled charcoal for chalk (Brooks). And as the participants shared their stories, the children, dressed in their Sunday best, listened. After the stories were read, the guests and authors visited over punch and cake. Families and parents were proud that their mother, grandmother, or child care provider had preserved an important story and shared it so beautifully.

These same participants later spoke on a television program and to community groups regarding the effect of being heard by others—of realizing that their stories had value. These women had never been on a television program, yet they confidently discussed the pride they felt when their day care children and their own children and grandchildren saw them as authors. They talked about their self-esteem being enhanced through their writing. Speaking again to a group of more than one hundred persons in Selma, Alabama, they told their stories, fielded questions from the audience, and urged everyone there to read and write and be proud of their own stories. Each of the participants had been taught by her own family or loved ones that language is important; each had held onto this belief and seized this opportunity to test its truth.

Following that June Sunday afternoon, more child care providers attended the workshops. During the summer, I held the workshops at day care centers during nap time in order for all child care providers to participate. In the fall, I held a workshop series in Chilton County, Alabama. The participants of this group were African American and White females. Three of the participants of the original group enrolled again, and one participant, Ida Stewart, told me that she had a story that was troubling her and that she needed to write it.

Ida had recounted, with pain, humor, and grace, her own Alabama history in every story she wrote. In front of another packed house at our Chilton County "Celebration of Reading and Writing," she shared, however, her most poignant story, *Old Plowgirl*, the story which had been surfacing for months. She recalled:

> I didn't go to school much because we would have to stay out to get the plowing and planting done. When it was just about time for the bus to come along on the road that ran by our house, I'd go way down at the other end of the field from the road to do my plowing because I didn't want the other kids to see me. But my stepdaddy would usually holler at me to come back, so I'd have to come over. . . . Every day that bus would come along that road and there I'd be, plowing. The kids would holler out, "*There's Plowgirl!*" Oh, that would just *hit me*. It was so embarrassing that I could have just went into the ground.

Upon hearing this story of a poor child who was not allowed to go to school, many African American and White adults in the audience quietly cried. A small White child, who had been sitting on the floor at Ms. Stewart's feet, rose innocently and patted Ms. Stewart's shoulder; in front of the audience the little girl told her that she was sorry those people on the bus had been so mean to her. The words of Ms. Stewart and the child's response *hit* those of us listening with incredible force. Most of us at some time in our lives had been made fun of, but more importantly, many of us knew that we were guilty of insensitively hurling insults at those who were less fortunate, those whom we perceived as being different. Again, in Pratt's words, "no one was excluded, and no one was safe" (39). However, Ms. Stewart finally had felt safe enough—perhaps "healed" enough—to share her feelings with African Americans and Whites who had lived in the same area for many years (40).

At this celebration, the participants had once again taken full charge. They had decorated the building with their own handmade quilts from home, and they served the guests a special punch made from their own Chilton County peaches. During the reception, participants shared stories of the quilts and their recipes— their "vernacular art forms" of survival and life (Pratt 37).

We adapted one story into a play; again, on a Sunday afternoon, child care providers, parents, and their children performed together. Everyone had copies of the play to read and practice at the day care center and at home; everyone had met at my office to practice and make cardboard scenery. One father, who good-naturedly became an "actor," announced to the audience at the end of the play that he had never been in a play before; he then autographed programs to everyone's delight. Fifty-four adults and forty children eventually authored their own stories. Three day care centers received sets of stories, which their own teachers and children had authored, for their libraries. One participant stated that she believed that true stories might help mothers and fathers be better parents and that she had found love and concern for others through the program. Another participant shared that she had made new friends and that her self-esteem had been improved, for she was perceived by her family and friends as an author who had something valuable to say. By sharing their drafts with family and friends, the writers clearly constructed "their interpretation[s] of past events from the vantage point of a particular present . . . [creating a life story which then became] a dialogical account of . . . . . [their] experience[s] rather than a chronological report of verifiable events" (Soliday 514).

Carol Burton, a day care director quoted in a local newspaper article, stated now that when the children in her day care center went to the library, they selected books and immediately read the title page to find the name of the author and illustrator: "They look at these things because they can relate to these people. They've done it themselves" (qtd. in Kuper 18). One day, while working with children whose child care providers had participated earlier in the program, I read a book by Faith Ringgold to the six- and seven-year-olds in the day care center; their child care provider sat with me. At the end of the book, I showed Ringgold's picture and read some information about the author. A young boy looked at his child care provider, and said, "Oh, *she's* an author just like you are." He then explained to me that his child care providers frequently read books which they had authored previously in the program. The day care provider beamed, and so did the child. He knew an author, and becoming an author of one's thoughts was perceived as an obtainable and desirable goal. The author had transmitted pride in authoring to a child, and she had proven that her thoughts were valuable and could safely make their way to the printed page.

When initiating The Joy of Telling Stories to Children, I was free to grow a reading and writing project which would respect the language and thoughts of the participants. By starting with *their* knowledge about child-rearing practices and stories, instead of my own, I took a risk, uncomfortable at times, and sacrificed the creation of an educational setting of my own making. Paulo Freire states that many professionals believe that it is

> absurd to consider the necessity of respecting the "view of the world" held by the people. The professionals are the ones with a "world view." They regard as equally absurd the affirmation that one must necessarily consult the people when organizing the program content of educational action. They feel that the ignorance of the people is so complete that they are unfit for anything except to receive the teachings of the professionals. (137)

Indeed, initially some people had questioned my pedagogical decisions. However, the participants confirmed, as had my students in Hawaii, that "story-telling [is] . . . a legitimate mode of knowing" (Knoblauch and Brannon 22). They proved that "one story does not falsify another. It is instead dialogical: stories beget stories; voices mingle and interanimate" (26).

The pedagogical arts of this contact zone focused on exercises in storytelling and personal histories—on "the redemption of the oral" (Pratt 40). We created a safe house where the stories could be heard and written, and then we created public arenas for their performance, interpretation, and critique. In our safe house, we redistributed power, and we redefined roles, creating "ways for people to engage with suppressed aspects of history (including their own histories), ways to move *into and out of* rhetorics of authenticity; ground rules for communication across lines of difference and hierarchy that . . . [went] beyond politeness but maintain[ed] mutual respect" (40). We respected, included, and examined "vernacular art forms."

In our contact zone, the stories conveyed the suffering and reality of those who had experienced prejudice, poverty, and injustice. The stories also conveyed the remembered wisdom of a grandfather, the unconditional love of a parent, and the humor necessary for human survival. The storytellers shared wisdom, learned in sometimes harsh circumstances: Be fair, be just, be kind, and believe in oneself and others. Persevere with dignity. And it was the *dignity* in the storytellers' faces that one saw at the workshops, at literacy celebrations, on television; that is what the women wanted me to see—their dignity. They wanted me to respect them.

This house-building left me humbled. The first group of participants gave me a plaque, which now hangs over my computer. Its message directs each new syllabus and writing assignment that I create, for the women taught me that my syllabi and my assignments must be flexible. My assignments must be designed to allow one's dignity to be seen. Their engraved message thanked me for "sacrificing enough to allow others to grow." These telling words jar me every day of my life, reminding me of my many challenges as a teacher: What did I sacrifice in Alabama? My assumed power, my self-righteousness, my insensitivity, my claim to knowledge, my time? These women, whom I consider to be my fellow teachers of life and language, showed me that no one "lost" when I made these sacrifices. I believe we all won. But now, when I meet my college classes, what must I *sacrifice*?

As opposed to some loud cultural clashes which rumble and ignite and over which few voices are heard, this dialogical sharing steadily and powerfully illuminated *our* self-respect, *our* understanding, and *our* precious stories with which we filled *our* house. The house was safe and tolerant enough for all voices to be heard. By contrast, the voices on the bus, engrained in Ms. Stewart's memory, were harsh, but during her recounting, we saw and heard her determination to overcome them; I saw and heard haunting reflections and echoes of myself. Alma Bennett had taught us earlier that it is "soft, sweet" voices which we wish to recall, which foster that which is good in all of us. Indeed, we recall many voices, and they all "mingle." But they have the power to make us stronger and wiser if we provide a safe house in which they can be heard, discussed, and respected—a house which honors human dignity.

Reflections

Paul Jude Beauvais, Patricia Bizzell, Katherine Gottschalk, Thomas Philion, and I have described institutional spaces in which we work or have worked. As I read and reread these essays, I realized that while I have never met these authors in person, I now have insights into their struggles and their hopes for voices to be heard and not silenced inadvertently in the institutional contexts in which we work and wield power. Also, I am struck by the many spaces where contact zone theory informs our thinking, our practices. But we have been privy to contact zone theory, a framework that allows us to ponder multiculturalism and diversity in educational settings in new ways. Our essays focus on the following institutional spaces: the first-year composition class and the college campus as a larger zone worthy of exploration as first-year students make their way into a new world of language and customs; curriculum within higher education and perhaps in K–12 schools; university writing programs; secondary schools in urban settings; and community literacy projects.

In each of these essays, voices emerge within the institutional contexts that are each situated in a larger place, shaped by history and constantly reshaped by the unique personalities we have introduced in our texts. Most of us chose to introduce real people who inhabit these spaces; most of us chose to deal with our limitations and struggles as facilitators in these spaces. I think we are all trying to give our students "space" to be respected, to be heard; however, as Beauvais, Gottschalk, Philion, and I noted, negotiating respectful discourse is not easy for our students or for us. We are quite human, and I think our texts reveal our desires to be good teachers, but also our own needs and weaknesses. Airing them is the first step toward ensuring that the spaces are safe spaces where all can be heard, and this is our challenge.

Immediately after reading these essays, I received correspondence from an elementary teacher who has stopped teaching. She is frustrated and angry. A seasoned teacher, she had an idea for an inner-city school program. She quit after one year; she felt paralyzed and could not teach. I have been introducing her to contact zone theory, but I wish she had been better prepared for the implications of a contact zone before entering it. She is now "clashing and grappling" with herself, her frustrations, her feelings of not being able to teach in a diverse setting (Pratt 34). As I work with her and think about my own teaching life (preschool, elementary, middle, high school, community college, and university), I realize that I have been privy not only to theory and research that helped me teach and navigate in potentially volatile contact zones but also to real experiences in these zones.

Perhaps we should make an effort to educate the teachers of young children about the realities of spaces that are not always homogenous, that are "contexts of highly asymmetrical relations of power" (Pratt 34). Perhaps then our job at the secondary and postsecondary levels would not be as overwhelming. Since I am currently working with future teachers and supervising student teachers, I feel an obligation to expose them to contact zone theory and diverse teaching experiences; I think Philion is on the right track and has written an essay that provides a door for practicing the arts of the contact zone even prior to entering the world of college. But as he poignantly notes, his future teachers must be able to navigate in the zone and facilitate the discourse. Interestingly, the voices of elementary and middle school teachers are omitted in our section, "Spaces." However, there can be no gaps in our dialogue if we are to ensure that all students are heard and respected. Those facilitating the important work in these varied spaces are critical to each human being's having a chance to reach his or her potential in a wonderfully diverse world.

Note

1. Participants' names and quotations from their stories are used with their permission.

Works Cited

Atwell, Nancie. *In the Middle*. Portsmouth, NH: Heinemann, 1987.

Bennett, Alma. *The Joy of Visiting the Country Every Summer with My Sisters*. Montgomery, AL: Family Guidance Center, 1993.

Bridwell-Bowles, Lillian. "Discourse and Diversity: Experimental Writing within the Academy." *College Composition and Communication* 43.3 (1992): 349–68.

Britt, Suzanne. "The First Person." *The Bedford Guide for College Writers: With Readings and Handbook*. 2nd ed. Ed. X. J. Kennedy and Dorothy M. Kennedy. Boston: Bedford, 1990. 221–22. Originally published in *Show & Tell* by Suzanne Britt. Raleigh, NC: Morning Owl, 1983.

Brooks, Jeanetta. *The Brown Paper Bag*. Montgomery, AL: Family Guidance Center, 1993.

Fine, Michelle. *Disruptive Voices: The Possibilities of Feminist Research*. Ann Arbor: U of Michigan P, 1992.

Freire, Paulo. *Pedagogy of the Oppressed*. New York: Continuum, 1993.

Gere, Anne Ruggles. "Kitchen Tables and Rented Rooms: The Extracurriculum of Composition." *College Composition and Communication* 45.1 (1994): 75–92.

Key, Daphne. *Literacy Shutdown: Stories of Six American Women*. Newark, DE, and Chicago: International Reading Association and National Reading Conference, 1998.

Knoblauch, C. H., and Lil Brannon. "Knowing Our Knowledge—A Phenomenological Basis for Teacher Research." *Audits of Mean-*

ing: A Festschrift in Honor of Ann E. Berthoff. Ed. Louise Z. Smith. Portsmouth, NH: Boynton/Cook, 1988. 17–28.

Kuper, Angela. "Family Guidance Center, Mother's Image Day-Care Publish Books." *East Montgomery Weekly* 26 Aug. 1993: 18.

Ogbu, John. "Cultural Diversity and School Experience." *Literacy as Praxis: Culture, Language, and Pedagogy.* Ed. Catherine E. Walsh. Norwood, NJ: Ablex, 1991. 25–50.

Pratt, Mary Louise. "Arts of the Contact Zone." *Profession 91.* New York: MLA, 1991. 33–40. (Originally presented as the keynote address at MLA's Responsibilities for Literacy conference in September 1990 in Pittsburgh.)

Shuman, Amy. *Storytelling Rights: The Uses of Oral and Written Texts by Urban Adolescents.* New York: Cambridge UP, 1986.

Soliday, Mary. "Translating Self and Difference Through Literacy Narratives." *College English* 56.5 (1994): 511–23.

Spellmeyer, Kurt. "'Too Little Care': Language, Politics, and Embodiment in the Life-World." *College English* 55.3 (1993): 265–83.

Stewart, Ida. *Old Plowgirl.* Montgomery, AL: Family Guidance Center, 1993.

II

CLASHES AND CONFLICTS

Fault Lines in the Contact Zone

RICHARD E. MILLER
Rutgers University

O n the cover of what has turned out to be the final issue of
Focus, a magazine "for and about the people of AT&T,"
there's a tableau of five happy employees, arranged so that their
smiling faces provide an ethnically diverse frame for a poster
bearing the slogan, "TRUE VOICE." Although the cover promotes the image of a harmonious, multicultural working environment, one gets a slightly different image of the company in
the "Fun 'n' Games" section at the back of the magazine. In the
lower right-hand corner of this section, beneath a quiz about
AT&T's international reach, there is a drawing of a globe with
people speaking avidly into telephones all over the world: there's
a woman in a babushka in Eastern Europe; there's a man with a
moustache wearing a beret in France; and, following this theme
and the telephone lines south, there is a gorilla in Africa holding
a telephone (50). A gorilla?

Although Bob Allen, AT&T's CEO, has acknowledged in a
letter to all AT&T employees that this was "a deplorable mistake on the part of a company with a long, distinguished record
of supporting the African-American community," he has so far
met with little success in his attempts to manage the crisis caused
by the distribution of this illustration to literally hundreds of thou-
sands of AT&T employees worldwide. First, the art director who
approved the cartoon and the illustrator who drew it were dismissed;
commitments were made to hire more minority artists, illustra-
tors, and photographers; a hotline was opened up for expressing

This essay was originally published in *College English* 56.4 (1994): 389–409.
Used with permission.

grievances and making suggestions; AT&T's Diversity Team was instructed to make recommendations "for immediate and long-term improvement"; and, as a cathartic gesture, employees were encouraged to "tear that page out and throw it in the trash where it belongs," since they wouldn't want "AT&T material circulating that violates our values"(Allen). Then, when the hotline overheated and the battle raging across the company's electronic bulletin board continued unabated, Allen pulled the plug on the entire *Focus* venture and assigned all its employees to other posts. This is certainly one strategy for handling offensive material: declare solidarity with those who have been offended (Allen's letter is addressed "To all AT&T people"); voice outrage (it was "a deplorable mistake"); shut down avenues for expressing such thoughts (fire or reassign employees, dismantle the magazine). While this approach undoubtedly paves the way for restoring the appearance of corporate harmony, does it have any pedagogical value? That is, does the expulsion of offending individuals and the restriction of lines of communication address the roots of the racist feelings that produced the image of the gorilla as the representative image of the African? Or does it merely seek to insure that the "deplorable mistake" of having such an image surface in a public document doesn't occur again?

"What is the place of unsolicited oppositional discourse, parody, resistance, critique in the imagined classroom community?" Mary Louise Pratt asks in "Arts of the Contact Zone" (39). In Pratt's essay, this question is occasioned not by an event as troubling as the cartoon discussed above, but by the fact that Pratt's son, Manuel, received "the usual star" from his teacher for writing a paragraph promoting a vaccine that would make school attendance unnecessary. Manuel's teacher, ignoring the critique of schooling leveled in the paragraph, registered only that the required work of responding to the assignment's questions about a helpful invention had been completed and, consequently, appended the silent, enigmatic star. For Pratt, the teacher's star labors to conceal a conflict in the classroom over what work is to be valued and why, presenting instead the image that everything is under control—students are writing and the teacher is evaluating. It is this other strategy for handling difficult material, namely ignoring the content and focusing only on the outward forms of obedient behavior, that leads Pratt to wonder about the place of unsolicited oppositional discourse in the classroom. With regard to Manuel's real classroom community, the answer to this question is clear: the place of unsolicited oppositional discourse is no place at all.

Given Pratt's promising suggestion that the classroom be re-conceived as a "contact zone," which she defines as a social space "where cultures meet, clash, and grapple with each other, often in contexts of highly asymmetrical relations of power" (34), this example of the kind of writing produced in such a contact zone seems oddly benign. One might expect that the writing Pratt's students did in Stanford's Culture, Ideas, Values course, which she goes on to discuss, would provide ample evidence of more highly charged conflicts involving "unsolicited oppositional dis-course, parody, resistance, critique." Unfortunately, however, al-though Pratt avows that this course "put ideas and identities on the line" (39), she offers no example of how her students negoti-ated this struggle in their writing or of how their teachers partici-pated in and responded to their struggles on and over "the line." Instead, Pratt leaves us with just two images of writers in the contact zone—her son, Manuel, and Guaman Poma, author of a largely unread sixteenth-century bilingual chronicle of Andean culture. Both, to be sure, are readily sympathetic figures, obvi-ously deserving better readers and more thoughtful respondents, but what about the illustrator who provided what might be con-sidered an unsolicited parody or critique of AT&T's "Common Bond values," which state that "we treat each other with respect and dignity, valuing individual and cultural differences"? What "Arts of the Contact Zone" are going to help us learn how to read and respond to voices such as this? And what exactly are we to say or do when the kind of racist, sexist, and homophobic sentiments now signified by the term "hate speech" surface in our classrooms?

In focusing on a student essay that, like the *Focus* cartoon, is much less likely to arouse our sympathies than Manuel's inven-tive critique, my concern is to examine the heuristic value of the notion of the contact zone when applied not only to student writ-ing, but also to our own academic discussions of that writing. The student essay I begin with was so offensive that when it was first mentioned at an MLA workshop titled Composition, Multiculturalism, and Political Correctness in December 1991, provisions were quickly made to devote an entire panel to the essay at the 1992 Conference on College Composition and Communication Convention, and this, in turn, led to a follow-up workshop titled The Politics of Response at CCCC in 1993. Thus, I would hazard a guess that this student essay, entitled "Queers, Bums, and Magic," has seized the attention of more teachers, taken up more institutional time, and provoked more debate than any other single piece of unpublished undergraduate writing in recent memory. Before beginning my discussion of "Queers, Bums, and Magic," I should note, however, that in what follows I have intentionally allowed the content of the student's essay and the wider sweep of its context to emerge in fragments, as they did in the contact zone of the national conferences, where competing modes of response served alternately to reveal and obscure both the text and information about its writer. This partial, hesitant, contradictory motion defines how business gets transacted in the contact zones of our classrooms and our conferences, where important questions often don't get heard, are ignored, or simply don't get posed in the heat of the moment, with the result that vital contextual information often is either never disclosed or comes to light very late in the discussion. I believe that following this motion provides a stark portrait of the ways in which dominant assumptions about students and student writing allow unsolicited oppositional discourse to pass through the classroom unread and unaffected.

"Queers, Bums, and Magic," was written in a pre-college-level community college composition class taught by Scott Lankford at Foothill College in Los Altos Hills, California, in response to an assignment taken from *The Bedford Guide for College Writers* that asked students to write a report on group behavior. One of Lankford's students responded with an essay detailing a drunken trip he and some friends made to "San Fagcisco" to study "the lowest class . . . the queers and the bums." The essay recounts how the students stopped a man on Polk Street, informed him that they were doing a survey and needed to know if he was "a fag." From here, the narrative follows the students into a dark alleyway where they discover, as they relieve themselves drunkenly against the wall, that they have been urinating on a homeless person. In a frenzy, the students begin to kick the homeless person, stopping after "30 seconds of non-stop blows to the body," at which point the writer says he "thought the guy was dead." Terrified, the students make a run for their car and eventually escape the city.

It's a haunting piece, one that gave Lankford many sleepless nights and one that has traveled from conference to conference because it is so unsettling. When Lankford discussed it at CCCC in his paper entitled "How Would You Grade a Gay-Bashing?" the engaged, provocative, and at times heated hour-long discussion that followed provided a forum for a range of competing commitments to, as Pratt might say, "meet, clash, and grapple" with one another. What was clear from this interchange was that part of what makes "Queers, Bums, and Magic" so powerful is that it disables the most familiar kinds of conference presentations and teacher responses. Here is writing that cannot easily be recuperated as somehow praiseworthy despite its numerous surface flaws, writing that instead offers direct access to a voice from the margins that seems to belong there. The reactions given to Lankford's request to know how those present "would have handled such a situation" (5) varied considerably, both in intensity and in detail, but most of them, I would say, fell into one of three categories: read the essay as factual and respond accordingly; read the essay as fictional and respond accordingly; momentarily suspend the question of the essay's factual or fictional status and respond accordingly.

In the first category, by far the most popular, I place all suggestions that the student be removed from the classroom and turned over either to a professional counselor or to the police. Such a response, audience members argued repeatedly, would be automatic if the student had described suicidal tendencies, involvement in a rape, or having been the victim of incest. To substantiate this point, one member of the audience spoke passionately about Marc LeClerc, saying that the Canadian gunman had revealed his hatred of women to many of his college professors prior to his murderous rampage. As compelling as such examples seem, it is important to realize that this line of argumentation assumes that the essay records a set of criminal events that actually occurred or, at the very least, evidences the fantasy life of a potentially dangerous person. This assessment of the student essay is striking because the audience members had little to go on beyond the kind of brief outline that has been provided here. In other words, although no one in the audience had actually read the student essay, many felt quite confident recommending that, based on brief excerpts and a summary of the essay's content alone, the student ought to be turned over to either the legal or the psychological authorities! These respondents, starting with the assumption of a stable and unified subjectivity for Lankford's student, went on to construct a student writer incapable of dissimulation. Within such a paradigm, the actual text the student produced was of secondary importance at best in relation to a hasty and, as we will see, partial summary of the text's contents.

Lankford chose another route entirely, electing "to respond to the essay exactly as if it were a fictional short story" (4). What this meant in practice was that he restricted himself to commenting on the student's word choice, querying the student about his imagined audience, acknowledging the text's "reasonable detail," and "favorably comparing the essay to A Clockwork Orange in its straightforward depictions of nightmarish 'megaviolence' and surrealistic detail" (4). According to these criteria, Lankford determined that the essay merited a low B. Although this strategy provoked the wrath of a large portion of the audience, Lankford argued that it was not without its virtues: by focusing only on the formal features of the essay and its surface errors, Lankford was able to successfully deflect the student writer's use of his writing to "bash" his professor, with the unexpected result that the student not only stayed in the course, but actually chose to study with Lankford again the next semester. Thus, despite Lankford's own assessment of his approach as "spineless," he was in a position to insist that it was nevertheless a "qualified success," since the student in question "learned to cope with an openly gay instructor with some measure of civility" (5).

Among those present who had access to the student's paper, there were those on the panel who agreed with Lankford's approach but disagreed with the grade assigned. These respondents spoke of the essay's faulty organization, the problems evident in its plot development, the number of mechanical errors. On these grounds alone, one panelist assured the audience, the paper ought to have received a failing mark. If the first category of response displays a curious willingness to dispense with the formality of reading the student's essay, Lankford's strategy asks teachers to look away from what the student's writing is attempting to do— at the havoc it is trying to wreak in the contact zone—and restrict their comments to the essay's surface features and formal qualities, affixing the "usual star" or downgrading as the situation warrants. Such a strategy itself invites parody: would changing the word choice/spelling errors/verb agreement problems/ organization really "improve" this student's essay? Would such changes help inch it towards being, say, an excellent gay-bashing essay, one worthy of an A?

I intend this question to be deliberately troubling and offensive. The problem, however, is not that this approach is "spineless." To the contrary, in Lankford's hands, this kind of response made it possible for both the teacher and the student to remain in the contact zone of his classroom, allowing them to negotiate the difficult business of working with and through important issues of cultural and sexual difference. By suggesting that his difficulty in responding to the student essay is a personal problem, that it revolves around a question of "spine," Lankford obscures the ways in which the difficulty that confronted him as he struggled to find a way to respond to "Queers, Bums, and Magic" is the trace of a broader institutional conflict over what it means for a teacher to work on and with student writing. Lankford and the others who spoke of responding to the essay as "a piece of fiction" did not suddenly invent this curiously decontextualized way of responding to writing, this way that can imagine no other approach to discussing a piece of writing than to speak of how it is organized, the aptness of the writer's word choice, and the fit between the text and its audience. Such an approach to writing instruction has been proffered in the majority of grammars, rhetorics, and readers that have filled English classrooms since before the turn of the century: it has been around for so long that, despite the grand "turn to process" in writing instruction, it continues to suggest itself as the most "natural" or "reasonable" way to define the work of responding to student writing. All of which leaves us with this profoundly strange state of affairs where the discipline explicitly devoted to studying and articulating the power of the written word gets thrown into crisis when a student produces a powerful piece of writing.

To sum up, then, these two lines of response to the student essay—one recommending the removal of the offending writer from circulation and the other overlooking the offensive aspects of the student text in order to attend to its surface and structural features—taken together dramatize how little professional training in English Studies prepares teachers to read and respond to the kinds of parodic, critical, oppositional, dismissive, resistant, transgressive, and regressive writing that gets produced by students writing in the contact zone of the classroom. This absence of training, I would argue, actually comes into play every time a teacher sits down to comment on a student paper: it's just that the pedagogical shortcomings of restricting such commentary to the surface features and formal aspects of the writing aren't as readily visible in a response to an essay on a summer vacation as they are in a response to an essay about beating up a homeless person. Unfortunately, recent efforts to reimagine the work of responding to student writing provide little guidance for addressing this particular problem. Edward White's *Teaching and Assessing Writing*, for instance, argues for holistic scoring, but offers no suggestions on how to go about holistically scoring essays that are racist, homophobic, misogynistic. And, similarly, NCTE's *Writing and Response: Theory, Practice, and Research*, which asserts that "real, substantive response is in one form or another fundamental to language development" (Anson 4), never gets around to the business of discussing how to produce a "real, substantive response" to the kind of unsolicited oppositional discourse discussed here. Since this is uncharted territory, it is not surprising that we often find ourselves at a loss, not knowing what to do, where to go, or what to say once we cross this line.

One has to wonder why it is that, at a time when almost all of the current major theories on the rise celebrate partial readings, multiple subjectivities, marginalized positions, and subjugated knowledges, nearly all student essays remain essentially illegible, offered forth more often than not as the space where error exercises its full reign, or, as here, the site where some untutored evil shows its face. There seems, in other words, to be little evidence of what one might call "poststructural" or "postcolonial" trickledown, little sign that the theoretical insights that carry so much weight in our journals actually make themselves known in the pedagogical practices deployed in classrooms across the country. There were, however, a few respondents to Lankford's presentation who saw a way to smuggle some of these insights into the classroom and thereby propose more fruitful responses than either expelling the student or ignoring the content of his essay. In proposing that "Queers, Bums, and Magic" be reproduced alongside legal definitions of hate speech for the entire class to read and discuss, one panelist found a way to pull the paper out of the private corridor running between the student writer and the teacher and move it into the public arena. This approach turns the essay into a "teachable object," enabling an investigation of the writing's performative aspect—how it does its work, what its imagined project might have been, and who or what might be the possible subjects of its critique. By situating the essay in relation to legal definitions of hate speech, this approach also puts the class in a position to consider both how words can work in the world and how and why that work has been regulated.

The prospect of having such a discussion would, no doubt, frighten some, since it would promise to be an explosive, tense, disturbing interchange. Some students would undoubtedly agree with the treatment meted out to the disenfranchised; others might speak of it as being funny; others might point to the references to "Elm Street," "nightmares," and "magic" in the essay to argue that it was a piece of fiction; and still others might be horrified by the essay and express their feelings to the class. Such a discussion would, in other words, place one squarely in the act of teaching in the contact zone where, as Pratt says, "No one [is] excluded, and no one [is] safe" (39). The point of having such discussions, however, is neither to establish a community where a simple pluralism rules and hate speech is just one of its many voices, nor to create an environment that is relentlessly threatening, where not feeling safe comes to mean the same thing as feeling terrified.

Pratt, in fact, is careful to maintain the importance of establishing "safe houses" in the curriculum, courses where a different kind of talk is supported and sustained. But for those courses that take as their subject how language works in the world, the central concern should be to provide students with moments taken from their own writing as well as from the writing collected in published texts where the written word is powerful. In such classrooms, "teaching the conflicts" is not simply an empty slogan plastered over a practice that means "business as usual," but an actual set of practices whereby the conflicts that capture and construct both the students and their teachers become the proper subject of study for the course.

This third category of response argues for the necessity of seeing the way we structure our courses and the kinds of texts we read with our students as potential resources for commenting on the writing our students produce. Thinking along these lines, another member of the audience suggested that the best way to respond to this essay was with a revisionary assignment, where the student would be required to rewrite the story from the perspective either of the gay man whom the students had harassed on Polk Street or from the perspective of the homeless person whom the students had beaten in the alleyway. This strategy of having the student do some more writing about this event seems particularly appropriate in a discipline that believes in the heuristic power of the composing process, and the further requirement to have the student shift perspective provides a meaningful avenue for reseeing the described events. As useful as I believe it is to see the assignment of revision as a way of responding to student writing, though, I think the response called for in this instance is so obvious that it is most likely to solicit a seamless parody, one of those acts of hyperconformity regularly produced by those writing in the contact zone. In other words, while producing a writing situation where the student is advised to mime the teacher's desired position would probably succeed in sweeping the most visible manifestations of the student's hateful thoughts and actions out of the classroom, it would not, I think, actually address the roots of that hatred. That hatred would simply curl up and go underground for the duration of the course.

At this point, it may seem that in assessing the range of reactions to "Queers, Bums, and Magic" I am holding out for some magical form of response that would not only make this student stop writing such things, but would actually put an end to his thinking them as well. My central concern, however, is not with this particular student essay or with what the student writer, as an individual, thinks, but with what this student essay and the professional activity that surrounds it can tell us about the cultural, political, and pedagogical complexities of composition instruction. With this distinction in mind, I would go so far as to argue that adopting any classroom strategy that isolates this essay and treats it as an anomaly misreads both the essay's cultural significance and its pedagogical possibilities. As the recent debate over military service has made abundantly clear, Lankford's student has not expressed some unique and private hatred of gays, nor, to be sure, has he voiced some peculiar antipathy for homeless persons. Rather, the homophobia this student articulates and the violence he describes himself as perpetrating against the disenfranchised are cultural commonplaces. For these reasons, it seems much more important to me to produce a classroom where part of the work involves articulating, investigating, and questioning the affiliated cultural forces that underwrite the ways of thinking that find expression in this student's essay—a classroom, in short, that studies the forces that make such thoughts not only permissible but prevalent.

From this perspective, one could say that the only truly surprising thing about "Queers, Bums, and Magic" is that it voices this particular set of cultural commonplaces in the classroom, since most students practiced in the conventions of reading teacher expectations know not to commit themselves to positions their teachers clearly oppose. In this regard, the following facts are not insignificant: the student writer grew up in Kuwait; English is his second language; he was writing during the onset of the Persian Gulf War. An outsider himself, Lankford's student almost certainly did not understand what was intended by the examples that accompanied the assignment in the *Bedford Guide* to do the following: "Station yourself in a nearby place where you can mingle with a group of people gathered for some reason or occasion. Observe the group's behavior and in a short paper report on it. Then offer some insight" (41). Following these instructions, the student is informed that one writer "did an outstanding job of observing a group of people nervously awaiting a road test for their driver's licenses"; another observed a bar mitzvah; another an emergency room; and another a group of people looking at a luna moth on a telephone pole "(including a man who viewed it with alarm, a wondering toddler, and an amateur entomologist)" (42). Unschooled in the arts of reading the U.S. textbook, this student failed to pick up on the implicit directions: when you write this essay, report only on a group from which you are safely detached and on behavior unlikely to disturb others. Had the student been able to read the cues in the suggested examples, he might well have selected a less explosive topic and thereby kept his most familiar ways of knowing the world out of view.

If the examples direct students to topics guaranteed not to provoke offense, the assignment, by refraining from using any kind of critical terminology, further guarantees that the students will not wander beyond the business of reporting their immediate experience. In lieu of inviting students to work with any of the central terms taken from anthropology, sociology, or cultural studies, say, the assignment merely informs the students that, after observing the behavior of their selected group, they are "to form some general impression of the group or come to some realization about it" (42). They can expect, the assignment concludes, that it will take at least two written pages "to cover" their subject. Grasping the import of these directives, Lankford's student did even more than was required, performing the kind of hyperconformity that, as I suggested earlier, characterizes one of the arts of the contact zone: he wrote, as required, for his "fellow students" (41); he handed in not two, but four typed pages; and he made sure his essay concluded with "some insight." His final paragraph reads as follows:

> Although this night was supposed to be an observation on the people of the streets, it turned out that we were walking on "Elm Street," and it was a "nightmare." I will always remember one thing, next time I see bums and fags walking on the streets, I will

never make fun of them or piss on them, or anything like that, because they did not want to be bums or fags. It was society that forced them out of their jobs and they could not beat the system. Now when I think about that bum we beat up I can't understand how he managed to follow us the whole time, after being kicked and being down for so long. I think it was one of two things; he is either psychic or it was just plain magic.

In miming the requisite better understanding that is supposed to come from studying groups, the student's essay concludes by disrupting all that has come before: did the beating actually take place or has the writer simply fabricated it, recasting the assignment within the readily available narrative frame of the movie *A Nightmare on Elm Street*? Is the student having one over on the system, manufacturing both the material for his response and his consequent realization, and thus, in one fell swoop, parodying, resisting, and critiquing the values that hold the classroom community together? Or, and this is obviously the more frightening possibility, is his conclusion some kind of penitential confession for events that really did happen?

These questions, slightly rephrased, are of central importance to any writing classroom: How does a writer establish authority? How does one distinguish between fact and fiction in a written document? What does it mean to read and to write dialogically? And yet, it is important to realize that, had the assignment worked as it was supposed to, these questions would never have surfaced with the urgency they have here. That is, had Lankford's student been a better reader of classroom norms and textbook procedures, he might well have written about beekeepers or people at hair salons and left the surface calm of the educational community undisturbed. If we step back from "Queers, Bums, and Magic" for a moment and consider the fact that the mixture of anger, rage, ignorance, and confusion that produced this student essay is present in varying degrees on college campuses across the country, what is truly significant about this event is not that it occurred, but that it occurs so rarely. This, surely, is a testament to the immense pressures exerted by the classroom environment, the presentation of the assigned readings, the directions included in the writing assignments, and the range of teaching practices which work together to ensure that conflicts about or contact between fundamental beliefs and prejudices do not arise. The classroom does not, in other words, automatically function as a contact zone in the positive ways Pratt discovered in the Stanford course, where, she asserts, "along with rage, incomprehension, and pain there were exhilarating moments of wonder and revelation, mutual understanding, and new wisdom—the joys of the contact zone" (39). As the conclusion of Pratt's article makes clear, and the foregoing discussion of "Queers, Bums, and Magic" vividly illustrates, there is still a great deal of work to be done in constructing the "pedagogical arts of the contact zone." Thus, in setting aside the important but what is for us irresolvable question of whether or not "Queers, Bums, and Magic" is a factual or fictional account, I would like in the remainder of this essay to discuss my own efforts to reconfigure the power relations in my classroom so that more contact between the competing interpretive systems of the classroom and the worlds outside the classroom might occur and become available for discussion.

There is a paradox, of course, in trying to establish a classroom that solicits "unsolicited oppositional discourse." There is, also, an attendant danger of a kind of "intellectual slumming," where investigating the disjunction between the ways of knowing fostered inside and outside the classroom might inevitably result in students deeming the former kind of knowledge "artificial" and the latter "authentic." Rather than perish in the abyss created by this killer dichotomy or put myself in the pedagogically questionable position of inviting my students to vent their feelings on the page for us to discuss afterwards, I have tried to develop a pedagogical practice that allows the classroom to function as a contact zone where the central activity is investigating the range of literate practices available to those within asymmetrical power relationships. My primary concern as a composition instructor, in other words, is with the kinds of issues raised in Pratt's article and Lankford's student's essay insofar as they shape the ways of reading and writing that occur inside and outside the classroom and our ways of talking about that reading and writing. Given the heightened racial tensions following the Rodney King beating, the ongoing fear and ignorance about AIDS and the means of its transmission, the backlash against feminism, and a climate of rising unemployment and violence, it has not been difficult to find material around my campus that meets these requirements.

Most recently, for example, I have become interested in a battle being waged at my campus along what I have come to call the "textual corridors"—the walkways to and from the main libraries, the mailboxes and newspaper dispensers, the bus stops and lamp posts. In these spaces, all well away from the classrooms, one or more students or perhaps competing groups of students have been carrying out a heated, accusatory, and highly coded discussion about rape, feminism, and sexual politics. Early in the semester, the following poster affixed to the lid of a garbage can caught my attention:

> DON'T MAKE
> YOUR
> MOTHER
> HAVE TO TELL
> HER FRIENDS
> THAT YOU'RE
> A
> RAPIST

Copies of this poster stayed up for a couple of days before being ripped down or papered over with campaign flyers for the upcoming student elections. Then, a few weeks later, the following poster appeared:

> WHO aRE ~~you? Go~~
> TRA~~de your~~ MoPs
> ~~for a~~ BIT ~~of~~ CHange.
> ~~Be a w~~HOLE ~~woman~~
> ~~becau~~Se LIT~~tle else~~
> ~~Will ev~~EN CHange.
> DefY, Kill, Even
> TrEAt SomE as
> DOGS.
> RevolUtioN
> RevolUtioN

While I found the rhetorical tactic of the first poster fairly straightforward, this one stumped me: I simply could not figure out how to read it or what it might be saying. Was it written by the same person or group of people who had distributed the first poster? Or was it written in response to the first poster, demanding to know who was making such anonymous accusations? What sense was to be made of the play between the text under erasure and the subtext placed in the foreground? And, how, finally, was one to read the question in much smaller type at the bottom of the poster: "what are you, a feminist?"

My inability to decode the interaction between these posters ceased to be a simple matter of curiosity for me that weekend, when I read in the local paper that one of our students had been abducted and raped on her way home from a party. Because I found this event so upsetting and felt that it, in some way, was connected to the posters, I brought the broadsides into my composition classroom as texts to be read. We had just finished working through what Pratt might mean when she defines autoethnographic texts as "heterogenous on the reception end as well as the production end" (36–37) and I felt that discussing these two posters might bring this definition to life. Here was writing from the contact zone that was simultaneously oppositional, parodic, resistant, and critical: How, I asked, were we to read it? One student described the first poster as "sneaky": instead of just coming out and saying that rape was wrong, it asked a rhetorical question. When I asked her to turn that rhetorical question into a statement, she replied: "It says, 'We know who you are and we're going to catch you,' but it says it in a way that makes you stop and think. It's like a threat, almost." While the students had up to this point expressed a healthy suspicion of "hidden meanings" in general and had specifically criticized Pratt for "reading too much into" the writings of her son and Guaman Poma, they found little to object to in this assessment of the first poster's strategy and its "message." And although there was some disagreement about whether the "you" in the poster signified all men or just those men who were or had the potential to be rapists—about whether the poster was produced by "one of those male-bashing feminists" or by a "politically committed artist" trying to make a better world—the students were united in condemning the act of rape. Given the combination of the context and the location of this discussion and the spell cast by the rhetorical structure of the first poster, it is hard to see how they could have said anything else.

The second poster problematizes the dependable uniformity of this response, however, since, to a certain way of reading, it seemed to make an open call for violence against women. From this perspective, the second poster responds to the first, asking, "Who are you?" in an effort to discover the identity of its anonymous and threatening author. The poster then parodies a feminist call to arms— "go trade your mops for a bit of change"—and culminates in a command to "defy, kill, even treat some [men presumably] as dogs." The poster, in effect, transforms the feminist revolution into license to talk back to, discipline, and, ultimately, kill their oppressors. This is a multivocal poster, however, deploying the clumsy Derridean device of erasure to speak its two positions simultaneously: beneath the parodic call to arms rests the undistilled anger of the author or authors, unleashed in the catalogue of derogatory terms for women as it builds to the frightening transformation of "revolution" into a command to "Run, Run." In the context of the kidnapping and sexual violation that had occurred on campus over the weekend, I was both convinced that this was what the poster intended and horrified by what I read. To my mind, and to some of the students in the class, the second poster openly defied the threat of the first poster, providing an involved, but nonetheless clear, assertion of the second writer's determination to go on a rampage.

A number of the students in the class resisted this take on the second poster, however, arguing that it was probably by the same person who produced the first one. Making a case for a wholly ironized text, these students insisted that the writer was miming the voice of "the angry male" and through this process mocking that voice. This reading, in effect, reverses the foreground and the background of the previous reading, making the list of derogatory terms the literal or surface meaning and the call to arms embedded in and amongst the letters of this list the hidden promise of a better world. Thus, where the voice of the "angry male" commands "Run, Run," the creative genius of the writer/artist sees the possibility of "Revolution, Revolution." As clever as I found this approach to the text and as persuasive as many of the members of the class deemed it to be, I was not, in the end, convinced that the second poster was just "more of the same" from the writer of the first poster. Although this discussion ended up releasing a flood of stories from the students about the daily acts of violence they experienced in the dorms and parking lots, at football games and dance parties, on and off campus, it did not lead to any sort of consensus about which reading of the poster was "correct." This is one of the hazards of allowing students to work with writing in the contact zone: the meaning of a text is seen to be up for grabs; the students, drawing on their local knowledge, may prove to be better readers of certain texts than their teacher; and the teacher's ability to insist upon a certain reading will be diminished. In place of a community of uniform and obedient students, one finds a contestatory space where the vertiginous possibilities of the multivalent, multivocal text become at least a momentary reality in the hands of a loosely federated, heterogenous group with widely divergent reading abilities and political commitments.

As exciting as it can be when students are arguing in an engaged way about how best to interpret a text, such moments mark for me a starting point in the work of a course on reading and writing rather than an end point. That is, while such exercises do serve to introduce students to the idea that texts may be interpreted to have a range of meanings, there is always the danger that such work will quickly produce a classroom situation where any reading is seen to be as good as any other reading. Thus, when the third poster appeared a month later, it was difficult to get the students to move beyond developing an interpretation of the poster to staking out a position in relation to their interpretation, despite the poster's deliberately provocative declaration:

NOT ALL
MEN RAPE
SOME OF US
JUST
WATCH

By this point in the semester, we were reading Stanley Fish's "How to Recognize a Poem When You See One," and the students had become fairly adept at detecting and exploiting ambiguities in a text. Some of the students had also read an interview with the author of the first poster, entitled "Guerilla Feminist Kicks Some Ass," in the university's self-described "common, degenerate tabloid." In this interview, the student, whose anonymity was maintained, stated, "I put these flyers up because art has an obligation to be dangerous and political" (Mulligan). With Fish and the interview in mind, the students quickly produced three overlapping readings of the third poster: the broadside, written by the author of the first poster, either accuses all men of being involved in rape in one way or another or, more inclusively, indicts an entire culture for standing by while rape occurs; or, conversely, some students suggested, the poster could have been written by a male parodying the feminist critique. What had started as an exciting discussion that led to a number of insights into the dynamics of the contact zone quickly devolved into a predictable trotting out of interpretations. The students, it seemed, had learned what they could *in the classroom* about the advantages and disadvantages of the conventions governing this particular interchange in a textual corridor outside the classroom. But they also recognized that the anonymity of the participants deprived the interchange of the kind of depth necessary to sustain discussion, with the significant result that a strategy to produce public art designed to be "dangerous and political," ended up being dismissed as the work of cowards afraid to make their positions clear. This, too, is one of the inevitable perils of writing in the contact zone: the rhetorical approach designed to deliver a critique or parody may simply lead to the material being cast aside as nonsense. There is always the possibility, as Pratt observes, that the letter will not reach its intended destination.

This is not an insignificant lesson to learn in a course devoted to thinking about writing as a process, since it both introduces the possibility of a range of ways of responding to a writing assignment and, at the same time, drives home the importance of balancing the strengths and weaknesses available within any given rhetorical approach. To return to the example of the posters, anonymity may buy the writer or writers the freedom to express opinions and prejudices openly, but it does so at the cost of undermining the credibility or significance of what is being said. It also, in the name of fostering a heightened awareness of violence against women, helps to create an environment of suspicion and hostility: "What if," one of my students asked, "the people producing these posters are in this class?" The conventions governing the interchange, in effect, guarantee only that the described situation will continue: in this sphere, anonymous threats and ambiguous slogans combine to produce a kind of political paralysis, where nothing happens because nobody knows where anybody stands. The value of pursuing such issues in a writing course is that it helps to illustrate the fact that no writing situation is without its conventions, nor is any writer ever fully able to control those conventions. Once the student writer recognizes that all texts, in this regard, are heterogenous in their production as well as their reception, it becomes possible to talk about the range and kinds of choices available during the acts of reading and writing, and this, I would argue, is the most important work that can be begun in a composition course.

If discussing the posters and the conventions of the interchange within this particular textual corridor allowed us to explore what can and cannot be achieved through the adoption of a uniformly confrontational stance, the assignment of Gloria Anzaldúa's "Entering into the Serpent" moved the class on to the business of developing alternate routes of response to a challenging and, for many of my students, threatening text. In "Entering into the Serpent," excerpted from Anzaldúa's *Borderlands/La Frontera*, Anzaldúa shifts back and forth between Anglo-American English, Castilian Spanish, Tex-Mex, Northern Mexican dialect, and Nahuatl, writing in a mélange of languages to express the diversity of her heritage and her position as lesbian, feminist, Chicana poet and critic. While Anzaldúa's multilingual text thus places special linguistic demands on its readers, it also makes relatively unique generic demands, moving between poetry and prose, personal narrative and revisionist history. Where the posters spoke in one or two voices, Anzaldúa occupies a range of positions, some of them contradictory, as she relates her efforts to reclaim the Aztec goddess Coatlicue, the "serpent goddess," split from the goddess Cihuacoatl by the "male dominated Azteca-Mexica culture" in order to drive "the powerful female deities underground" (26–27). After the Spanish Conquest, Cihuacoatl was further domesticated by the Christian Church and transformed by stages into the figure now known as the Virgin of Guadalupe. While Anzaldúa admires *La Virgen de Guadalupe* as "the symbol of ethnic identity and of the tolerance for ambiguity that Chicanos-*mexicanos*, people of mixed race, people who have Indian blood, people who cross cultures, by necessity possess" (29), she nevertheless insists on the importance of regaining access to Coatlicue, "the symbol of the dark sexual drive, the chthonic (underworld), the feminine, the serpentine movement of sexuality, of creativity, the basis of all energy and life" (33). Recovering this contact with the supernatural provides one with "*la facultad* . . . the capacity to see in surface phenomena the meaning of deeper realities, to see the deep structure below the surface" (36). Anzaldúa concludes this section by asserting that "those who are pounced on the most have [*la facultad*] the strongest—the females, the homosexuals of all races, the darkskinned, the outcast, the persecuted, the marginalized, the foreign" (36).

Here's how one of my students described his experience in reading "Entering into the Serpent":

> Even though I had barely read half of the first page, I was already disgusted. I found myself reading onward only to stop and ask "What is she trying to prove?" Scanning the words and skipping over the ones that were not english, I went from an egocentric personal story to a femo-nazi account of central american mythology that was occasionally interrupted by more poems . . . .
>
> From what I gather, she is trying to exorcise some personal demons. Her feelings of inadequacy and insecurity drove her to project her own problems not only onto the world, but into history and mythology. I'm surprised she didn't call history "herstory." It seems that she had no sense of self or worth. To overcome this, she fabricated a world, a past, and a scapegoat in her own image. Although her accusations do hold some truth, her incredible distortion of the world would lead me to believe that she has lost touch with reality and is obsessively driven by her social psychosis. She views herself as a gallant and brilliant member of a great culture that has been oppressed by the world. Her continuous references to females, sex, and the phallic symbols of snakes is most likely brought out by the lack of a man in her life. Rather than admit her faults, she cherishes them and calls them friends.

This is not an uncommon response to my assignment that began by asking the students to discuss the difficulties they encountered in reading Anzaldúa's essay. This student, having made his way past the language barrier of the text, confronts the description of a world and a way of being in that world that he finds personally repugnant. Beginning with a variant of the Rush Limbaughism "feminazi," the student then proceeds to document the many ways that "Entering into the Serpent" offended him: it contains Anzaldúa's effort to "exorcise some personal demons"; it includes "her incredible distortion of the world"; the writer claims to be "a gallant and brilliant member of a great culture" of which the student is not a part. Given this reading, it is not too surprising that the student concludes that all the faults in the text are produced by "the lack of a man in [Anzaldúa's] life."

Taking offense at this student's response to Anzaldúa's essay strikes me as being exactly the wrong tactic here. It is of paramount importance, I believe, to begin where students are, rather than where one thinks they should be, and this student, by my reading, is trapped between the desire to produce a stereotypical critique of any feminist text ("I'm surprised she didn't call history 'herstory'") and the necessity of responding to this particular feminist text. He negotiates the tension between this desire and this necessity by producing a fairly detailed outline of Anzaldúa's essay and, simultaneously, mocking its argument ("Rather than admit her faults, she cherishes them and calls them friends"). However rudimentary or sophisticated one deems this kind of multivocalic writing to be, it is, as I've said above, only a starting point for beginning more detailed work with Anzaldúa's text. For this reason, the assignment that solicited this response does not simply ask the students to revel in the difficulties they experienced in reading Anzaldúa's essay, but also requests that they outline "a plan of action for addressing the difficulties [they] encountered." The goal, thus, is not to invite students simply to record their various levels of rage, incomprehension, and despair with an admittedly difficult text, but rather to have them reflect on how their own ways of reading are disclosed and complicated during this textual transaction.

The results of having the students read their own readings and chart out alternative ways of returning to the text can be startling indeed. Although this writer began by accusing Anzaldúa of being a "femo-nazi," he concluded by reflecting on what he had done with her text in the following way:

> If not for searching for her hidden motives and then using them to criticize/bash Anzaldúa and her story, I would not have been able to read the story in its entirety. Although my view is a bit harsh, it has been a way that allows me to counter Anzaldúa's extremities. In turn, I can now see her strategy of language and culture choice and placement to reveal the contact zone in her own life. All of my obstacles previously mentioned, (not liking the stories, poems, or their content) were overcome by "bashing" them. Unfortunately, doing that in addition to Anzaldúa's ridiculous disproportionism and over-intense, distorted beliefs created a mountain which was impossible for me to climb. This in effect made it impossible to have taken any part of her work seriously or to heart. I feel I need to set aside my personal values, outlook and social position in order to escape the bars of being offended and discouraged. Not only must I lessen my own barriers of understanding, but I must be able to comprehend and understand the argument of the other. It is these differences between people and groups of people that lead to the conflicts and struggles portrayed and created by this selection.

This strikes me as being an extraordinarily astute assessment of the strengths and weaknesses of this writer's initial reading strategy: "bashing" Anzaldúa enabled a certain kind of work to be accomplished (the reading was completed, the writing assignment could be fulfilled), but it also prevented the writer from taking "any part of her work seriously or to heart." The writer's approach, in effect, only verified feelings he already had: it did not allow him to see or learn anything he didn't already know. Reflecting on his own reading practice, the writer finds himself compelled to reassess Anzaldúa's strategy, seeing at the end of his work that she has written in a way that will show "the contact zone in her life." Thus, by "bashing" Anzaldúa, the student inadvertently ended up showing himself that her description of her trying experiences within the straight Anglo world was, at least partly, accurate. The writer's proposed solution to this problem—setting aside his "personal values, outlook and social position"—attests to the magnitude of the challenge Anzaldúa's position holds for him. Whether or not this proposed solution proves in practice to be a workable plan is something that emerges when the writer returns to Anzaldúa's essay to begin his revision. What is important to notice here, however, is that the writer's plan does make returning to her text an imaginable activity with an unforeseeable outcome. Given the way this student's essay began, this is no small accomplishment.

Required self-reflexivity does not, of course, guarantee that repugnant positions will be abandoned. At best, it ensures only that the students' attention will be focused on the interconnections between the ways they read and the ways they write. This can be a salutary experience as in the example above, where it provided the student with an avenue for renegotiating a relationship with a difficult text and the wide range of concerns affiliated with that text, but it does not mean that this approach wields sufficient power to transform the matrix of beliefs, values, and prejudices that students (and teachers) bring to the classroom. This kind of wholesale transformation (or, to be more precise, the appearance of this kind of wholesale transformation) is possible only in classrooms where the highly asymmetrical relations of power are fully reinstated and students are told either implicitly or explicitly (as I was during a course in graduate school), "No language that is racist, sexist, homophobic, or that degrades the working class will be allowed in our discussions." Reimagining the classroom as a contact zone is a potentially powerful pedagogical intervention only so long as it involves resisting the temptation either to silence or to celebrate the voices that seek to oppose, critique, and/or parody the work of constructing knowledge in the classroom. By dismantling *Focus*, Bob Allen did not address the roots of the problem that produced the offensive cartoon; he merely tried to make it more difficult for another "deplorable mistake" of this kind to further tarnish the image of multicultural harmony the company has been at such pains to construct. Scott Lankford, on the other hand, achieved the kind of partial, imperfect, negotiated, microvictory available to those who work in the contact zone when he found a way to respond to his student's essay that not only kept the student in his course, but eventually led to the student signing up to work with him in another course as well. By having my students interrogate literate practices inside and outside the classroom, by having them work with challenging essays that speak about issues of difference from a range of perspectives, and by having them pursue this work in the ways I've outlined here, I have been trying to create a course that allows the students to use their writing to investigate the cultural conflicts that serve to define and limit their lived experience.

In the uncharted realms of teaching and studying in the contact zone, the teacher's traditional claim to authority is thus constantly undermined and reconfigured, which, in turn, enables the real work of learning how to negotiate and to place oneself in dialogue with different ways of knowing to commence. This can be strangely disorienting work, requiring, as it does, the recognition that in many places what passes as reason or rationality in the academy functions not as something separate from rhetoric, but rather as one of many rhetorical devices. This, in turn, quickly leads to the corollary concession that, in certain situations, reason exercises little or no persuasive force when vying against the combined powers of rage, fear, and prejudice, which together forge innumerable hateful ways of knowing the world that have their own internalized systems, self-sustaining logics, and justifications. For teachers who believe in education as a force for positive social change, the appropriate response to these new working conditions is not to exile students to the penitentiaries or the psychiatric wards for writing offensive, antisocial papers. Nor is it to give free rein to one's self-righteous indignation and call the resultant interchange a "political intervention." The most promising pedagogical response lies, rather, in closely attending to what our students say and write in an ongoing effort to learn how to read, understand, and respond to the strange, sometimes threatening, multivocal texts they produce while writing in the contact zone.

Note

I thank Scott Lankford for making this student essay available for discussion, Jean Ferguson Carr for providing me with materials related to this panel, and Mariolina Salvatori for introducing me to the idea of the "position paper" that appears here, in modified form, in my discussion of my students' responses to Gloria Anzaldúa's essay. None of these parties is, of course, to be understood as endorsing the position I have staked out here. I also wish to thank Judy Karwowski for her invaluable assistance in helping me to prepare this manuscript.

Works Cited

Allen, Bob. Letter to all AT&T employees. 17 Sept. 1993.

Anson, Chris M., ed. *Writing and Response: Theory, Practice, and Research*. Urbana, IL: NCTE, 1989.

Anzaldúa, Gloria. "Entering into the Serpent." *Ways of Reading: An Anthology for Writers*. 3rd ed. Ed. David Bartholomae and Anthony Petrosky. Boston: Bedford, 1993. 25–38. Rpt. from *Borderlands/La Frontera: The New Mestiza* by Gloria Anzaldúa. San Francisco: Spinsters/Aunt Lute, 1987.

Fish, Stanley. "How to Recognize a Poem When You See One." *Ways of Reading*. 3rd ed. Ed. David Bartholomae and David Petrosky. Boston: Bedford, 1993. 140–52.

Focus. AT&T. September 1993.

Kennedy, X. J., and Dorothy M. Kennedy. *The Bedford Guide for College Writers: With Readings and Handbook*. 2nd ed. Boston: Bedford, 1990. 41–42.

Lankford, Scott. "'Queers, Bums, and Magic': How Would You Grade a Gay-Bashing?" Conference on College Composition and Communication Convention. Cincinnati. 19 Mar. 1992.

Mulligan, Bartley. "Guerrilla Feminist Kicks Some Ass." *The Medium* 29 Sept. 1993: 1.

Pratt, Mary Louise. "Arts of the Contact Zone." *Profession 91*. New York: MLA, 1991. 33–40. (Originally presented as the keynote address at MLA's Responsibilities for Literacy conference in September 1990 in Pittsburgh.)

White, Edward M. *Teaching and Assessing Writing*. San Francisco: Jossey, 1985.

Reconstitution and Race in the Contact Zone

ROBERT D. MURRAY

St. Thomas Aquinas College

In its pedagogical context, Mary Louise Pratt's anthropological notion of a "contact zone" is essentially a theory of representation that allows writers and their teachers to recognize how a piece of writing manifests itself in layers of meaning. Each layer is analogous to a "voice," each of which is invented, learned, or parodistic. This analogy allows us to describe the writing as "multivocal," especially when it is done by a member of a subordinated group. That is to say, a writer's subordination, even repression, makes it easier to notice and identify these vocalized layers. Therefore, Pratt's analysis of Guaman Poma's autoethnographic *New Chronicle and Good Government* is fascinating because she is able to demonstrate how Guaman Poma is both able and unable to resist the rhetorical and political power of the Spanish metropolitan ruling class. Because of the asymmetrical power relationship between Spanish colonizers and Andeans living in Cuzco, Guaman Poma enters a "contact zone" once he attempts the task of self- (and cultural) representation. Pratt also tells us about another text, *Royal Commentaries of the Incas*, written in Spanish by a mestizo (born of a Spanish official and an Inca princess) named Inca Garcilaso de la Vega, who, apparently, chose to write it in the language of the colonizers and who "coded the Andean past and present in ways thought unthreatening to colonial hierarchy" ("Arts" 37). Inca Garcilaso, because of this more favorable political positioning of his rhetoric, produces a text that is accepted by the colonial government and therefore is endowed with a textual authority which it still carries today; Pratt describes it as a "staple item on Ph.D. reading lists in Spanish" ("Arts" 37).

We might be tempted to view Inca Garcilaso as a tool of the colonial hierarchy, as a person *not* in a contact zone because he writes from a position above the asymmetrical power relations of colonial domination. However, Pratt corrects this view in a footnote, saying that "it is far from clear that the *Royal Commentaries* was as benign as the Spanish seemed to assume. The book certainly played a role in maintaining the identity and aspirations of indigenous elites in the Andes" ("Arts" 40). Therefore, it seems that Inca Garcilaso may have had something up his sleeve after all. In fact, it might be the case that, despite having been written from a position relatively close to the seat of power of the colonial enterprise (and in its language), Inca Garcilaso's work still evidences some of the characteristics and effects of the contact zone. This is not to suggest that the contact zone does not exist, or is so broad a topic as to be useless, but that, like the effects of slavery, the effects of colonialism are widespread and include persons in, or close to, the seats of power. This claim has two implications. First, like the recursive effects of slavery noted by Frederick Douglass, colonialism corrupts its enforcers, and, thus corrupted, their attempts at self-representation may well be produced in zones where they must "grapple" with problematic political asymmetry.

The second implication—and the one on which this essay is based—sends us back to the basic premises of Pratt's definition of a contact zone. It is helpful to remember that Pratt herself sees the term as "a way to reconsider the models of community that many of us rely on in teaching and theorizing" ("Arts" 34). It is also noteworthy that the selective process of self-representation created in the contact zone is a deliberate strategy of intervention:

> Autoethnographic texts are not, then, what are usually thought of as autochthonous forms of expression or self-representation (as the Andean *quipus* were). Rather they involve a selective collaboration with and appropriation of idioms of the metropolis or the conqueror. These are merged or infiltrated to varying degrees with indigenous idioms to create self-representations intended to intervene in metropolitan modes of understanding.

> Autoethnographic works are often addressed to both metropoli-
> tan audiences and the speaker's own community. Their reception
> is thus highly indeterminate. ("Arts" 35)

A number of oppositions are indicated here. The production
of autoethnographic texts seems to serve the interests of both
creating and destabilizing a sense of community. It seems to want
to undermine the conqueror, and yet it seems intended to circumscribe a large sense of community, in which the conqueror is included. Again, these oppositions do not threaten the theory of
transculturation or the notion of the contact zone itself. Rather,
they reveal the possibility that the indeterminacy of the reception
of the works produced in it may indicate that the "zone" itself is
a place where indeterminacy is a necessity. That is, the
multivocality of self-representation produced in the contact zone
is a byproduct of one's willingness to imagine one's identity as
indeterminate. Therefore, it makes sense that the "literate arts of
the contact zone" include "autoethnography, transculturation,
critique, collaboration, bilingualism, mediation, parody, denunciation, imaginary dialogue, vernacular expression" ("Arts" 37).
Each of these methods of communication depends upon the existence of oppositions and can work (or work best) only by rejecting a single and set "vocal range" and attempting (or
pretending) to be fluent in a language other than one's own.

The second implication of Inca Garcilaso's text is, therefore,
that the indeterminacy of the contact zone, and of the communities that inhabit and surround it, makes it possible that the asymmetry of power works both ways. Perhaps people in power are
capable of producing such works too, and thereby reinscribing
and further empowering the colonial rulers. Thus, a person in
the dominant ruling position, or one who subscribes to the ideas
of that position, is able to cast his or her rhetoric in ways that
exploit the necessary indeterminacy of the contact zone in order
to serve the ruling interests by simultaneously pretending to serve
(or at least share) the interests of the subordinated group.

I call this rhetorical process "reconstitution," and I mean to
use it in ways that are informed by Foucault's use of the term in
The Order of Things. There, writing about Velasquez's *Las
Meninas*, Foucault describes the indeterminate activity wherein

the gaze of an observer of the painting meets the gaze of the painter represented on the canvas:

> The painter is looking, his face turned slightly and his head leaning towards one shoulder. He is staring at a point to which, even though it is invisible, we, the spectators can easily assign an object, since it is we, ourselves, who are at that point: our bodies, our faces, our eyes. The spectacle he is observing is thus doubly invisible: first, because it is not represented within the space of the painting, and, second, because it is situated precisely in that blind point, in that essential hiding-place into which our gaze disappears from ourselves at the moment of actual looking. And yet, how could we fail to see that invisibility, there in front of our eyes, since it has its own perceptible equivalent, its sealed-in figure, in the painting itself? We could, in effect, guess what it is the painter is looking at if it were possible to glance for a moment at the canvas he is working on; but all we can see of that canvas is texture, the horizontal and vertical bars of the stretcher, and the obliquely rising foot of the easel. The tall, monotonous rectangle occupying the whole left portion of the real picture, and representing the back of the canvas within the picture, reconstitutes in the form of a surface the invisibility in depth of what the artist is observing: that space in which we are, and which we are. (4)

The back of the canvas, facing us on its easel, reconstitutes—makes visible and therefore available for comment and analysis—the invisible space wherein our gaze merges with the painted artist's gaze because our position is that of his model. That is, if we could see the front of the canvas, there would be no question about what the subject of the painting is. However, because we cannot see the front of the canvas, we are forced to look into the painter's eyes in a more reflexive and recursive way. Thus Velasquez's desire to explore the issues of subjectivity and reception are enacted by the positioning of the "monotonous rectangle" in ways that reconstitute an *invisible* indeterminate activity into a *visible* indeterminate activity; it does not resolve the indeterminacy, but, by making it apparent, transforms it into a powerful rhetorical strategy.

Foucault's concept of reconstitution can also be used to explain the rhetorical strategies of writers—Inca Garcilaso as well as student writers—who similarly desire to make visible the indeterminacy of the contact zone in order to stake their own claim within in it. However, before I locate this concept within student writing, I need to describe more fully the terms of "contact" in the "contact zone" in order to better understand the ways in which this space is perceived as asymmetrical by students and by teachers. Most frequently, this asymmetry of power is discussed in terms of "teacher authority," on the one hand, and "student resistance," on the other. Yet, typically, the discussion is not about power in the sense of classroom discipline; what is at stake is ideological power, frequently involving an agenda of (actual or perceived) political conversion. Therefore, classrooms tend to become contact zones when the topics discussed in them, like Guaman Poma's *New Chronicle and Good Government* or Inca Garcilaso's *Royal Commentaries of the Incas*, overtly address identity politics, especially concerning racial and ethnic identity.

Authority and Resistance

Student strategies of contravention appear in many forms but usually come as the result of a convergence of student assumptions into a construction of a teacher with multiple meanings, texts, and subtexts.[1] Questions about contested teacher authority are, of course, numerous and complex, and the implications for classroom practice are immense: What happens to a teacher's authority in a class that cannot construct it—cannot believe in it—in traditional ways? Let me ask this in another, more theoretically familiar, way: What becomes of the concept of teacher authority when you intentionally place your class in a contact zone? When you demand that your students "meet, clash, and grapple with each other"—and with you—and that they "put ideas and identities on the line," as Pratt suggests, chances are good that the students' constructions of you and your authoritative role in the classroom may suffer some erosion.

Let me clarify somewhat what I mean by this complex term "authority," before I consider the nature of student resistance and its manifestation in the form of reconstitution, and before I finally explore ways to continue—and refine—the process of institutional liberatory "decentering" often typified by the work of Paulo Freire.

I say we must "refine," and even adapt, Freire's ideas because his ideas of a "problem-posing" education, while extraordinarily useful as a general model of student-teacher interaction and student self-actualization, are considerably narrowed once we consider the specific relationship between the students and the teacher on which he bases his ideas. Freire the teacher seems not to have the same authority problems I have in my class; resistance is less likely when, from the very start, teacher and student agree on their asymmetrical power relationship. His students are, on the whole, aware of their oppression and powerlessness, are eager to be empowered, and clearly see him as the means to that end. Look, for example, at Freire's observations about his students' self-deprecation, their belief in his ability to change it, and their acceptance of his definition of education as the act of helping to improve their conditions:

> Not infrequently, peasants in educational projects begin to discuss a generative theme in a lively manner, then stop suddenly and say to the educator: "Excuse us, we ought to keep quiet and let you talk. You are the one who knows, we don't know anything." (45)

Gradually, however, and through Freire's agency, the peasants become aware of their oppression and begin to resist *external* systems, but not the implicit system that is their educational experience. This is a demonstration of the kind of power Patricia Bizzell calls "persuasion," that which is "exercised by A over B only with B's consent, which is given only if B is convinced that doing as A suggests will serve B's best interests" (56).[2] I tend to agree with Bizzell's desire for a different way of constructing classroom power relationships; for her, useful power is a two-stage process which she calls "authority." Dialogic at first, this process becomes less so after the student works through the "persuasion" stage, coming to a collaborative agreement that the teacher has expertise, and has her best interests in mind. At that point, the relationship enters the second stage—the student empowers the teacher to direct the course of study without, but not exclusive of, any further dialogue. Freire's students eventually reach this point.

It is that early collaborative dialogue that I find compelling and useful. Bizzell is interested in sharing with her students "the problematic nature of our relation as liberatory teachers to an oppressive system" (58). This is a kind of classroom authority that assumes nothing:

> The teacher cannot ask students to grant him or her authority simply on the grounds that anyone appointed to the position of teacher is thereby certified to be worthy of authority. . . . Rather I am imagining a form of argumentation in which the teacher demonstrates links between his or her own historical circumstances and those of the students, to suggest that their joining together in a liberatory educational project will serve all of their best interests. (Bizzell 58)

This seems to me to be an ideal rendition of classroom; the equality in the classroom is complete and thoroughgoing; the student and the teacher each reveal, and learn, something about their situated positions. If clearly articulated and enacted, this kind of authority might have simple manifestations, such as getting work handed in on time or having assignments read by the due date, but its more important synonym is a kind of intellectual trust that the students place in their teacher. They can clearly define their own interests as represented in the classroom, and they know that the teacher respects and privileges these interests. Though it might seem paradoxical, part of this self-interest consists in granting the teacher expertise: you know how to help them to write and think more clearly, and they do not.

On the other hand, however, where matters of racial identity are concerned, this construction of authority becomes problematic: resistant White students may assume a smaller gap, if any at all, between a teacher's authority and theirs. What they feel that they have learned about African Americans from their own experiences may outweigh anything that their teacher, from his or her reading, or that the texts, from their own reading, have to tell them about Black oppression. Therefore, the teacher's "authority" is suspended here because the students resist and disallow that collaborative persuasion with which Bizzell begins the process. Instead, authority in this circumstance must be construed as a more elastic set of practices.

One now-famous, and admittedly extreme, example of resistance leading to a teacher authority crisis is the case of Scott Lankford's student who wrote a gay-bashing essay that included a scene of students beating a homeless person in San Francisco. The questions usually raised by this essay, "Queers, Bums, and Magic," are all about propriety of response: Should Lankford have considered the work fictional, criticizing its surface with little regard to content? Or should he have assumed the events were real and reported the student to the police, or at least lectured the student on appropriate social conduct? Lankford treated the essay as fiction, assigning it a low B, an approach used to deflect the student writer's attempt to "bash" his professor. In this way, the student "learned to cope with an openly gay instructor with some measure of civility" (qtd. in Miller 393).

Thus, the student in the contact zone of Lankford's class learns that his resistant opinions are not automatically dismissed by the teacher in ways that he assumed—even hoped—that they would be; by heightening and then challenging these assumptions, Lankford is able to meet with "qualified success" because the student develops a coping strategy that serves his own interests.[3] However, as Richard Miller suggests, there is a third way of responding: to make the writer revise the essay from the beaten man's point of view. But even then the problem will not go away: the student, according to Miller, will more than likely produce a work of "seamless parody," which successfully masks the student's hatred under a veneer of "hyperconformity."

Lankford's student's essay illuminates the relationship between resistance and teacher authority because it attempts to exploit the distinction between the writer's interests and those of the teacher. This type of student resistance is at the far end of the spectrum of responses found within the classroom contact zone; at the other end are what we might call "the converted"—those students either already in accord with the principles of multiculturalism, or who quickly see an opportunity to "give the teacher what he or she wants" by producing conformist texts. David Rothgery calls this range of response the "continuum" of possible answers, which, to him, ultimately reinforces the need for a "necessary directionality" of ethics (243). However, the classrooms in which we are likely to see acts of reconstitution are made up of those students in the middle. They don't "hate" like Lankford's student; their resistance is more subtle, confused, and often self-interrogating, and it poses the most insidious threat of subversion of the teacher's authority.

This type of resistance seems closest to the concept of reconstitution because the student discerns the subjective indeterminacy behind the topic and makes it a visible and viable means to reconfigure the authority in the classroom, to manipulate the asymmetry of power, and thereby make his experiences compete with the textual expressions of authors whose messages he resists. Reconstitution is, in fact, an inversion of Bizzell's notion of "authority." First the student determines the politics of those who disagree with her in a kind of "collaborative" effort of dissuasion (Bizzell 59). Next, she repositions herself within the framework of that opposition, thereby redefining the terms of the opposition itself. As a result, in her textual presentation, though her position has not changed, she reassigns the terms of what she sees as the teacher's smugly "correct" view into a text that is at once, to use consciously simplified terms, "conservative" and "progressive." This is not the same as giving the teacher what he or she wants; it is a strategy which seeks to further the interests of both parties simultaneously. Cheryl Johnson puts it this way: "readers who encounter a racially, culturally, or linguistically different text may read their perceptions of these differences into the text, manipulating the language to conform to their culturally learned assumptions" (412).

Thus—and this is certainly not new to anyone who teaches about difference—classroom discussions and writing assignments about race do not automatically change students' minds about racism. Instead, their responses tend to perform the act of "sweeping" that Miller describes; their spoken and written texts reinscribe, or reconstitute, their previously held views on race. This method of reconstitution is similar to the coping strategy of Lankford's student, but through it the student manipulates the teacher into a strategy of cocreation. It is also similar to what Miller calls "miming," but it does not aim at hyperconformity. Reconstitution is a different, and I think common, kind of student production in the contact zone. Miller is closest to describing what I am talking about when he recognizes the existence of contestatory "multivocal texts" rather than "a community of uniform and obedient students" (402). "Multivocal," then, may be the best alternative word for the rhetorical moves I am trying to examine here, especially if considered in the same sense as the multilingual writings Pratt analyzes.

"Jean": A Study in Reconstitution

As my primary example of reconstitution, I would like to talk about a student who was in a first-year research class I taught on the topic of Race and Rights. We read Patricia Williams's *The Alchemy of Race and Rights*, Richard Wright's *Uncle Tom's Children*, and selections from Booker T. Washington and W. E. B. Du Bois. One day in the earliest weeks of the semester, one of the White students—I'll call her Jean—came up after class and asked belligerently: "Do we have to talk about Blacks in our essays?" In a class whose stated purpose was to discuss race and rights, I explained to her, she could examine any race she chose, but since the readings were by African American writers, she might find it difficult to ignore "the problem of the color line." She was no less resistant in the next few weeks, and while she did not manifest this resistance vocally in class, I overheard a few comments which she confided to the students in her all-White peer review group.

I do not wish to present Jean's work as part of a "conversion narrative," evidence that the contact zone works by making students "grapple" with things they don't understand or value, by exposing them to real-life situations that realize and resolve the problems of asymmetrical power relations. Rather, I believe that she is representative of a group of students with whom most composition teachers are familiar: White, middle-class, from a homogeneous suburban or rural background, and uncomfortable talking about race. Her comments clearly could be interpreted as racist at the outset of the course; her written text, on its surface at least, was less so by the end. But I am not convinced that her position changed by the end of the course. Rather, I suspect that she discovered a way to articulate her views on race in

"multivocal" ways, one "vocalization" of which might be interpreted as racial tolerance.

For example, in her final research project, Jean told me she
wanted to write about her workplace, where she observed dis-
criminatory work practices. When I asked her to describe these
practices, she told me that there were two kinds of jobs—full-
time with benefits and part-time without benefits—and that the
part-time jobs were regularly given to Black candidates. The full-
time, full-benefit jobs were reserved for Whites. As I began to tell
her how to proceed with this project, which I thought to be a
classic case of racially motivated employment discrimination, she
corrected me by revealing that the "discrimination" she perceived
was that it was too difficult for White candidates to get any of
these part-time jobs. By overlooking the restrictions against Blacks
and emphasizing instead White difficulty—by conflating affirmative action and reverse racism—she reconstitutes these into a
"personal" definition of affirmative action that simultaneously
accommodates two opposing viewpoints—one (to appeal to my
interests) an outcry that discrimination is wrong, and the other
(to address her own) that it is especially unfair when it affects
"everyone," i.e., the White middle class.

Jean's attitude here is explained by David Roediger, who suggests how the concept of reverse racism "grows out of [an] assur-
ance among Whites that they have transcended race" (14). Further,
according to Roediger, White students like Jean are sure that they
see the world based on merit and that "multiculturalists, affirmative action officers, Native American fishermen, Black nation-
alists and pointy headed liberals 'bring in race'" (14).

By looking at the language of Jean's essay, we can see how
this reconstitution—this belief in merit—makes its appearance
as her desire for a paradoxical affirmative action policy which is
based on the concept of earned rewards. She writes:

> At some point the employer should observe the applicant's abili-
> ties, as opposed to focusing on the expectations portrayed by the
> affirmative action program. Williams believes that she became a
> successful law professor based on her abilities to perform her job
> adequately and not because of affirmative action. Although af-
> firmative action qualified her for admission to law school, Patricia

Williams would state that her true capabilities can be observed in her being a studious individual the first semester she entered college.

By glossing over the hiring issue ("at some point"), and by confusing the expectations of the employer with those of affirmative action, Jean focuses instead on the idea of performative accountability and aligns her interests with those of the employer. It is fine, she says, for an African American student such as Williams to be admitted to law school on the basis of her race, but after that, performance should be the determining factor. This reading contrasts with Williams's own sense of getting through Harvard Law School, "quietly driven by the false idol of White-man-within-me, and absorb[ing] much of the knowledge and values that had enslaved my foremothers" (155).

For Williams, affirmative action is a response to a complex set of sociocultural forces, leading her to this straightforward conclusion: "I strongly believe not just in programs like affirmative action, but in affirmative action as a socially and professionally pervasive concept" (121). Yet to this student, and to many other White students in that class, Williams was "unclear" about the standards issue at the heart of affirmative action, and, in effect, apologetic for having taken advantage of it.[4]

I do not wish to demonize Jean, or any of my students, most of whom found themselves facing a very real cultural dilemma: talking about that which is uncomfortable in an academy which places great value on "opening one's mind." Placed in a class with a teacher who assumed, as Henry Giroux does in *Schooling and the Struggle for Public Life*, that each student would show trust, sharing, and commitment to improving the quality of human life (Giroux 107), my students saw a critical thinking pedagogy as repressive and stifling. In their reading of my agenda, I was expecting a shocked, leftist taking of offense at racial discrimination, and they resisted what Bizzell would call my "coercion," not by loudly articulating their opposition, but by repositioning this opposition within the dominating and subordinating terms of my discussion.

Such strategies are, to Patricia Bizzell, evidence that students can be "stunningly successful at normalizing or defusing material that we might have thought was politically explosive," an activity that should not surprise us since leaving so much of the class up to the students "sends the message that what one does with politically explosive material is entirely a matter of personal choice" (66). Yet these multivocal acts of "coping," "defusing," or "reconstituting" are more than just ways of making room for students' views in the class; they are also, in a strange and unexpected way, "transcultural" in the broadest sense of Mary Louise Pratt's use of the term. To Pratt, transcultural texts are those where members of "subordinated or marginal groups select and invent from materials transmitted by a dominant or metropolitan culture" ("Arts" 36). My students, feeling isolated and threatened by the demands of an academic privileging of a multicultural agenda, saw themselves as "marginalized," as in Jean's construction of herself as the victim of discrimination in her workplace.[5] In a sense, then, Jean's text operates somewhat like Guaman Poma's *New Chronicle and Good Government*, but even more like Inca Garcilaso's *Royal Commentaries of the Incas*. All are products of working within a contact zone; all three writers determine which elements of a culture that they view as dominating, and even colonizing, them will become "absorbed into their own and what it gets used for" ("Arts" 36).

This application of the term "contact zone" seems close to the intent of Pratt's original source, linguistics, where the idea of a contact language "refers to improvised languages that develop among speakers of different native languages who need to communicate with each other consistently" (*Imperial* 6). "Contact," in this regard, emphasizes all the things a resistant student is interested in creating: interactive, improvisational texts which assert the copresence of separated and distinct subjects. Further, my student's writing can be viewed not only as transcultural, but also as generating works of "anti-conquest," as are all texts by people who, according to Pratt, "secure their innocence in the same moment as they assert [their] hegemony" (*Imperial* 7).

Seen in this regard, Scott Lankford's student produces a response which is neither anticonquest nor transcultural in its approach, given that he does not identify himself as "marginalized" by the "oppressive" and dominating force of multiculturalism.

Rather, he considers himself one of the majority of "right-think-ing" people. His text sets its own hegemonic agenda, leaving his teacher to consider the implications. On the other hand, Jean's approach, which I believe to be a more common one, is subtler, more willing to make the kinds of cultural compromises that constitute what Pratt refers to as acts of self-consciously resistant "anti-conquest." Here, again, is Jean staking out a position that simultaneously subscribes to the principles of affirmative action and attacks them as unfair:

> Affirmative action can be viewed as a political scam for whites and a conspiracy against blacks. Racism still exists in today's society through many equal opportunity programs. Although we as a society are working towards equality between the multiple races, it is difficult to put away the past experiences of racism because our parents educate young people on their views. The views presented to the young people by their parents were in turn carried on by the generation before. Young people adopt the views and morals taught to them by their parents, which can lead to inherited racism by having preconceived ideas without getting to know the actual situation.

What does it mean for affirmative action to be at once "a political scam for whites" and a "conspiracy against blacks"? Clearly, Jean believes that as a social policy affirmative action serves no one, and is, in fact, a disservice to all. The end of this paragraph similarly shows the writer seemingly pulled in two different directions: she begins by seeming to justify the continu-ance of racism on grounds of a naturalized, domesticated histori-cal precedent, but then shifts to a realization that this "inherited racism" has, at its heart, an ignorance of the "actual situation." Nowhere does Jean reconstitute the discussion about race into a piece of anti-conquest rhetoric more clearly than in her essay conclusion:

> As a white female, I feel that affirmative action is a positive beginning towards creating equal opportunities for everyone and diminishing racial bias within the work force. It is impor-tant that more [African Americans] achieve top management positions to create an atmosphere in which people can be hired on their abilities to perform, rather than their sex or race. Once

there are an equal amount of "preferenced" people as white males at the top management levels, then today's society may not need to depend upon affirmative action programs as a means of achieving equal opportunities within the workforce.

Though her initially stated position is, at first, in favor of affirmative action, her motive for wanting to see such a program succeed is so that we can finally, and without guilt, do away with it. Her wish for its success seems more motivated by the desire for the elimination of yet another social program than by her attraction to social justice. After aligning herself with a marginalized group—women—she appeals to a utopian future of race neutrality that Williams herself says is determined by "reference to an aesthetic of uniformity, in which difference is simply omitted" (48).

My experience with Jean is reminiscent of Elizabeth Ellsworth's experience at the University of Wisconsin–Madison. Attempting to work against a rising tide of racism on her campus, Ellsworth held a graduate seminar entitled Media and Anti-Racist Pedagogies that would "not only work to clarify the structures of institutional racism underlying university practices and its culture in Spring 1988, but that would also use that understanding to plan and carry out a political intervention within that formation" (299).

However, according to Ellsworth, far from being liberating, the course was debilitating:

> When participants in our class attempted to put into practice prescriptions offered in the literature concerning empowerment, student voice, and dialogue, we produced results that were not only unhelpful, but actually exacerbated the very conditions we were trying to work against, including Eurocentrism, racism, sexism, classism, and "banking education." (298)

Further, students "expressed much pain, confusion, and difficulty in speaking because of the ways in which discussions called up multiple and contradictory social positionings" (312). For example, White students in the class found it difficult to speak about race because it meant subordinating their own oppression as people "living under U.S. imperialist policies" (312).

A Possible Solution: Reconstituting Classroom Power

No matter how many versions of subordination we consider, no matter how noble our aims in addressing the diverse needs of diverse student groups, questions remain: What does student resistance do to our desires for students to engage in heuristic learning? How can we work it so that self-instruction, which is based on their belief that I will look out for their interests, is not voided by their rejection of my authority? Can we solve these problems in a way that maintains our authority—their intellectual trust in us?

The first answer is that we need to conceive of authority dialectically, as a recursive power given to teachers by students, constructed in equal parts of their assent to our control of the classroom and their resistance to that control. Therefore, the use of authority is a fluid, constantly shifting process. Classrooms as sites of resistance operate best when the authority in them is exposed, shared, and therefore malleable.

The second answer, which is clearly related, is that perhaps teachers might resolve the authority issues that produce works of reconstitution by reconstituting the very notion of classroom asymmetry. The space, largely imagined, between the painter and the viewer in Foucault's reading of *Las Meninas* is itself a contact zone. There, the contest seems to be about who or what is the real subject of the painting. The problematic classroom can be described in this way, too: In the space between a student's gaze at the teacher and the teacher's gaze at the student, they translate and transform each other into something they probably are not. Informed and distracted by traditional concepts of teacher and student, each may construct himself or herself as subordinated to the political intentions of the other.

Student resistance is an unavoidable characteristic of the contact zone of the multicultural classroom, and this is not necessarily a bad thing. In saying that "required self-reflexivity does not, of course, guarantee that repugnant positions will be abandoned," Richard E. Miller reassures us that creating a pedagogy of the contact zone is worthwhile—that by having students "interrogate literate practices inside and outside the classroom" and by having them "work with challenging texts that speak about issues of difference from a range of perspectives," we must continue to seek to create courses that "investigate the cultural conflicts that serve to define and limit [students'] lived experience" (407).

By exposing and situating the historical similarities between, on one hand, the invisibility of the teacher's power and, on the other hand, dominant, and frequently unquestioned, power constructs, we add to the range of perspectives that all of our students must address, and we further their comprehension of new ways to interrogate power and authority, in and out of the classroom.

Notes

1. Such resistance is certainly more problematic when the teacher is a woman, a person of color, or both. As Cheryl L. Johnson says, "When students encounter a professor enclosed in a racial/gendered body, her very presence in the classroom inaugurates the creation of another decipherable text" (410). Students tend to decipher this text in ways which essentialize Black experience; White students assume that teachers of color have a specific brand of authority over the subject of race, just as students of color are often asked to represent a typically "racial" classroom position. Rejecting this "authority of experience" model, bell hooks assumes that everyone brings experiential knowledge into the classroom which, when "invoked . . . as a way of knowing that coexists in a nonhierarchical way with other ways of knowing," can be used as a means to distribute authority more equitably (83).

However, just as Johnson points out the error beneath the assumption of an ideological harmony between Black professor and Black student because both "locate themselves culturally, socially, politically, historically, and intellectually at an all encompassing Black/African-American site" (416), discussions about racial identity are no less of a classroom authority problem when both the teacher and the students are White. Like Johnson, I am trying to understand "how my race and gender construct my role as professor, my pedagogical style, and my ideology" about the teaching of race (415).

2. Bizzell also details a form of power that she calls "coercion," which more closely fits the Pythagorean form I describe in the opening paragraph: "One sort of power might be imagined as exercised by A over B,

regardless of B's consent or best interests. Here A uses B to benefit A, and there's nothing B can do about it" (56).

3. "Coping," of course, is a controversial term. It is Richard Rorty's word for one of the aims of knowledge (325). It is also the concept which Kurt Spellmeyer locates in the work of Rorty and Kenneth Bruffee and finds to be ahistorical (see pages 193–224 of Spellmeyer's *Common Ground*).

4. This perception of a lack of clarity on Williams's part was due not to reading comprehension problems, but rather to a more complicated system of resistance to what such students might have seen as "the teacher's agenda," which is, to them, a subset of the larger reformation project they correctly or incorrectly think the writing program endorses.

5. See Charles A. Gallagher's "White Reconstruction in the University."

Works Cited

Bizzell, Patricia. "Power, Authority, and Critical Pedagogy." *Journal of Basic Writing* 10 (1991): 54–70.

Ellsworth, Elizabeth. "Why Doesn't This Feel Empowering? Working Through the Repressive Myths of Critical Pedagogy." *Harvard Educational Review* 59 (1989): 297–324.

Foucault, Michel. *The Order of Things: An Archaeology of the Human Sciences*. New York: Random, 1970.

Freire, Paulo. *Pedagogy of the Oppressed*. Trans. Myra Bergman Ramos. New York: Continuum, 1993.

Gallagher, Charles A. "White Reconstruction in the University." *Socialist Review* 24 (1995): 165–187.

Giroux, Henry A. *Schooling and the Struggle for Public Life: Critical Pedagogy in the Modern Age*. Minneapolis: U of Minnesota P, 1988.

hooks, bell. *Teaching to Transgress: Education as the Practice of Freedom*. New York: Routledge, 1994.

Johnson, Cheryl L. "Participatory Rhetoric and the Teacher as Racial/Gendered Subject." *College English* 56.4 (1994): 409–19.

Miller, Richard E. "Fault Lines in the Contact Zone." *College English* 56.4 (1994): 389–408.

Pratt, Mary Louise. "Arts of the Contact Zone." *Profession 91*. New York: MLA, 1991. 33–40. (Originally presented as the keynote address at MLA's Responsibilities for Literacy conference in September 1990 in Pittsburgh.)

———. *Imperial Eyes: Studies in Travel Writing and Transculturation.* New York: Routledge, 1992.

Roediger, David R. *Towards the Abolition of Whiteness: Essays on Race, Politics, and Working Class History.* London: Verso, 1994.

Rorty, Richard. *Philosophy and the Mirror of Nature.* Princeton, NJ: Princeton UP, 1979.

Rothgery, David. "'So What Do We Do Now?' Necessary Directionality as the Writing Teacher's Response to Racist, Sexist, Homophobic Papers." *College Composition and Communication* 44.2 (1993): 241–47.

Spellmeyer, Kurt. *Common Ground: Dialogue, Understanding, and the Teaching of Composition.* Englewood Cliffs, NJ: Prentice, 1993.

Williams, Patricia J. *The Alchemy of Race and Rights: Diary of a Law Professor.* Cambridge: Harvard UP, 1991.

CHAPTER EIGHT

"Can't We All Just Get Along?" When a College Community Resists the Contact Zone

DIANE PENROD
Rowan University

Excitement in higher education was viewed as potentially disruptive of the atmosphere of seriousness assumed to be essential to the learning process. To enter classroom settings in colleges and universities with the will to share the desire to encourage excitement was to transgress. Not only did it require movement beyond accepted boundaries, but excitement could not be generated without a full recognition of the fact that there could never be an absolute set agenda governing teaching practices. Agendas had to be flexible, had to allow for spontaneous shifts in direction.

BELL HOOKS, *Teaching to Transgress*

Silence is an important marker in any college community. It acts as both a point of acceptance and a point of resistance, a cultural space that is continually invented and reinvented. Sometimes when silence acts as a point of acceptance, the receiver garners public affirmation of her or his ideas, which may indeed include a material reward of some kind. Conversely, when silence acts as a point of resistance, the recipient of the "silent moment" is always wondering what went wrong and strives to reinvent herself or himself. For college composition instructors, silence can be more deafening, as well as more defining, than voice. We waver between silence as acceptance and as resistance whenever we teach. However, this dilemma over silence is never more acute than when we enter contact zone discussions in our classes and in our faculty endeavors. In contact zones, those places in language where various levels of race, gender, and social pressures are engaged, we often find shifting cultural spaces where points of acceptance and resistance occur almost simultaneously, depending on who is involved in the conversations. Moreover, at times we can also find those gaps—silences—where the emptiness of words and phrases is overwhelming and leaves us feeling as if a "fight or flight" situation may exist.

While linguistic gaps are expected, anticipated, and even encouraged in contact zones, particularly in classroom experiences, it is the silence that sometimes underlies those pressure points and gaps that is most disturbing. Silence is the representation of the "great abyss" of ideas, a great void that can be filled with anything. Commonly, though, a room filled with silence becomes the cultural space where one invents and reinvents oneself in order to receive affirmation and reward based on a rhetoric of tolerance supported by the community at large. We see not only our students doing this, but also periodically ourselves, as we scramble to save face in faculty meetings or colloquia where contact zones emerge. This paper, then, explores how a college community fills the abyss created by language and how the potentially productive disruptiveness of a certain cultural space, the contact zone, is endangered when we aim for collective public affirmation and reward—tolerance—and not for critical exploration of those issues underlying the language we use.

Where I teach now, as well as in the various institutions where I have taught before, contact zones, gaps, and silences exist. There is a difference, however, in the kinds of gaps and silences I face in the classroom now as compared with those I faced in the past when entering contact zones. The silence I see currently is based on the use of the term "tolerance" by many of my colleagues, as well as the use of the phrase famously coined by Rodney King and now appropriated by my students—"Can't we all just get along?"—to dismiss critical discussions raised by and in language. What follows in this essay is a series of personal observations taken across several campus situations to illustrate what happens in a college community when it "zones out" (Janice Wolff, personal correspondence) and resists entering contact zones at any discourse level.

For me, "zoning out" is an intriguing model of resistance in the college community. It seems to manifest itself in two different forms: the benign approach and the backlash approach. The most obvious form, the backlash approach, is the reactionary accusation of "political correctness" whenever issues of language and ideas intersect with racial, class, gendered or sexual domains of the status quo. As a professor, I prefer that students adopt the backlash mode of resistance when I teach issues of language use in my classes. Entering these conflicts can produce enlightening, teachable moments. Once the class engages in discussing such ideological challenges to an existing state of affairs, we all find ourselves enmeshed in one or more contact zones, and we begin to sift through the linguistic fragments to negotiate ways of understanding the dynamics that form around the words and/or phrases in question.

But, while much has been written about the backlash forms of resistance to the contact zone, perhaps because of their vehemence, vitriol, and sensational effect on an audience, little is spoken about the other form of resistance. This is a form of resistance I find to be more insidious in the development of a college community than the backlash approach: the benign resistance found in "tolerance," the silence that simultaneously appears to accept and resist those ideas or individuals who run counter to the status quo.

Benign resistance to contact zone issues—that is, the claims of tolerance and "getting along" that exist in polite discourse—can be far more damaging to a college community. Quite simply, if a person tolerates *everything* or wants to get along with *everybody* just to keep the peace, then we cannot truly discuss anything with this person. A conversation is almost impossible to have because we cannot engage in debate with someone who, apparently, does not want to see that inequalities exist anywhere. These individuals "zone out" of the discussion, which can reduce a discourse situation to something bordering on nothingness. If dialogue is reduced to accepting everything one says, then there is nearly nothing to say, no point to discuss, as there is no point of contention to act as the catalyst for discourse. As teachers committed to working in contact zones, we need to think about what is (and is not) accepted and acceptable in order to facilitate conversations in the classroom and in our daily faculty activities. Clearly, some ideas and some language will not encourage solid argument and exchange of thought, regardless of whether a student or a colleague proffers the line of reasoning. When pressed on their issues, practitioners of benign resistance techniques adopt the language and ideas of the status quo in whatever form it takes at a given time. Is following the mainstream being *tolerant* or being careful of one's step to make sure a person doesn't have to save face and reinvent himself or herself? Is following the expected a way to "just get along" with any group of people? I wonder. Though I wonder even more about the reasons why some folks refuse to enter contact zone discussions.

Why is it after thirty years of what has been called "diversity building" on American college campuses that we have the problem of resisting the contact zones we've been creating for three decades? While the backlash response claims that people who resist contact zones are tired of "victim theory" in which individuals allege they are victims against larger social forces, I don't tend to view the problem in the same manner—particularly when we address these issues on campus. Perhaps Mary Louise Pratt best points to the crux of this problem in her discussion of Benedict Anderson's "imagined communities" (37). Colleges and universities are direct creations of imagined communities in Anderson's use of the phrase: sites where language and literacy can preserve a sense of national culture and where, regardless of whatever actual inequalities or exploitations may prevail, the institution is always visualized as a place of great, level solidarity (Anderson 7). The style in which academic communities are imagined noticeably follows Anderson's three features for creating binding communal ties: they are limited; they are sovereign; and they are fraternal (Anderson 6–7; Pratt 37). Thus, contact zones regularly poke at what we have envisioned for ourselves on campus and, more specifically, in our classrooms. Contact zones suggest that college communities, like college classrooms, are not as limited, sovereign, and fraternal as we might believe. As Mary Louise Pratt indicates, the intention of contact zone theory is to "contrast with ideas of community that underlie much of the thinking about language, communication, and culture that gets done in the academy" (590).

The primary mode for discussion of issues that matter to college and university institutions concerning the communication of their public image is one of *tolerance*. *Tolerance* for presumably everyone's ideas creates the imagined level playing field that colleges and universities are built upon. However, the "tolerant" mode in academic discussions tends to cause more difficulties than it solves.[1] That is because tolerance's blind acceptance of *all* positions as being equally legitimate renders talk into mindless parroting of any and all ideas, regardless of their soundness or their effect on those outside the majority. Contact zone theory clearly jabs at the notion of this supposed homogenous, fraternal community built around the language of tolerance.

There is a strong social and economic root to the legitimacy of "tolerance" as a discourse position that must not be ignored, as it is ingrained so deeply in America's collective consciousness. Because "tolerance" and its connection to economics are so embedded in American cultural memory, we must recognize that this notion will also be infused throughout our higher educational system. There are profound reasons that it is easy for our colleagues and students, as well as for ourselves, to be so accepting of certain economic systems that produce or maintain social problems, but not of certain individuals who reap the benefits from systems like capitalism. Capitalism is rife with power and class inequities, so it becomes easy to stand for the continuation of specific social conflicts because we are raised with the tacit understanding that "these things exist" in a capitalist system. Those persons who transcend power and class inequities, especially if they are persons of color, are looked at skeptically. Speculation runs rampant on the question of how one who is outside of the spheres of power and class succeeds. In higher education, for instance, many faculty wonder about the value of affirmative action, special admissions, and legacy policies on campus. Rarely, though, do professors interrogate the central reasons as to why each of these guidelines needs to exist in their community. Instead, most tolerate these admissions actions as being equivalent to each other even though they are clearly separate and unequal.

Tolerance as a form of benign resistance within contact zones has its origin in the European bourgeoisie model that Mary Louise Pratt presents to us in her essay "Arts of the Contact Zone." The English economist R. H. Tawney argues that there is an economic and moral connection to tolerance tracing back to the Restoration (17) and that this economic-moral connection to tolerance flourished during the English upper class's turn to Calvinism in the seventeenth century (100). Tolerance becomes an accepted compromise, suggests Tawney, because of the pressure brought to bear by commercial interests to construct a balance of power based upon the conflicting views of the current authorities (100). In short, the societal pressures fed by the rise of capitalism and laissez-faire in Europe, and later in America, required a practical solution: encourage individuality to a point in order to maintain what we think is a level playing field. This is exactly what many of us in composition find in our classrooms and in our academic communities—individuality is encouraged and tolerated *to a point*. Beyond this unwritten, unvoiced "point," individuality becomes equated with "deviancy." And deviancy tends not to be tolerated in most college communities. But why is this so? Why is there an unspoken limit to individuality in classrooms and committee meetings that we dare not transgress without shattering "tolerance"?

A rhetoric of tolerance avoids the "messiness" of confrontation and conflict that individuality brings: individuality frequently points up the illusions conjured by the imagined "level playing field" in colleges and universities. Likewise, tolerance helps those in power keep decorum, which keeps us all focused on our productivity, regardless of whether that productivity is educationally or economically based. A tolerant view of individual cultural diversity in a college community, then, increases (educational or economic) capital. We need only look at an op-ed piece in the *Wall Street Journal* entitled "Paymasters of the PC Brigades" to find a more current example of Tawney's proposal. The author,

Evan Gahr, a reporter for the conservative magazine *Insight*, discussed how first-year mandatory readings for rhetoric courses at the University of Iowa dealing with ageism and sexism, as well as how math courses can be made more "attractive" for women at Nassau Community College in Garden City, New York, are funded by "mainstays of the American establishment": philanthropic groups like the Ford and Rockefeller foundations (A10). Gahr took exception to the ways in which these two educational institutions directly addressed contact zones in the teaching of writing and math.

While Gahr's underlying message in "Paymasters" that philanthropies (using money donated by wealthy corporations and individuals) are funding politically correct ideas is obvious, and is another overt form of backlash resistance to critical teaching in the contact zones, there is a far more important message in the language being used by philanthropies funding everything from curriculum development to scholarship. This is a point Gahr completely misses.

Academic projects funded by foundations like Ford and Rockefeller generally have the intent of "mainstreaming" those individuals who have been "shortchanged" in American culture. This funding is promoted as a way to level the playing field for minorities and women. I find the use of business terms in Gahr's article relating to the education of diverse on-campus populations to be quite telling. Promoting an impression of tolerance, of inclusion, on college campuses for minorities and women makes sense for the business world. Using philanthropy, one can bankroll certain ideas or positions that "pay off" in the longer term by drawing upon a rhetoric of diversity that is disingenuous. The rhetoric of diversity in these instances results in a tolerance of these "underrepresented" folks and looks for ways to get them into the mainstream of being economically productive citizens, of being on that level playing field. Women, gays and lesbians, and people of color who feel accepted in a community will be better workers later on, especially if they are mainstreamed into sponsored ideas. Many professors on college campuses already have the perception that a student's self-improvement comes from emulating those in power; that is, students want to become like their professors. Philanthropically funded academic projects play even more into this perception. This is a point similar to what Mary Louise Pratt raises in her essay, as she questions whether teachers are successful when they erase any and all oppositions to the ideal image, thus creating students who are, to some degree, constructed in the teacher's own image (39).

If Pratt's view relates to the relative comfort in which some professors live, as compared with many of their students, and to the types of ideas the professors promote according to their respective comfortable lifestyles, then "tolerance" *does* contain the economic message Tawney argues for in his article. Under the rhetoric of tolerance in this respect, the closer a student emulates the appearance and demeanor of the professor, the more successful the student becomes—regardless of race, class, gender, or sexuality—because the student has accepted the limits of individuality set by those in power. Theoretically, as Tawney implied, individuality is acceptable *to a point*. So, a woman, or a working-class White male, or a Black male, or a gay Asian, or a lesbian Latina, *could, conceivably*, make career choices based on her or his individual interests and capabilities. However, those choices may be limited and constrained because the individual does not know any other possibilities than what is tolerated by those who are above him or her in the chain of power. Given the construction of the rhetoric of tolerance, when one's distinctive characteristics contest or breach the collective consciousness of a community, that individualism is not tolerated. The community's lack of tolerance for a person's or a group's behavior translates into a lack of individual success. But, with respect to Mary Louise Pratt, success is not a matter of who wins or who loses in the mode of tolerance, because in these relationships the one with more power always wins: success is determined by *who marks the point of contestation*. More precisely, success depends on who can determine what "acceptable level" the playing field takes.

Reading "tolerance" as a rhetorical strategy used by a dominant majority in a community, and as a strategy connected to economics, directs us toward seeing that there are many important contact zone elements contained within the term *tolerance* itself. One must be in the position of power to tolerate—to accept or willingly endure—something or someone. Therefore, we should recognize that "tolerance" also has a blindness created by the nexus of power and knowledge that exists within the community that permits members to be tolerant toward those defined as Others.

The power of tolerance as a mode of benign resistance and as a form of rhetoric within the college community demonstrates that the academy is clearly an example of Benedict Anderson's primordial village. Tolerance based on the primordial village approach creates a bandwagon effect that quickly descends into what semanticists call a "we/they" dichotomy: *Everyone wants to be like us.* Dichotomous thinking clearly typifies the fact that the imagined community's playing fields are not in fact level. *We* relate to the ideal. Those who want to be recognized for their individuality aren't like *us*. *They* aren't part of the community. *They* don't respect *our* ideal. *We* "can't get along with *them*" until *they* think more like *we* do. This type of thinking regularly occurs within the administrative, faculty, and student ranks in a college community. It fosters adversarial relationships at multiple points. Dichotomous thinking provides fertile ground for contact zones to grow. However, a rhetoric of tolerance that runs throughout a campus allows for quiescence, ignorance, and denial of any rhetoric of diversity, multiculturalism, and/or individuality, because the claim of "tolerance" permits people to defer to an ideal that promises (but may not deliver) economic benefit. Anyone can "zone out" of a discussion if he or she thinks the conversation infringes upon his or her image or perception of future success in the community. And, as I explain in the following two examples, "zoning out" occurs more often than we care to admit in college communities—sometimes to the detriment of all the participants involved.

"Tolerance" in Action: An Example of "Zoning Out" in a Faculty Meeting

I can only say this doesn't sound like liberation to me.
BELL HOOKS, *Teaching to Transgress*

In October 1994, I was asked to join our campus's Multicultural Resource Team. As a then-new faculty member, I did not have historical knowledge of this committee's rise, nor did I have much background surrounding the rhetorics of diversity on my campus. Therefore I had no knowledge of the ideals the college community had for presenting multicultural issues on campus. Since I am of Native American and working-class descent, I was eager to find out where the college stood relative to multiculturalism. Our first meeting of the year was in early November, a luncheon to meet everyone and discuss the future of multiculturalist issues in the classroom.

What I heard was stunning. Rather than have serious interaction in contact zones along disciplinary lines at the meeting, I heard how an older, White (male) religion professor said multiculturalism helped him teach Roger Williams's religious theories better to his (primarily working-class, racially mixed, religiously diverse) students, and how a young, Ivy League–educated, White (female) English professor could really teach the heart of African and Caribbean literature to the same student population by applying multicultural ideas. To me, these people's rhetoric sounded like missionary work, a kind of "let's bring civilization to the natives" rhetoric, full of good intentions but leading us down the pavement to Hell. As I looked around the room, there were about thirty of us. Except for five of us in the room, it seemed that the composition of the group was of White, upper middle-class, European descent—paralleling both the European bourgeoisie's communities Pratt discusses in her essay and Anderson's imagined community that Pratt draws on in her work. The idea that kept repeating itself in the rhetoric was that *if we learned the language of multiculturalism*, we could understand our students better. *If we learned the language of multiculturalism*, then we could form a stronger campus community. As if there were a single language of multiculturalism to learn . . . to colonize . . . to govern . . . to create new consciousness of group identities. Contact zones show us that there is no single language to learn in any community. A community, whether it is a class or a meeting group, is characterized by multiple languages competing for attention and voice, not for blind acceptance and mindless parroting of words and ideas. As story after story repeated the theme of *if we learned the language of multiculturalism*, it became apparent that we in the room were in the great abyss of benign resistance. We were "zoning out."

In front of me, nearly thirty people who were extremely serious about the need to bring multiculturalism to our campus sat discussing "multiculturalism" and "minority students" as objects of study rather than as concerns involving real individuals with real pressures and demands concerning their studies. The more I heard, the more I was irritated. At first, my exasperation grew because I could see myself as one of "those students" being classified to be dissected: a first-generation college student from a blue-collar rural community, female, of Native American heritage who was often told throughout her academic training that she was "lucky to be in school." Second, I felt the group members were objectifying students; that is, the participants in the discussion spoke of students not in terms of their diversity, but in terms of the meeting-goers' own literacies and how "those students" fell short in comparison. In the process of scrutinizing various student populations, the group created a monolithic, homogenous Minority Student based on the group's imagined vision of who, or what, that might be. The committee's language that created this Minority Student and the Multicultural Classroom was, as Pratt puts it, "analyzed as a social world unified and homogenized with respect to the teacher," which could easily result in "whatever students do other than what the teacher specifies [being] invisible or anomalous to the analysis" (39).

I couldn't believe what I kept hearing—a discussion of multiculturalism that did not address difference, struggle, or border crossing in its rhetoric. Pratt's observations of teachers feeling their most successful when they eliminate oppositional discourse and unify the social world in their own image (39) never seemed so clear to me as at this meeting. Indeed, success surely can be defined by who marks the points of contestation. In this instance, the Multicultural Resource Team's success was defined by their perceptions of how the Minority Student fell short of the members' own personal literacies and expectations. *Of course, if we learned the language of multiculturalism* . . . except, as the discussion continued, I began to feel it was the minority faculty who had to learn the language of the majority. And the actual minority students who take our classes might never want to learn the language of either faculty group in the room.

Then one man spoke. A newly hired assistant professor in foreign languages and literatures suggested that courses in European languages (Spanish, French, Italian, and so on) have demonstrated that "tolerance" can be taught. So, in his opinion, all students should be required to take a European language. His statement about European languages encouraging tolerance reminded me of Benedict Anderson's argument, quoted in Pratt's essay, that the European bourgeoisie believed their literacies would "achieve solidarity on an essentially imagined basis" (Anderson 74) although that solidarity was never really achieved. However, like the European bourgeoisie before him, this young male professor set in motion a utopic understanding of community based on language—and it opened into a contact zone exchange.

Immediately, from across the room, one of my colleagues from my department entered the contact zone exchange that had been unintentionally opened up by this male assistant professor. A woman of Bahamian descent, she quickly responded, "Perhaps I don't want to be 'tolerated.' In my community, we argue. We have conflict. And no one leaves with hard feelings." *Yes!* I understood this well. Growing up in my family and in my hometown, I experienced conflict as a commonplace at the dinner table, on the playground, and in the schools. Though people were rough with their language and their actions, rarely did anyone leave the conflict with hard feelings. As Pratt points out, vernacular expression, denunciation, and critique are important literate arts in some linguistic communities, and conflict is how some folks mediate and resolve differences (37). Still, these linguistic styles are not part of the ideal college community based on the model of the European bourgeoisie. Nor are outbursts accepted in the model of European tolerance. Those faculty and students who aren't raised in this European bourgeoisie environment will not always follow the expected rules of orderliness or scripted literate interactions (Pratt 38). In all likelihood, their alternative discursive styles will, when juxtaposed with a dominant style accepted in a given setting (e.g., a faculty meeting), foreground contact zones.

With my colleague's words, the tenor of the discussion

changed. Tensions began to rise in the room. An adjunct professor from my department responded. "What is wrong with *tolerance?*," she asked. Most in the room nodded their heads in assent. That was enough for me. I chimed in. I could not stay silent. As Pratt offers, "when speakers are from different classes or cultures, one party is exercising authority and another is submitting to it or questioning it" (38). I needed to enter the contact zone that had emerged in our discussion. I refused to submit to an illegitimate authority that refused to recognize the sentiments of Others, and I felt it was important to interrogate this professor's use of "tolerance."

I explained that no one wants to be "tolerated." "Tolerance" implies that an individual or group in question is a bother, a pest, perhaps to the point of being a "White man's burden." "Tolerance" carries the message of *indulging* in a set of beliefs or practices that *differs* or *deviates* from one's own set values. Furthermore, "tolerance" implies *a limit of variation permitted* by a group or an individual, as well as an ability to endure the effects of the variation. Given the messages transmitted to people by the word "tolerance," who would *want* to be "tolerated"?

The instructor, a woman who has taught in my department part-time for nearly two decades, then asked me: "Well, then, what *do* you want?"[2] The contact zone's pressure bore down on many of my colleagues at that moment. All eyes turned toward me. My response: "Recognition." Those few in the room who were aware of having a direct stake in this discussion by virtue of their ethnicity or class affiliation nodded in agreement. *Recognition* is what is wanted by many engaged directly in contact zones: *Recognize* fully the identities that comprise the entire community, not just the dominant ones. A community is not unified and homogenized solely around a singular, majority point of view, but is made up of differing views and heterogeneous ideas.

The woman tersely answered back: "Well, I certainly don't see the difference between *tolerance* and *recognition*. You're a semanticist." At this point, the chair of the day's activities moved the discussion along to less inflammatory matters about how to bring multicultural classes to our departments. Clearly, the line of accepting individuality had been breached in the contact zone and it was time to save face in the community. We who spoke from a minority position did not play the discourse games in the same way as those who spoke from the majority position based in the European bourgeoisie model of discourse. Since our discourse norms were not the same as theirs, we didn't obey the established rules. Therefore, any points the minority faculty tried to make were rendered invisible, an anomaly, in the day's conversation. As we divided into our respective subgroups, the meeting came to an abrupt close because many members suddenly had to leave the room for one reason or another. Time to "zone out" again. Meanwhile, the contact zone lingered upon the edges of the abyss known as "tolerance" and filled the emptiness with meaning for those who stayed. However, in this instance, the abyss was a stronger force. People were able to "zone out," to withdraw, before some kind of resolution could be negotiated.

Sometimes in journal articles and in teacher lore, contact zones are celebrated spaces. Teachers are encouraged to seek out those spaces to push for critical dialogue. We must remember, though, that in practice contact zones can be harsh, unforgiving places. We're challenging students'—as well as our own—literacies, language usage, and home cultures. This confrontation can be painful and not as neat or as clean as some may suggest. What transpired in the faculty meeting that November afternoon showed me how disruptive contact zone engagement can be with colleagues.

I want to return to the adjunct instructor's response before moving on. She is absolutely correct in one aspect of her charge: I *am* a semanticist. I teach semantics as well as composition and other courses for our program, so I am acutely aware of the inherent power of words. And there *is* a significant difference between the meanings of *tolerance* and *recognition*. This is especially so in the context of a college community. When one is *recognized*, others admit to that person or group being entitled to have a voice in the discussion. With acknowledgment of the right to have a voice comes an admission to having a particular status within the community, an acknowledgment of the existence of and the sovereignty of those thoughts, ideas, and words carried by one's voice. Recognized languages and ideas are given space to be heard and discussed, without limitation. *Recognition* carries the implication of one's having the power and the right to speak and be heard by the community. For all these reasons, *recognition* leads to a sense of an individual or a group belonging to a community.

Tolerance, however, implies none of this. The implications of the meaning of *tolerance* reflect Pratt's "highly asymmetrical relations of power" (34) that exist in many communities. Under the guise of tolerance, one must still speak within the limits and sovereignty of those above who allow the individual or group to speak. Speech that goes beyond the variations that those in power permit—in language or ideas—is considered transgressive and thus unacceptable. Therefore, in a system based on tolerance, not everyone has the same stake in the outcomes of ideas or in the language that is used to frame those ideas. So if a college community, whether one rooted in the classroom or one rooted in the meeting room, constructs a rhetoric of diversity and a multicultural curriculum based on tolerance, then what is expressed by the community is that *certain* types of representation and *certain* rights are permitted. But, whose representations and rights will be permitted under this system of *tolerance*? Clearly, those representations and rights that are closest (and safest) to the imagined vision of community that exists in the minds of those who have the greatest voice. In these instances, individuality works as long as it reinforces the view of the imagined primordial society. Should a person or a group deviate too far from this imagined vision of community, those who have the greatest voice (hence the greatest level of power) will enforce the limits of the acceptable level of deviance permitted if one is to remain part of the community.[3] This is *tolerance in action*.

Pratt raises an important question in her essay that I will paraphrase here to end this section: Are faculty members supposed to feel their collegiality is most successful when they have eliminated unsolicited oppositional discourse, resistance, and critique and united the college or university's social world, probably in their own image? (Pratt 39). What I learned from this particular faculty meeting is that underlying quiescence frequently gives way to a differing range of stakes and issues which require cultural mediation in order to become fruitful discussions. Otherwise, the temptation to zone out becomes too great on all sides.

When Students "Zone Out" in Class:
Writing and Responding to bell hooks

> Sometimes it is difficult to find words to make a critique when
> we find ourselves attracted by some aspect of a performer's act
> and disturbed by others, or when a performer shows more inter-
> est in promoting progressive social causes than is customary. We
> may see that performer as above critique. Or we may feel our
> critique will in no way intervene on the worship of them as a
> cultural icon.
>
> BELL HOOKS, Teaching to Transgress

Students innately understand the concepts I have presented
throughout this paper. They understand that emulating the
"teacher" drives success; in turn, the payoff for success in the
classroom is the promise of future economic success—a college
degree, a job, perhaps graduate school. In short, the payoff is the
"American Dream." Why else would instructors hear the common student refrain, "What do *you* want?" when discussing a
writing assignment. If students give us what we want, then presumably we, in turn, will be tolerant of them and their idiosyn-
crasies when issuing grades or writing recommendations for jobs
or graduate school. Many students want to adopt stances similar
to the ones we present in the classroom because they hope for
our recognition. Sometimes a student's reticence to speak in ways
contrary to the professor's is interpreted by the instructor as the
student's striking of a "cool pose" (Denis Mercier, personal correspondence) in order to avoid being engaged in an intellectual
debate. However, while trying to be cool or suave in front of
their peers certainly may be important for some students, I'm not
sure this perception holds true for most students. When some
students hold back their comments, I find it is more often the
case that they do not want to anger us (show us intolerance,
perhaps) because "we" are the "authority" and "they" are the
"students"—and, of course, asymmetrical power relations being
what they are in the classroom, students who are intolerant of
professors' positions run the risk of being punished. For many
more students I have taught, it appears that students are afraid
to articulate their positions in the classroom because of real or

perceived repercussions from the professor or the students in the classroom, such as bad grades, inappropriate side comments, or being shunned by peers. Most of my work in contact zone classroom debates is spent in dissipating the students' fears of speaking out and, in turn, in creating a space where they can voice their positions without retaliation from me or others. Sometimes my attempts are successful, and sometimes, clearly, they are not.

When contact zones press students in a piece of writing, the class is faced with situations that estrange the familiar boundaries of "we/they" and "teacher/student" in ways that I, the instructor, cannot easily address. An excellent example of this difficulty comes from teaching bell hooks's essay "Madonna: Plantation Mistress or Soul Sister?" where a popular figure in society, the singer Madonna, is connected to pressures of race, gender, and sexuality. For most students in the class, Madonna the celebrity icon is constructed quite differently in hooks's essay from what students expect. Rather than being a labeled "a star" in the essay, Madonna is characterized as an oppressor of Black women, a dominatrix of Black men, an exploiter of Black sexuality. In a text like hooks's essay, the students' images of Madonna, which are picked up from the mass media and with which students are quite familiar, are suppressed. Instead, the images of the plantation mistress, the soul sister, the materialistic girl, which also coexist in Madonna's videos, are put front and center for examination. And students find hooks's discussion of Madonna in this light difficult to take. Students see hooks's representations of Madonna as paralleling the media's iconic representations, yet they do not want to acknowledge hooks's position. After teaching hooks's essay for more than seven years, I often wonder why the unfamiliarity of hooks's images of Madonna confronts students so?

I think Mary Louise Pratt points to this action of resistance in students when she describes Guaman Poma's mirroring back to the Spanish their own images. In her essay, hooks writes often in the students' own language, and inherent in that language are images that students frequently attempt to suppress in their academic discourse. More pointedly addressed in hooks's essay are the images of Madonna's success. In the popular media, Madonna is presented as an extremely wealthy individual, as representative of a contemporary Horatio Alger story with a female character. However, in hooks's essay, Madonna is a sycophant looking to profit from minority culture. hooks's writing forces all these images to the foreground in contact zones.[4] The clash of the students' ideal images (of the icon, of a successful entertainer, of education, perhaps even of the professor in the room) with hooks's critique creates confusion and chaos for many students. Rather than recognizing that those ideal images exist and discussing how they become transculturated—"the process of selecting and inventing linguistic and conceptual materials transmitted by a dominant or metropolitan culture" (Pratt 36)—in society, many students opt for "zoning out." When students zone out, they allow themselves to suppress their images for the promise of acceptance by and success in the dominant culture. In essence, these students become "passive stenographers" (Denis Mercier, personal correspondence) of their surroundings. Their transcription of hooks's essay goes something like this: Madonna is to be tolerated by us because she has made a "success of herself" (Monday 8:00 A.M. College Composition I class, November 15, 1994).[5]

In effect, these students create ideal primordial villages or communities about celebrities, college, and life, too, just like the faculty and administration do. This is not a difficult concept for us to understand. Many students, especially in larger American colleges and universities, are similar to their professors or administrators in that most never know their fellow members of the campus "village." Rarely do students in a given class meet outside of a classroom setting to talk. And very few ever get to know their professors or instructors as living, breathing human beings. Still others carry with them an understanding of life based on their parents' experiences. Many have their views of celebrity shaped by an ever-present media culture. As a result, most students create imagined communities concerning the "college experience" and the "real world." These student-imagined communities are as equally as "limited . . . fraternal . . . and sovereign" (Pratt 37) as any faculty- or administration-imagined entity. As with the faculty and the administration, students also generate images of the college community based on a particular discourse style that is, for the most part, imagined.

I think hooks's writing shatters the imagined community some students build about their worlds. Her work is rife with contact zone interactions. hooks fragments the solid camaraderie that students believe they have in the college community. Because her writing mixes "street" and academic English as well as vernacular and academic topics, hooks demands that students account for their linguistic and literary skills as they might exist in worlds beyond the classroom. Sometimes I think the linguistic mix shatters the image students have of the classroom community. Many students have responded to hooks's writing with statements like, "I didn't know teachers talked like that!" In hooks's writing the class finds that some professors don't have a unified, homogenous linguistic code—no positive reference for "tolerating" actions, words, and images that are driven by economics. When hooks writes, the social world is not on a level playing field. Inequities exist. hooks *recognizes* that these inequities exist and puts them forward for full interrogation. And while that may speak to most students, only a few respond. The others, regardless of race, class, gender or sexuality, attempt to zone out.

Unlike in the faculty experience where "zoning out" meant either leaving the room or trying to recuperate a discussion, zoning out for students appears to be a process of staying neutral; that is, to attempt to maintain a sense of quiet classroom decorum ingrained in many students' minds. This seems especially to be the case when the topic of classroom discussion centers on someone or something attractive to students by virtue of her, his, or its status or purpose in society. hooks's words sting and hurt the status quo that many students want, and so it is highly unlikely they would adopt a cool pose to avoid intellectual debate. Still, as angry as students might be during, after, or before class regarding the words hooks writes, some students believe responding to her is "not worth it."

Dantae, a twenty-five-year-old Black male in one of my Comp I classes, said that talking about Madonna and Black culture "ain't a big deal. She's gonna make money off anyone she can" (November 13, 1994). The denunciation of others who appropriate Black culture for economic gain while marginalizing Black people in society threatens many students, regardless of race, who equate hooks's critique with jealousy. In his class response to the piece, however, Dantae wrote that "while its wrong Madonna found a way to make money and live the American Dream, people have to respect her for what she does" (in-class written response, November 21, 1994). Presumably, Dantae refers to Madonna's making money. While some instructors may interpret Dantae's words as vague or as striking a "cool pose," I don't. Dantae progresses from his original position during class discussion that what hooks is discussing "ain't a big deal" to his realization that hooks makes a point about Madonna (since both Dantae and hooks acknowledge that Madonna is "wrong" in appropriating Black culture), but Dantae then justifies Madonna's actions because of economics. Dantae's position moves only a matter of degrees because of a class discussion that ends with a student-based "consensus" response to hooks that appropriating a culture is "wrong," but since Madonna is making so much money, her actions are okay.[6]

Dantae's response is the clearest example I can provide to illustrate a point I made earlier in the theoretical section of this essay: Students like Dantae can acknowledge the idea that a system which appropriates a culture for exploitation is "wrong"; however, it is far more difficult for students to acknowledge certain individuals who carry out the exploitation (like Madonna) are also "wrong" in their actions because these people have benefited handsomely from the system. Rather than question or critique the situation—which would mean that the student would have to examine his or her own (and one's classmates') actions, desires, and attitudes in light of what is discovered in the contact zones that someone like hooks provides—it is far more desirable to be tolerant of wrong actions because of the highly visible payoff. And, what we come to find is that economic success, not musical talent, is the real appeal Madonna has for students.

Yet the difficulty for students in zoning out as a response to hooks's writing is that this movement toward tolerance and its economic ramifications becomes painfully obvious. As the epigraph from hooks that opens this section explains, there is a problem in critiquing a cultural icon like Madonna. Scores of people are attracted to a particular aspect of her act, or they find Madonna personally attractive. These two elements of celebrity seem to erase, or at the very least have the potential to transculturate, any acts of cultural exploitation that hooks or any other author points out. However, in class discussions, several students frequently can and do reveal the complex hierarchical structures at work in society and how those hierarchies are threatened by hooks's words as they make public the students' suppressed images of Madonna or any popular cultural object. A few students in a different College Composition I class, for example, conceded hooks's point that Madonna "can't sing, can't dance, can't act" (Tuesday 9:30 A.M. College Composition I class, November 14, 1994). For others, the vernacular language hooks employs is irritating, and they see hooks as the one who exploits.

Of the forty students who took my College Composition I that semester, a majority responded in their writing that hooks's critique is a sign of jealousy over Madonna's economic success. When I told students that bell hooks is, indeed, a very successful professor, many responded, "Not as successful (monetarily) as Madonna!" One student in particular, Jay, wrote in an in-class essay,

> I feel that after reading Hook's essay that she seems to be somewhat of a facist. All through the essay the word fascist is thrown around. It seems to me that everything Bell Hooks wrote about had to be believed as true. This is why I feel she may be the facist of the essay. It also appears that Bell Hooks is jealous of Madonna's success. (November 21, 1994)

Jay's response is an interesting reinterpretation of hooks's words. hooks places Jay in a contact zone based on race, gender, and economics, and Jay sees hooks as being intolerant of Madonna and her success. Specifically, hooks's minor use of the term *fascist* places Jay into a contact zone. In carefully reexamining hooks's essay, I found only one instance of hooks's use of the term *fascism*: two lines in the fourth-from-the-last paragraph of the essay where hooks writes, "Some of us do not find it hip or cute for Madonna to brag that she has a 'fascistic side,' a side well documented in the film [*Truth or Dare*]. Well, we did not see any of her cute little fascism in action when it was Warren Beatty calling her out in the film" [*Dick Tracy*] (196). hooks addresses a characteristic that Madonna uses to describe herself; however, Jay's reinterpretation of how hooks uses the term in the essay explains more about Jay's ability to accept a system when it benefits certain individuals economically than about his ability to critique an example of the system gone awry.

Jay finds himself tangled in a contact zone because of hooks's skilled use of many of the contact zone's literate arts—critique, parody, denunciation, vernacular expression—in her essay. His written response, full of miscomprehension and incomprehension, illustrates Pratt's points about the perils that exist for writers in the contact zone. Jay attempts to play the same linguistic game hooks does by referring to denunciation—the repeated use of the word *fascism* or *fascist*—to describe his interaction with and questioning of hooks's essay. However, Jay's lack of skill in the literate arts of the contact zone leaves him dependent on "what workings of language [he] want[s] to see or want[s] to see first, on what [he] define[s] as normative" (Pratt 38).

hooks's talent with the contact zone's literate arts expresses many ideas that students bring with them from people in their home communities, yet these students frequently resist such words and concepts because the language and ideas posed by writers like hooks generally place students in opposition to a world or mode of life that they consider to be successful.[7] Some students resist with silence or with cynicism, as in Dantae's case, or with misinterpretation, as in Jay's response. Or, students respond with a retrenched view of the idealized imagined community, as in the case of my Tuesday morning College Composition I class, where several students responded to hooks's essay with the cry made famous by Rodney King, "Can't we all just get along?" I felt this to be an ironic response coming from my students, since King's beating, trial, and verdict made contact zones public to an entire nation. King's plea attempted to squelch the chaos and disruption that filled Los Angeles's streets. Now his words were once again being used to silence debate. Unfortunately, this irony was lost on my students, as most of them never realized Rodney King once uttered those words.

In both classes, my observations of the student reactions to the discussions and their written responses to hooks's essay came to the same points: If students did not see an immediate, usually career-based or financial connection to the ideas presented in the text, then it was easy to resist reading or responding to the essay. If students did not agree with what was being said by an author, it was far more tactful (and less open to debate by other students) to maintain silence by saying the author's issue wasn't important and keep an image of tolerance—read as proper decorum—in the classroom. If students see their ideal image of community being threatened, they respond with the plea for all people to "just get along" and be tolerant of each other. These student positions are not cool poses to look good in front of their peers, but survival skills that allow many students to succeed without violating any unwritten limitations on their individuality that may mark them somehow as being "deviant" from the status quo and thus deny them a move forward in their careers. Years of schooling have taught many students not to bite the hand that feeds.

No Clear Solutions, Only Considerations

> If and when this radical critical self-interrogation takes place, she will have the power to create new and different cultural productions.
>
> BELL HOOKS, *Teaching to Transgress*

Tolerance fosters a climate where struggle, conflict, and confrontation in a group of people is erased in favor of decorum, obedience, and a future promise of success through a shared, albeit imagined, vision of community. Moreover, blind tolerance for everything in this imagined community wipes away an environment where engagement with ideas, discussion, and individual thought challenges the status quo.

I am not sure where we begin to stem the tide of, to challenge, benign resistance and the rhetoric of tolerance in faculty, student, and administrative attitudes and discourse. Perhaps some of this benign resistance can be lessened by engaging in discussion entire college or university participants, from administrators to students, on what the term "community" means. This action suggests dismantling the unified social view many bring to the conversation. In the exchange, the concepts underlying the term "community" need to include the struggles and conflicts some have, as well as the common aims and goals individual participants have, as they try to enter into a shared experience. In short, *community* must be reimagined.

At the faculty and administrative levels, that means we need to rethink the word *community* as being something more than a "safety" or "comfort" zone *of* ideas; rather, *community* needs to be a "contact" zone *with* ideas. To build a community as contact zone, we all need to think that ideas and language become provocative tools used to develop a literate public citizenry, not to create better mousetraps or more effective production managers. Students, in turn, need to rethink *community* not in terms of a place where like-minded people congregate, but in terms of a place where connections are made and companions challenge each other with the hope of legitimating multiple ideas and positions.

For me, *community* has come to mean that we, as faculty, encourage students to develop a critical voice and to learn how to articulate that critical voice in society. Sometimes it means showing students how to tap into the literate arts of the contact zone. More frequently, it means I must authorize students in class and in their assignments to step away from tired models of thinking—regardless of how hard and painful the process may be—when students confront the many worlds they live in.

Is my view of what *community* needs to be in contact zones an idealistic one, an imagined one? Not necessarily. Rather than keep this form of *community* in the realm of the imaginary, we need to infuse the contact zone's literate arts and scope of historical relationships into our actual daily practices of teaching writing. It begins in the college classroom by calling out the dissonant voices and ideas that exist in the world—recognizing them in our students, in ourselves, and in the readings we select for our courses. And, in turn, we need to ask if those voices and ideas we hear tell us things we might not want to know about ourselves, and if so, we need to reflect upon what is being said and why we want to "zone out" when we hear these messages. To tolerate the words and ideas before us without critique is to zone out in the worst way. It is to affirm everything blindly and without question, to fall prey to a seduction by predictable images, a seduction that builds and reinforces imagined communities.

Zoning out creates social amnesia on a campus, whether it is in the administration, the faculty, or the student population. Resistance based on social amnesia seems to me to be the most insidious type of opposition in a society driven by massive amounts of information. It promotes a rhetoric of virtual nothingness, where every point and every idea is given equal merit, even if those points and ideas are unworkable, insufferable, and/or banal. If a community wants to resist information, we need to provide the models of resistance that are, as hooks suggests, acts that transform the community rather than seduce it (*Teaching* 197).

The final consideration is this: Let us begin to build college communities that use the discourse of recognition that dwells in contact zones rather than the rhetoric of tolerance. In the discourse of recognition, we need to identify which voices are heard (and which voices are not) as well as identify why those voices are or are not heard. Recognizing the sound of another's voice can bridge the abyss of silence. We need to ask, then: Are these voices in our presence suppressive or expressive of desires, choices, and motivations of a given constituency? Until we ask, we are left to live in imagined communities—and to tolerate and presume that which we do not really know.

Reflections on Turf and Teaching: Getting Along Six Years Later

Since writing this essay, I must have walked one or two hundred square miles of campus space and sat in on at least as many meetings of various importance. In this same time span, I also must have taught at least five hundred students in eight different classes—most at the undergraduate level, but many in graduate programs as well. To varying degrees, many of the attitudes and actions I described in my essay still exist on our campus. "Getting along" on our campus seems just as distant in the new imagined paradigm of learning communities as it did in the old imagined paradigm of multicultural communities.

Snippets overheard in some of my most recent travels:

From a class discussion in my Mass Media & Their Influences course in summer 2000: "You ever hear how some of these [nonnative] people speak? I work in a Philly bakery and I can't understand what the Hell they're saying. They don't understand me. Why do we hire people who can't speak the language? If you're gonna come work in America, you gotta speak English. Plain and simple."

From the graduate course Communication Research in fall 1999: "I'm never going to be hired [by a good PR firm]. There's going to be a minority or a woman who will get the job before I will. It doesn't matter that I come from a very good graduate program in PR."

From a hiring committee discussion: "The Administration can't force us to take a minority applicant for this job. If I don't think the person is qualified, I don't want him or her on the job."

For me, what is common to walking around campus, sitting on committees, teaching classes, and the overarching theme of contact zones is the notion of *turf*. Turf defines who *we* are in university or public life, regardless of whether *we* are students or faculty or members of any cultural group. Turf marks our cultural, ethnic, geographic, or disciplinary roots. Turf also demands a homogeneity of its inhabitants—a homogeneity that, upon closer examination, often is more imagined than not. Thus, when *we* share turf with others, we assume that a deep-seated level of confederation exists, even though there are inequalities and exploitation spread among the participants. However, because *we* visualize our turf to be comprised of shared consciousness, we believe others inside our turf boundaries—marked by classroom, department, committee, discipline, college of study, university structure, block, town, geographic region, and so on—maintain similar beliefs. As a result, professors surmise that the students in their classes really want to be like them; committee members presume their peers think like they do; townspeople trust that the colleges and universities within their borders will preserve the ideals of the town that provides the land the college or university rests upon. *We* maintain faith in these notions because each of us believes the linguistic and spatial boundaries constructed around these ideas come from kindred spirits. In this way, turf is indeed a powerful thing. When we act in shared ways, tolerance abounds and turf is respected. But turf also blinds us to other possibilities, other ways of seeing the world.

More fragments of conversation from my travels around campus:

From a discussion with a colleague in our College of Education during our negotiations to start a Master's in Writing program and an undergraduate specialization in Writing Arts: "What I like about your program is that you respect our department as professionals. You contact us and we talk about how to proceed. You just don't go off and do something and tell us later."

From a student sitting in my office: "What I like about your class is you treat students as equals. You are 'real' in the way you talk to us."

Contact zones are equally as powerful as turf, however. In classrooms or meeting rooms, or even across town, so I've found, contact zones shatter those imagined, homogenized turf boundaries and the communities we've created around them. Whether through the use of language or nonverbal action, contact zones disrupt the unified fields we believe exist in our classrooms, conference rooms, hallways, and boroughs. Students, colleagues, and townspeople do not always think or act as *we* do or as *we* expect, nor do *we* always think or act as they do or as they expect. Contact zones make us see the world from a different, albeit unexpected, lens. Sometimes, depending upon the severity of the contact zone's effect upon our turf, each of us can develop amnesia about the rupture, and tolerance returns quickly. Other times, though, the contact zones estrange us and force us to see that these identities and communities we've imagined—created in our own images, really—are not "natural" at all. The more genuine identities that arise from a contact zone rupture demand recognition, a new identification, to be acknowledged in the turf. Consequently, contact zones push turf boundaries in important, critical ways that require participants to admit that differences do exist in our imagined classroom or college communities. Depending on the situation, *we* just can't sweep away race, gender, sexuality, physical ability, language use, or social class from the conversation.

During my walks across campus and my times sitting in meetings, one part of my earlier discussion still resonates: Economics drives many contact zone disruptions. Turf disputes, whether in class or in committee, never seem so vehement linguistically or culturally until economic factors emerge. In those moments, the personal and cultural (or disciplinary) identities connected to a particular group become heightened. Economics pulls in issues of race, ethnicity, region, gender, sexuality, and disability. Economic concerns shape our language use and how each of us views the world. I see this happen repeatedly in my students' responses to critiques of popular culture, just as I see it when an economic issue is raised in a departmental or all-campus committee. Similarly, reading the companion essays in this section of the present collection, I see that turf concerns and economics permeate the discussions—from Mary Harmon's recounting of her midstate Michigan university students coming to terms with colonization and ethnicity, to Richard Miller's account of student reactions to sexual difference that emerge from assigned course readings, to Robert Murray's observations of how students confront race and civil rights. For a society that imagines itself as being "classless," as America often does, there is an incredible amount of discursive and physical hostility connected to race, gender, sexuality, and physical ability each time economics rears its head.

So, can we all just get along? Perhaps I am less optimistic about this possibility now than I was when I wrote my original essay back in 1994. As Benedict Anderson observed in his *Imagined Communities*, the book that spurred Mary Louise Pratt's discussion of the "arts of the contact zone" in 1991, communities are susceptible to time, space, language, history, and economics. Most of us realize that turf battles and boundaries are also susceptible to these same factors. Certainly classroom discussions are open and vulnerable to changes in time, space, language, history, and economics. That suggests contact zones will always be with us on college campuses. Maybe professing in the contact zone means not just "getting along" but discovering how to continually negotiate and restructure these factors in our pedagogies to include new identities and new boundaries to overcome the ignorance and shortsightedness that result when we hold on to our turf too long or too intensely. Learning how to profess in the contact zone not only requires that we tend to our intellectual and personal agendas, but also that we recognize that those plans need to be flexible as we—and our students—grow and change.

Notes

1. When I wrote the original draft of this paper, the President of Rutgers, the State University of New Jersey, Francis L. Lawrence, was under fire from segments of the student body of his institution and in some national media outlets for his comments on the "genetic hereditary background" of Black students (*Philadelphia Inquirer* B1). Lawrence's defense of his statements: He has worked hard to foster a cooperative community (B8).

2. The most ironic element of this exchange is the fact that, as an "adjunct" in a college community, this woman does not realize her own marginalization in the existing power relations of the academy. As harsh as this may sound, "adjunct" implies that one is joined to, but not essentially part of, a group or main structural element of the community. The "adjunct" teacher occupies an extremely subordinate position within the college community; it is one that suffers greatly from asymmetrical power relations while simultaneously being one of the more highly visible and economically driven positions in the academy. Having been an adjunct at several schools, I realized that my words were rarely heard or heeded by anyone except possibly my students or my peers, and my primary purpose for being an adjunct was economic survival during my graduate school career. Adjuncts are "tolerated" in many departments because they service classes no one else wants to cover or has room for in their schedules to cover. Likewise, adjuncts often relieve full-time faculty of the "burden" of tutoring, lab work, and so on in programs without graduate assistants. Usually, adjuncts work long hours for little pay and few thanks. Given all this, why would an adjunct want to be tolerated?

3. At times, I think it is hard to say which group in a college community can have the greatest voice. So much depends upon the issue at hand and what exigencies shape the participants' views. In this particular faculty exchange, the "adjunct" had the greater voice over the full-time minority faculty members because her views corresponded more favorably with those who had more power. One cannot judge who holds

greater power in the community based on title alone; sometimes we must look at the construction of the discourse being used and notice how closely the lines of discourse reflect the image(s) of the status quo.

4. A good example of student resistance came from a Tuesday morning College Composition I class that I taught in 1994, when a young woman said that hooks did not have to write a line like "The bitch can't even sing" ("Madonna" 191). When I asked the young woman why hooks shouldn't use a vernacular judgment like this in her writing, the student responded that the line made the piece sound "bitter" and "mean-spirited." This was a point that many of the females in the class agreed with. When I pressed again as to why the students felt that hooks was "jealous" of Madonna, the response was based on the students' perception that hooks was jealous of Madonna's economic success.

5. Pseudonyms have been used for all students quoted in this section. Because of the delay between the writing of this essay and its subsequent publication, the students cited either have left campus or graduated without forwarding addresses. Attempts were made to contact these students; however, none returned my letters seeking permission. The course hours and dates are correct.

6. I have thought about this particular class's "consensus" position for some time now. I placed "consensus" in quotes because I don't share their viewpoint, nor did I feel a few others in the classroom shared the dominant view. The dissenting students' voices were drowned out by Dantae's and two football players' voices, which kept pointing to Madonna's monetary success and hooks's lack of popular success in the mainstream. Because of Dantae's personality and the status of the football players, many students refused to voice their opinions or nodded their heads in agreement. Thus, we didn't truly have a consensus in the classroom.

7. Here I think of LaKeisha's response paper. As she begins her essay, LaKeisha explains that hooks's position is one taken by the women in her family. LaKeisha acknowledges that hooks's view is shared by many older Black women in her Newark, New Jersey, neighborhood. She discusses the fact that the feelings hooks expresses are shared so strongly by her mother and her aunts that she, LaKeisha, is not allowed to play Madonna's music in the house. LaKeisha's classmate, Nick, totally agrees with hooks, as he argues in his response that "minorities" in America are constantly appropriated by the dominant White culture, music being just one particular aspect of the appropriation. (Tuesday 9:30 A.M. College Composition I class, November 22, 1994).

Works Cited

Anderson, Benedict. *Imagined Communities: Reflections on the Origin and Spread of Nationalism*. 2nd ed. New York: Verso, 1991.

Gahr, Evan. "Looking at Philanthropy: Paymasters of the PC Brigades." *Wall Street Journal* 27 Jan. 1995: A10.

hooks, bell. "Madonna: Plantation Mistress or Soul Sister." *Signs of Life in the USA*. Ed. Sonia Maasik and Jack Solomon. New York: St. Martin's, 1994.

———. *Teaching to Transgress*. New York: Routledge, 1994.

Martin, Jay. In-class writing assignment. College Composition I, Rowan University, Glassboro, NJ. 21 Nov. 1994.

Mercier, Denis. Letter to the author. 23 Feb. 1995.

Philadelphia Inquirer (New Jersey/Metro section) 5 Feb. 1995: B1.

Pratt, Mary Louise. "Arts of the Contact Zone." *Profession 91*. New York: MLA, 1991. 33–40. (Originally presented as the keynote address at MLA's Responsibilities for Literacy conference in September 1990 in Pittsburgh.)

Tawney, R. H. *Religion and the Rise of Capitalism*. New York: New American, 1954.

Turler, Dantae. In-class writing assignment. College Composition I, Rowan University, Glassboro, NJ. 21 Nov. 1994.

Tyrell, LaKeisha. In-class writing assignment. College Composition I, Rowan University, Glassboro, NJ. 23 Nov. 1994.

Wolff, Janice. Letter to the author. 19 Jan. 1995.

CHAPTER NINE

Contact, Colonization, and Classrooms: Language Issues via Cisneros's Woman Hollering Creek and Villanueva's Bootstraps

MARY R. HARMON

Saginaw Valley State University

In 1995, newspapers throughout the United States carried the story of Texas District Court Judge Samuel Kiser. Reportedly, he scolded a mother for speaking to her daughter in Spanish and ordered her to speak to the child only in English. Failure to do so would relegate the child to life as a housemaid, contended the judge, and he warned the mother that he could take the child away if the girl did not do well in school ("Judge Scolds"). More recently, my local paper ran an article titled "'English, or Adios, Amigo.'" According to the *Argus Press*, the proprietor of the Old Town Pump in Union Gap, Washington, asked three pool-playing customers to speak in English, not Spanish. When they responded irately, she told them to leave. She stated, "We have the right to refuse service to anyone. This is America, where English is supposed to be the main language. We don't want Spanish gibberish here, and we mean it." The article takes its title from a sign hanging over the Old Town Pump's bar.

As shocking as these incidents seem, they are all too typical of daily occurrences in the linguistic and cultural contact zones which make up the United States. Last semester I encountered similar commentary, not from faraway strangers but from students in my composition/literature class as they read Sandra Cisneros's *Woman Hollering Creek* and as they entered the cultural and linguistic zones the text both contains and creates. What follows will tell the stories of their and my experiences in those zones and of some of the "arts of the contact zone" which resulted.

In 1988, Mary Louise Pratt called for a "linguistics that focused on the modes and zones of contact between dominant and dominated groups, between persons of different and multiple identities, speakers of different languages, that focused on how such speakers constitute each other relationally and in difference, how they enact differences of language" ("Linguistic Utopias" 60). About the same time, Michael Spooner recommended the study of "contact literature in English" and noted that, "as English becomes institutionalized in nations that do not share its Western cultural traditions, the language is broadening. . . . English produced in new contexts takes on the flavor of its surroundings, delivering a blend of native and Western linguistic features, semantic and pragmatic qualities, literary heritages and the like" (38). By 1991, in her now well known "Arts of the Contact Zone," Pratt had broadened her original call for the study of a linguistics of contact to include documents, records, journals, and literary and other oral and written texts and proposed the value of studying "contact zones," which she described as "social spaces where cultures meet, clash, and grapple with each other, often in contexts of highly asymmetrical relations of power, such as colonialism, slavery, or their aftermaths as they are lived out in many parts of the world today." (34). And in 1994, Patricia Bizzell suggested that English studies be organized in terms of "historically defined contact zones, moments when different groups within the society contend for the power to interpret what is going on" (165).

In light of this commentary on contact zones and a linguistics of contact, it occurred to me that I have been involved in contact zone pedagogy for sometime in my Themes in Literature/ Composition II course, a combined course in which I frequently feature sociolinguistic issues among the many topics discussed as I teach first-year university students from the Thumb and Saginaw Bay areas of Michigan. Most of my students are White and are small-town or rural dwellers; most have not traveled away from central Michigan for any real length of time; few possess readerly sophistication; and a significant number are the first to attend college in their families. Some of the texts we have read and/or viewed, and the language issues each has given rise to, are as follows:

Woman Hollering Creek, by Sandra Cisneros

> Bilingualism, dialects, an English-Only amendment, gender and language, students' home languages, story modes, language chauvinism

The Autobiography of Malcolm X, by Malcolm X with Alex Haley[*]

> Derogatory ethnic labels, other names and labels, language and social class, code switching

Fried Green Tomatoes, by Fanny Flagg[*]

> Names and labels, language and gender, home languages, dialect, the power of language

Animal Dreams, by Barbara Kingsolver

> Language as constraint and assist, the power of language, dialect, labels, language and the media, erasure via language, home languages

The Joy Luck Club, by Amy Tan[*]

> Bilingualism, erasure via language, language intolerance

Ironweed, by William Kennedy[*]

> Taboo language, slang, dialect, social class and language, registers, gender and language

The Color Purple, by Alice Walker[*]

> Alternative literacies, language and literacy, one's right to one's own language, dialect, names and labels, language standards, the power of language, finding one's voice

Ceremony, by Leslie Marmon Silko

> Story modes, the value of oral story, the necessity of language (and story) change, names and labels, language as assist and/or constraint, one's right to one's own language

Night, by Elie Wiesel, with the film *Schindler's List,* by Steven Spielberg

Hate language, the language of oppression, dehumanization via language

* Denotes the use of the film version as well as the print version.

As the above list makes apparent, the contemporary texts read in my class contain linguistic and cultural contact zones. But, even more interesting to me, for my students within the space of my classroom, and in their larger worlds as well, these texts not only contain, they also create linguistic and cultural contact zones as students encounter Englishes and other languages with which they are unfamiliar and which they often have been taught either to dismiss or to regard as inferior—and as students grapple with lifestyles and cultures much different from most of their own, lifestyles and cultures that some of my students, as discussion begins on a text, label as "other," substandard, immoral, or illiterate.

Thus, I prepared to write an article about my students, texts, and classroom in response to Bizzell's call for a pedagogy of the contact zone, even though I had a number of difficulties with Pratt's and Bizzell's term *contact zone.* When used alone without its accompanying descriptors, it tends to objectify and remove the political forces and power differentials inherent in such contact, as well as the suffering, dehumanization, and constraints caused by it. Hence, although I share Pratt's and Bizzell's notions of the contact zone with my students, I couple them with current thought on *colonization*, a term which by its very nature disallows dismissal of its political implications.

I began by promising the article in February, which blurred into March and April. As spring came to Michigan, I was still procrastinating; the article just didn't seem ready to be written. Then, on April 19, 1995, the world exploded in Oklahoma City as images of the bombing and its carnage flooded the media. Mid-Michigan, my and my students' home, seemed to be directly involved in the Oklahoma City events as news revealed possible Michigan connections as well as the rhetoric and maneuvers of the Michigan Militia. I was more than distressed; I was numbed into inactivity. As I mulled over events, a sense of isolation and impotence arose. So instead of the article, I wrote the following poem:

Midstate Contact Zones

I live midstate
    in a town Malcolm called "the white city,"
    forty miles from Howell, sixty miles from Hell.
At the Dam Site Inn, an old Klan hot spot,
    pickups with gun racks line the lot;
    bellies hang over the pool players' belts;
    a big-breasted, slack-armed waitress
    wearing flip flops
    sidles up to refill their orders.

Fifty miles to the north
    and a little to the east
    the Michigan Militia
    harangues
    and, dressed for combat,
    stockpiles guns,
    perfecting tactics
    for the coming government showdown.
Their kin sit in my class, where
    a twenty-five-year-old tells me the Klan
    is really just "nice guys."

Every morning, closer to home,
    a guy in fatigues pickets the high school
    carrying larger than life posters
    of aborted fetuses: "Jesus is coming to judge you,"
    "Stop murder now," they read.
A mile away,
    the regulars gather at J. Oliver's
    to drink their daily dose
    in the Rush Room.

And I wonder,
    how can I,
    nonnative to these parts,
    make my way through minefields
    to my students' minds?
How can I . . . can I . . .
    make contact?

Now, still shocked, but less paralyzed, I have come to realize that I do not have to travel, nor have I traveled, through potentially explosive minefields alone. I have been in the company of and assisted by the work of Geneva Smitherman (*Talkin'*; *Discourse*), Deborah Tannen, Robin Lakoff (*Talking*), Haig Bosmajian, and Harvey Daniels and all of the contributors to his *Not Only English*, to name only a few scholars, as well as some of my students, and, especially, most recently, Victor Villanueva and his *Bootstraps*.[1]

Many of my students can identify with Villanueva's efforts as they also strive to "pull themselves up by their own bootstraps." Many struggle economically as they hold part-time jobs and pay for part or all of their schooling. Many are returning students, often single parents working at full-time, low-paying jobs while going to school and raising a family. For a variety of reasons, most were not among the top students in their high schools, and many find the world of academic discourse and practices a foreign one. Some are persons of color, primarily African Americans and Mexican Americans.

Although they do not yet read Villanueva's full text, students are introduced to him early in the course as they read and view Alex Haley's and Spike Lee's reconstructions of Malcolm X's life. They note the assertion in *Bootstraps* that autobiography is a political act and they read Villanueva's succinct discussion of colonization, a term and a process named and decried by Malcolm X in Lee's film version of his life (*Malcolm X*). They learn that Villanueva (30) preserves John Ogbu's distinction between "immigrant" and "castelike minorities" and that he states further:

> Colonial theory refines the concept of the castelike minority by looking to the common features of the castelike's histories—colonization or colonization's explicitly commodified form, slavery. ... Minorities remain a colonized people. Sociologist Gail Omvedt sees colonization as "the economic, political, and cultural domination of one cultural-ethnic group by another. . . ." Gonzales Casanova goes a step further, writing in terms of "the domination and exploitation among heterogeneous groups," thereby accounting for a colonialism even when the colonized live and work among the colonizers . . . an internal colonialism. (31)

Thus Villanueva's comments define, distill, and clarify Lee's use of "colonized." After spending time in small groups discussing these comments, students had little problem relating Villanueva's statements to Malcolm X's comments, as recorded by Haley, on the bleaching and whitening of history and culture (162–64). They suggested that Malcolm X, through Haley, describes colonization in action along with some of the processes through which it occurs. Following discussion and sharing of examples from the Haley text and from students' lives, as well as my own, students no longer saw Pratt's and Bizzell's descriptions of contact zones as foreign to them. I began by telling them a rather revealing personal story about my own mixture of shame at and love for my family as I grew up on the fringes of a middle-class, Protestant neighborhood as a member of a Catholic, working-class family, two of whose members are mentally disabled, and all of whom were somewhat unconventional by the standards of my classmates. I confessed that as a teen and early adult, I had spent a great deal of energy trying to eradicate all vestiges of my background around friends and colleagues. My story, with its mixture of conflicting emotions, seemed to open up my students. They were willing to think about themselves and to share. Some saw themselves as inhabiting cultural and/or rhetorical contact zones as they worked at the university and found clashes between the conventions of academic expression and those of home; others spoke of the contact zones in their personal and professional lives as they moved between home, school, and jobs; still others could apply the concept of internal colonization to themselves as they strove to achieve "a better" life and remove themselves from their own backgrounds yet sometimes felt ashamed or tried to make others feel ashamed of family customs and ways of speaking. Some acknowledged having applied cultural pressure by silent or open mockery or by excluding others. Sometimes they saw themselves as colonizers, sometimes as colonized. In the process, some White students were surprised to discover that one Mexican American and one African American student had been accused of speaking, acting, or looking White by their families, and that the accusation had hurt and insulted both of them.

This past semester, two texts later, as we came to Sandra Cisneros's *Woman Hollering Creek*, many of the new insights that students appeared to have internalized about colonization, contact zones, and cultural dominance seemed to dissipate as students read her text. Perhaps repression was especially strong this term, as we had completed *The Autobiography of Malcolm X* just as the O. J. Simpson verdict was announced and had begun to read Cisneros amidst the media reconstruction of the Million Man March. Regardless, as students read *Woman Hollering Creek*—a wonderfully complex work that rides the borders between a collection of short stories and a somewhat more unified long fiction, as well as the borders between cultures, between religions, between past and present; a work that diverges widely from conventional linear plotting; a work that features both Spanish and English; and one that introduces readers to such a wide variety of characters that stereotypes and generalizations are confounded—some students responded with irritation, intolerance, frustration, ethnocentrism.

"Because I don't know Spanish," wrote one of my students, "I was just forced to skip big parts of the book as I read it."

"How many of you know speakers of Spanish," I asked during class discussion; many did. We live in an area populated by a significant number of Americans of Mexican heritage. "Why didn't you seek help," I asked, "Why at least not consult a Spanish/English dictionary?" (At that point, Jeremy, a student in our bilingual program, held his dictionary up.)

"Well," said a woman, "I hate to admit it, but if I couldn't figure it out from context, since it wasn't written in English, I figured it couldn't be very important." Said another, "I felt excluded and frustrated; but I really didn't go out of my way to figure it out; I don't have time." Another suggested that since "this is an English-speaking country, everyone should speak and write English." Nearly all of the students, in their initial responses to the text, disparaged Cisneros's inclusion of Spanish and her storytelling style. One went so far as to declare that writing so many stories to prove a single point, which she felt she had identified and which she quoted from "Bien Pretty" was "stupid." Another added that vignettes like "Bread" made no sense. And still another asked why Cisneros didn't just write a regular novel instead of "channel-surfing through her characters' lives." My Mexican American students sat silent.

At this point, one of my students, Ter-Ri, had had it. She spoke loudly:

> I can't figure you out. Whenever something's new or different or hard for you, you decide it's stupid—or you just don't get it— you don't understand it. Why don't you try to understand it? When we did Malcolm X, at first you all wanted to say that everything he said before Mecca was racist or stupid—how do you think that made me feel? [Ter-Ri is African American.] How do you think it makes him feel [pointing at Steve, a Mexican American student] when you call these stories about his culture or his language stupid, or not important? You say things like this when we're here; I wonder what you say when we're not here. I'd hate to be Dr. Harmon—you expect her to lay it all out for you, to make it all easy. You don't even want to try to understand somebody else's culture for yourselves. You liked the last book we did—it was about White guys and cars and poker (Paul Auster's *The Music of Chance*). You get that. But you don't seem to want to get anything you don't know yet.

Silence. Heavy silence.

"Well," I said, "do any of you wish to respond to Ter-Ri?" Steve said he sort of agreed with Ter-Ri—though it wasn't all the fault of the students in the class. Their high schools had been "so Eurocentric," he added.

"They're not in high school anymore!" Ter-Ri responded. Slowly, some of the students who had been sitting by quietly began to speak. They were interested, they insisted—but they needed help—Steve's help, Jeremy's help, Ter-Ri's help. And, to "provide a systematic approach to cultural mediation" (Pratt, "Arts" 40), I offered them Villanueva's help.

As they read his circuitous account, they responded warmly to his academic struggles and to his life as an emerging and developing scholar and as a person of color. I asked them to pay special attention again to his comments on colonization and their contextualization and positioning among the several theories he presents which have been put forward to explain the differences between the immigrant and the minority person (15–31). To students interested in further study of colonization, I recommended

Frantz Fanon's *The Wretched of the Earth* along with Edward Said's "Yeats and Decolonization," *Orientalism*, and *Culture and Imperialism*. As my students read farther in *Bootstraps*, I pointed to Villanueva's chapter "Spic in English," where he exposes the racism which too often underlies the English Only movement and where he discusses the cultural and linguistic "racelessness" which results from choosing to speak the dominant language and abandoning one's own. They acknowledged the colonialism inherent in racelessness and stated that he had introduced most of them to contact zone concepts they'd not thought about before when he asserted that:

> Racelessness, then, is the decision to go it alone. And it is most clearly marked linguistically, sometimes even by denying that one is choosing to learn to speak White English, by asserting that one is choosing to speak "correct" English. . . . Choosing to speak the language of the dominant, choosing racelessness, bears a price, however. And that price is alienation—the loss of fictive kinships without being fully adopted by the White community (40).

As they read his *"Ingles* in the Colleges," I asked my students to note particularly his account of the effects of the sophists and the Second Sophistic on the rhetorical style of Spanish-speaking peoples, a style alternative to the content-driven style of Aristotelian rhetoricians with their emphasis on linear logic with minimal rhetorical flourish and elaboration, which is the rhetorical style that dominates academic (and much nonacademic) writing in the United States. As presented by Villanueva, characteristics of the sophist-influenced rhetorical style of Spanish-speaking peoples include: the use of long sentences linked coordinately rather than subordinately; digressive tendencies; amplification of a single point by repeating it several times in different words; nonsequential sentences where the logical connections between sentences are not always readily apparent; less emphasis on linear logic, plotting, and progression; and an emphasis on patterns and sounds (79–90).

After reading and discussing Villanueva, some of my students began to resee Cisneros linguistically and rhetorically. Maybe, some of them suggested, she maintained the Spanish of her characters to assert the importance of their and her own ethnicity.

Maybe, her storytelling modes and her language use reflect what Villanueva refers to as "social and historical preferences, traditions, [and] rhetorics" (86) which differ from most of theirs. If, as my student had earlier suggested, many of Cisneros's stories do, indeed, seem to point toward Lupita's advice in "Bien Pretty" (163)—"We're going to right the world and live. I mean live our lives the way lives were meant to be lived. With throats and wrists. With rage and desire and joy and grief, and love till it hurts, maybe. But Goddam, girl. Live."—then perhaps Cisneros is reflecting the sophistic tendency to argue a point by repeating it several times in different reconfigurations through the stories of characters like Ines, Rosario, Felice, and Cleofilas.

I asked students to look carefully at Cisneros's arrangement of stories and to note any similarities they found between stories. After some thought, a quick-write, and small-group sharing, students suggested that as Cisneros allows readers only brief glimpses of people's lives in numerous short pieces like "Bread," "Los Boxers," "There Was a Man There Was a Woman," and "Anguiano Religious Articles Rosaries Statues . . .," she creates episodes and vignettes which operate in coordinate fashion with each other and with the longer pieces in the text. Constructed with their own titles, white space, and positions in the table of contents, they possess their own identity even as they augment the pieces which surround them, rather than being subordinated to those pieces as subplots or mere passages of description within larger, longer pieces. Some students, after a whole-class discussion of these issues, wondered if what others had described as Cisneros's "channel surfing" might in fact illustrate her use of an alternative mode of storytelling, yet a mode equally valid and effective as those to which they were more accustomed. Perhaps her "channel surfing" could be compared to writing sentences that feature coordination rather than subordination. For even though each seems constructed as a separate piece, Cisneros's stories appeared to many of my students to be more than the random and disconnected moments which result from switching channels. Rather, my students added, they possess links that, although they may not be readily apparent to readers initially, can be constructed by readers as they find similarities of tone, narrative style, and issues explored, and as they find evidence of a sometimes circuitous and always roundabout growth in Cisneros's characters and storytellers as they progress in age and in a sense of their own self-worth and agency as women and as border dwellers.

Bootstraps alerted my students to new possibilities as they reread Cisneros. Some of their written responses revealed that they now had entered, to some extent, into the contact zones she depicts in her writing and in her language choices rather than standing judgmentally on the outskirts. Wrote one, "I guess not always being able to translate the text encouraged me to feel more deeply for the characters. . . . After a woman had been dumped on—her language changed—and I said to myself—that's terrible; her words and feelings must have been too deep for English, her borrowed language." Wrote another, "Cisneros alerts her readers to the fact that languages other than English are just as important to their speakers." A third, a Spanish speaker, noted that "Cisneros's characters live on the borders of cultures and nations. Their language also rides those borders. She uses Spanish words and phrases as well as Spanglish. Her English speaking Mexican Americans sometimes speak in the rhythms of Mexican Spanish even when they speak English." A fourth writer, one who has shown a consistent interest in language throughout the course, took a different approach. She stated:

> Cisneros displays her belief in the power of language. Ines in "The Eyes Of Zapata" says that "Words hold their own magic. How a word can charm, and how a word can kill (105). Ines and her mother have both been called *perra* (bitch) and *bruja* (witch). Ines states that people "hurled those words." Cisneros's use of the word "hurled" lets readers know just how much the words hurt. When referring to *hombreriega*, Ines says, "the word is flint-edged and heavy, makes a drum of the body, something to maim and bruise, and sometimes kill" (105). Clearly Cisneros recognizes the harm words can cause. My mom says something which really sums what Cisneros knows about the power of language. She says, "Sticks and stones can break your bones but words can break your heart."

About ten days after finishing our reading of both Cisneros and Villanueva, in response to an open writing assignment featuring *Tejano* border cultures, the following developments occurred:

a. Jeremy, the student in our bilingual program, who up until a few weeks before had been silent about his Mexican American heritage, sang and played four songs he had written in Spanish, English, and Spanglish. One spoke from the point of view of the children in Cisneros's "Mericans"; a second chose the voice of Flavio, the poet, insect exterminator, and artist's model featured in two of Cisneros's stories.

b. Steve (Esteban that day), played some *Tejano* music for the class, described its musical style and its instruments, and demonstrated some dances. He also spoke of the importance to him of both the music and the dances; of his family, who moved from Mexico to Chicago by way of San Antonio twenty years ago; and of his sense of his family's culture.

c. Kris reported on Emiliano Zapata's and Pancho Villa's roles as revolutionaries and on current *zapatista* groups.

d. A fourth student read four riddling poems he had written featuring speakers from *Woman Hollering Creek*. In them, he experimented with mixed English and Spanish phrasing.

e. Jamie called for four volunteers to play a version of Jeopardy she'd constructed which queried Mexican and Mexican American history and culture. Others shared their diary and journal entries, children's books they had written, collections of recipes, explorations of the English Only controversy, and examinations of the economics of the border area between Mexico and the United States. Thus, my students had begun to engage in the "arts of the contact zone" of which Pratt writes: "Storytelling; identifying with the ideas, interests, histories, attitudes of others; experiments in transculturation; . . . comparisons between elite and vernacular cultural forms; the redemption of the oral" ("Arts" 40). Smiles, applause, and appreciation filled the room.

Had my students become fully transcultural? Of course not—not in a few short weeks. But many of them had changed. My students of Mexican heritage became, for the first time, active, visible, vocal members of the class. Nearly all students demonstrated more thoughtful, less judgmental, more open responses to the languages, story modes, and cultures of the texts which completed the course—*The Joy Luck Club, Ceremony, The Color Purple,* and *Ironweed.* In short, they no longer so readily retreated into the boundaries of the familiar; rather, they began the process of immersion in the contact zones these works depict.

Texts like *Bootstraps* amplify and extend Pratt's and Bizzell's work and assist students as they negotiate the contact zones that are contained in and created by works like Cisneros's *Woman Hollering Creek,* and as they negotiate the cultural, linguistic, and rhetorical contact zones in which many of them find themselves as they engage in their own academic development. With students like those depicted here, and with thinkers like Villanueva serving as experienced guides, I hardly need to feel hesitant or immobile as I ask students to grapple in unfamiliar zones; nor can I allow myself to retreat for fear of the very real frustration and conflict that sometimes arise as students read about and traverse contact zones.

Note

1. Since this article was drafted, a number of texts have been added to those I rely on as guides. They include Geneva Smitherman's *Talkin that Talk*; Alleen Pace Nilsen's commentary, as well as the contributed essays, in her collection *Living Language*; Walt Wolfram, Carolyn Temple Adger, and Donna Christian's *Dialects in Schools and Communities*; Theresa Perry and Lisa Delpit's collection *The Real Ebonics Debate*; and Robin Tolmach Lakoff's *The Language War*. As a text readily accessible to my students, I now refer them to John McLeod's *Beginning Postcolonialism*, in addition to work by Edward Said and Frantz Fanon. And the reading list for the course selects from additional entries, including Sherman Alexie's *The Lone Ranger and Tonto Fistfight in Heaven*, Edwidge Danticat's *Breath, Eyes, Memory*, Julia Alvarez's *In the Time of the Butterflies*, David Treuer's *Little*, David Henry Hwang's *M. Butterfly*, Joan Didion's *The Last Thing He Wanted*, and Tim O'Brien's *In the Lake of the Woods,* all of which both contain and create contact zones.

Works Cited

Bizzell, Patricia. "'Contact Zones' and English Studies." *College English* 56.2 (1994): 163–69.

Bosmajian, Haig A. *The Language of Oppression*. Washington: Public Affairs, 1974.

Cisneros, Sandra. *Woman Hollering Creek*. New York: Vintage, 1991.

Daniels, Harvey A., ed. *Not Only English: Affirming America's Multilingual Heritage*. Urbana, IL: NCTE, 1990.

"'English, or Adios, Amigo.'" *Argus Press* 5 Jan. 1996: A1.

Fanon, Frantz. *The Wretched of the Earth*. New York: Grove, 1965.

"Judge Scolds Mom for Speaking in Spanish." *Ann Arbor News* 30 Aug. 1995: A6.

Lakoff, Robin Tolmach. *Talking Power: The Politics of Language*. New York: Basic, 1990.

———. *The Language War*. Berkeley: U of California P, 2000.

Malcolm X. Dir. Spike Lee. Perf. Denzel Washington. Videocassette. Warner Brothers Home Video, 1992.

McLeod, John. *Beginning Postcolonialism*. New York: Manchester UP, 2000.

Nilsen, Alleen Pace, ed. *Living Language: Reading, Thinking, and Writing*. Boston: Allyn, 1999.

Perry, Theresa, and Lisa Delpit, eds. *The Real Ebonics Debate: Power, Language, and the Education of African-American Children*. Boston: Beacon, 1998.

Pratt, Mary Louise. "Linguistic Utopias." *The Linguistics of Writing: Arguments between Language and Literature*. Ed. Nigel Fabb, Derek Attridge, Alan Durant, and Colin MacCabe. New York: Methuen, 1987. 48–66.

———. "Arts of the Contact Zone." *Profession 91*. New York: MLA, 1991. 33–40. (Originally presented as the keynote address at MLA's Responsibilities for Literacy conference in September 1990 in Pittsburgh.)

Said, Edward W. *Culture and Imperialism*. New York: Vintage, 1993.

———. *Orientalism*. 2nd ed. New York: Penguin, 1995.

———. "Yeats and Decolonization." *Nationalism, Colonialism, and Literature*. Terry Eagleton, Fredric Jameson, Edward W. Said. Minneapolis: U of Minnesota P, 1990.

Smitherman, Geneva. *Talkin' and Testifyin': The Language of Black America*. New York: Houghton, 1977.

———. *Talkin that Talk: Language, Culture, and Education in African America*. New York: Routledge, 2000.

Smitherman-Donaldson, Geneva, and Teun A. van Dijk, eds. *Discourse and Discrimination*. Detroit: Wayne State UP, 1988.

Spooner, Michael. "Foreign Affairs: Contact Literature in English." *Expanding the Canon: Bridges to Understanding*. Ed. Faith Z. Schullstrom. Urbana, IL: NCTE, 1990.

Tannen, Deborah. *You Just Don't Understand: Women and Men in Conversation*. New York: Morrow, 1990.

Villanueva, Victor, Jr. *Bootstraps: From an American Academic of Color*. Urbana, IL: NCTE, 1993.

Wolfram, Walt, Carolyn Temple Adger, and Donna Christian. *Dialects in Schools and Communities*. Mahwah, NJ: Erlbaum, 1999.

X, Malcolm, with Alex Haley. *The Autobiography of Malcolm X*. New York: Grove, 1966.

III

COMMUNITY

CHAPTER TEN

Teaching in the Contact Zone: Multiple Literacies/Deep Portfolio

CYNTHIA LEWIECKI-WILSON
Miami University Middletown

The curriculum in Developmental English breeds a deep social and intellectual isolation from print; it fosters attitudes and beliefs about written language that, more than anything, keep students from becoming fully, richly literate. The curriculum teaches students that when it comes to written language use, they are children: they can perform the most constrained and ordered of tasks, and they must do so under the regimented guidance of a teacher. It teaches them that the most important thing about writing—the very essence of writing—is grammatical correctness, not the communication of something meaningful, or the generative struggle with ideas . . . not even word play.

MIKE ROSE, *Lives on the Boundary*

Like Mike Rose, I have long felt that the simplified and formulaic curriculum often deployed for students formerly called basic writers shortchanges and paradoxically deprives them of "fully, richly literate" experiences of writing as instructors strive at remediation. But it has taken me a while to put my feelings into practice. The way I teach basic writing has undergone a number of changes over the course of more than twenty years, as I

An earlier version of this essay appeared in *Teaching English in the Two-Year College* 21.4 (1994): 267–76. Used with permission.

have moved toward developing a pedagogy based on multiple literacies. I offer my own experience, not only because I suspect many writing teachers have gone through the same stages I have, but also as a context for understanding the deep portfolio approach. The deep portfolio is a classroom practice that I believe provides a way for basic writers to plunge into that rich "generative struggle with ideas" (to borrow Rose's words), allowing them to experience the "play," as well as the struggle, of writing.

Explaining the context of the deep portfolio approach requires three narrative strands. One strand of this narrative braid weaves in the composition theorists who have influenced my teaching, and the other two are stories about people I have worked with, a student and a colleague with whom I have had productive collaborations. First, my collaboration with a student, whom I will call Mark, led me to rethink the way I was teaching revision. Next, collaborative writing with a colleague led me to reconceptualize my writing pedagogy, classroom practices, and use of portfolios. Rather than thinking of the portfolio as a container for an accumulation of single papers, as I used to, I have begun thinking of it as a place—a zone, if you will—where reinvention occurs. Before I explain how a deep portfolio works, I would like to touch on several writers who have influenced my thinking, beginning with Mary Louise Pratt, from whom I have borrowed the term "contact zone" in my title.

The term comes from Pratt's "Arts of the Contact Zone," in which she suggests that classrooms at their best function very much like "contact zones," those spaces where dominant and colonized cultures intersect and influence each other, "often in contexts of highly asymmetrical relations of power" (34). I teach at a two-year open-admissions campus of a four-year state university. When I read Pratt's article, it immediately struck me that two-year writing classrooms are very much contact zones. The students in my classes are culturally and linguistically diverse. They are of all ages, with a high proportion of older, nontraditional students. Supporting this anecdotal evidence, a February 1994 column in NCTE's *Council Chronicle*, "Two-Year College English Teachers Face Many Challenges," reports that one quarter of students in two-year colleges are over thirty-five, that "open enrollment policies mean some two-year college students lack a high school education or its equivalent, and that the goals of two-year college students . . . vary widely" (Flanagan 3).

I would add, too, that almost all the students I encounter are members of the first generation in their family to attend college, so when they come into the classroom, they really are entering an entirely new place. However this culture of the classroom is defined, students often perceive it as alien, other, different from the communities they feel comfortable in and know better, such as their homes, workplaces, churches, and neighborhoods. In the context of the classroom culture, they frequently think of themselves as deficient, and often teachers do too. In "Arts of the Contact Zone," Pratt points out that when colonized cultures meet and grapple with the dominant culture, they produce writing that may appear—by the dominant culture—deficient, although Pratt, in fact, celebrates the kinds of writing that she calls the arts of the contact zone: heterogeneity, parody, unfinished writing, dialogue, autoethnography, multiple literacies, and texts written to mixed audiences—to the home community and in partially appropriated form to the dominant community. Her list of genres seems to describe the kinds of writing my students often produce.

When I first started teaching writing in 1977 as a graduate teaching assistant, I was committed to a student's right to her or his own language and freshly inspired by Mina Shaughnessy's *Errors and Expectations*. From her work, I learned to respect where my students were coming from and to analyze their errors for insight into the motives of their mistakes. My goals then were to help them correct their mistakes and learn academic writing. In the 1980s I became a fervently process-based teacher, expanding my pedagogy to include the stages of the writing process. Rather than emphasizing the correcting of individual errors, I stressed the importance of invention, drafting, peer workshop, and revising as the way to "correct" writing. Around 1990, I added the portfolio approach to process theory, seeing the portfolio as a further refinement of process that provided an extra inducement for students to revise their work.

In the course of these years, I moved from a conception of teaching writing as teaching remediation (the remedying of errors), to teaching the process of writing, to especially emphasizing revision.

I am not renouncing that path. Certainly teaching writing as a recursive process marks an advance on the older view of writing as some (often fatal) accumulation of discrete mistakes. However, I see now that I still was thinking about the teaching of writing in terms of single papers. Even when I stressed revision and then worked in a portfolio approach, the point was for students to produce revised, polished papers to go into their portfolios. The portfolio was like a gift-wrapped container, guaranteeing that what was inside was the finest work a student could produce that semester.

I see now that a focus on error, or what Glynda Hull, Mike Rose, Kay Losey Fraser, and Marisa Castellano call "deficit thinking," was still driving my approach to teaching writing. In "Remediation as Social Construct: Perspectives from an Analysis of Classroom Discourse," these authors report on an ethnographic study they conducted on the teaching of basic writing. They note "the ease with which older deficit-oriented explanations for failure can exist side by side with . . . new theories . . . turning differences into deficits, reducing the rich variability of human thought, language, and motive" (313). Hull, Rose, Fraser, and Castellano warn that explanations which locate inadequacies within the mind of the individual are so deeply ingrained in us that critical analysis of student performance always "runs the risk of being converted to a deficit theory" (324).

How are the revised papers of a portfolio a holdover of deficit thinking? In the portfolio approach I was using, my assessment of student writing still focused on single, completed products, albeit three or five papers rather than one. Even though these papers were revised (perhaps even more so because they were), my evaluation for a grade generally came down to what was "not there."

Let me illustrate how the deficit thinking sneaks in by telling a story about how I responded to a paper Mark wrote in a portfolio classroom. Mark was a student in a first-semester College Composition course I taught several years ago. I first began to rethink how I use portfolios from my interactions with him. Mark, a nontraditionally aged student, was probably then in his mid-thirties. He is African American, married, and the father of two.

He works a full forty-hour week, the three-to-eleven shift, in steel-making, an industry which dominates the small Ohio city where our regional campus of a state university is located. Mark tells me he also has a part-time entrepreneurial business, like an Amway distributorship, that he and his wife run from their home. Mark also takes college classes each day of the week, from 8 A.M. until noon. And I might add that he is a very good student. As you can see, he is a busy and competent person, a person of energy, and a student who straddles diverse communities. Mark was born in the South and migrated northward. He attended schools in Ohio but wasn't very impressed with education in his early years. He told me that when he graduated from high school, he just wanted to work and never thought about going to college.

The first assignment of the semester was to write about a family story, "one your family tells about itself or about you," I told the students, "and reflect on how it has shaped you." Students worked through invention, drafting, and peer-group evaluating of drafts, then revised their papers before they passed them in for teacher evaluation. I read and responded to their writing, but I did not give these intermediate drafts a grade since students were going to select three assignments to revise further for inclusion in their final portfolio.

Mark's paper, entitled "Homecoming," was a vivid narrative about his great-grandmother. He did not explain her relationship to him in the draft but instead focused on her character, conveyed through scenes rendered dramatically in direct dialogue that captured vernacular speech and through an omniscient narrative voice that had a poetic effect, like the choral voice of the community. I prided myself for not focusing on errors and for appreciating the strengths of this draft, clearly coming from an ear well trained in an oral tradition. His draft offered such a promising approach to the assignment that I used it as a class model, putting it up on the overhead projector and sharing my evaluation of it with the whole class. I pointed out how he had used evocative speech and explained meanings of perhaps unfamiliar words, paying attention to his audience and educating us about history and language in his community. If the paper were revised for the final portfolio, I suggested, Mark should develop his own connection to his great-grandmother more explicitly. In revising he might reflect more directly on how she had influenced his life.

No doubt these suggestions seem commonsensical enough. I thought I was not evaluating Mark's writing by focusing on error, although I see now I was still operating by deficit thinking. While I praised what was there, many of my comments constructed what was "not there." All my suggestions for revising were cast in terms of a single, unitary, complete essay and were suggestions for turning the draft really into a different kind of paper—the all-too-familiar "The Person Who Most Influenced Me" essay. Even though I was using a portfolio approach, I was not really conceiving of the portfolio writing space as a zone for creative reinvention, but merely as a container for corrected papers.

How would my response be different today? Instead of directing Mark's revising toward formal completeness of a predictable type, today I would probably suggest that a student try developing a variety of new writing subjects from the strengths and interests uncovered in the draft. New writing ideas might connect to the writer's interest in community, an aspect of Mark's draft I initially overlooked in my comments. I might now suggest that a student try a journal writing or try drafting an altogether different paper, perhaps an ethnography based on observation. Or I might suggest that the student collect some interviews on related subjects—on different generational ties, or on ways of parenting, or on the differences between Southern and Northern communities—all topics suggested by the earlier draft.

I didn't make these suggestions to Mark, however, and when he passed in his final portfolio, he had not revised the draft as I had suggested. He was a good writer, he had done good work for the semester, but I still judged his final writing performance on whether or not the papers in the portfolio were complete and unified. I was using the portfolio as an assessment tool; granted, a portfolio provided a fairer way of assessing writing than did a test or a single paper, but the portfolio was still for my (the teacher's) benefit, not the student's. Although it was compiled by the student near the end of the semester, it was passed in to the instructor for that final, all-important term grade. I gave Mark a B for the semester, and then right after I turned in my grades, I felt terrible, as though I had betrayed his writing skill, enthusiasm, and performance with that B.

There is a somewhat happy ending to this story. I invited Mark to participate in a joint faculty/student roundtable discussion on revision, and I eventually learned from our further collaboration that he and the other students liked portfolios in general. They reported that they initially feared writing and lacked confidence, that they found peer evaluations and opportunities for revision helpful, and that they preferred to exercise choice and control over the writing on which they would be judged. I also learned, though, how difficult it is for students to revise. Mark talked again and again about how hard it was to revise, that he worried he would ruin his fairly strong drafts. As I listened, I began to see that my students perceived revising within the whole scheme of correctness; that is, as a way to an error-free paper rather than as a process for inventing new ideas and better ways of communicating them.

In "Inventing the University," David Bartholomae argues that revision is not nearly as simple as we may seem to imply to our students, not merely a matter of applying a little more elbow grease to a task. Revision requires an act of imagination in which the writer more clearly conceptualizes the reader's goals, the context she or he is writing in, and the textual strategies which will embody those goals and fit those contexts. Most of all, really revising means the writer must be able to position herself or himself comfortably within a discourse community (to understand its conventions) and outside it too (to understand its boundaries and thereby control the text). Bartholomae stresses the difficult and long-term nature of learning to revise. One recommendation he makes is that teachers involve students in more scholarly collaborative projects so they get experience being positioned across the boundaries of different discourse communities.

I had done just that with Mark and the other students, and they expressed great enthusiasm for our faculty/student collaboration. They were very good at it too, but that is not so surprising given that two-year college students are already quite experienced with multiple perspectives. Even though students in two-year college composition classes may be unfamiliar with academic writing conventions, they do straddle many boundaries and operate effectively across different literacies. Mark, for instance, successfully operates in his work world at the steel mill, in his own entrepreneurial business, and in college classrooms. Rather than seeing two-year college students as deficient, I became even more convinced that we need to design writing activities that use and affirm the many literacies our students have already mastered. And we need to organize the classroom so that we give students opportunities to reflect in writing on their own transculturation, writing across and about these multiple discourse communities.

"Transculturation," Mary Louise Pratt argues, is what occurs when classrooms really work. Created by Cuban sociologist Fernando Ortiz, the term offers a less "reductive" way of thinking about "acculturation and assimilation" (Pratt 36). Subordinate groups may not control discourse, culture, values, but these are not entirely determined by the dominant group either. To some extent, Pratt believes, subordinate groups can determine what they accept and reject and how they absorb and use "what emanates from" the dominant culture (36). To me, the concept of transculturation offers the hopeful possibility that in learning to write in college, students do not necessarily have to suppress or give up their own cultures and languages in encounters with the dominant discourse. Instead, transculturation suggests the inventive work of constructing new relations of self to multiple cultures with the goal of becoming bicultural and bilingual.

My rethinking of the teaching of writing and the use of portfolios began with Mark and that joint student/faculty roundtable discussion on revision. But it didn't end there. I was also influenced by a collaboration with a colleague, Jeff Sommers. We decided to use our day-to-day knowledge of teaching writing at a two-year campus to create a writing textbook especially for two- and four-year open-admissions students. We selected readings and created class and group activities and journal and writing assignments with the goal of creating a writing course that would draw on the two-year college student's multiple literacies as rich resources for classroom writing. As we worked on this project, a new conceptualization of the portfolio started to emerge. Rather than a container for individual papers, we realized the portfolio could be used to create a recursive relationship among the elements of a class—reading, journal, and paper writing assignments, as well as classroom interactions—and to reflect on these elements. I might add that this discovery or invention, which I am calling the deep portfolio approach to distinguish it from the more established use of the portfolio as a final assessment tool, was unplanned and unanticipated.

In searching for a name to designate this new way of thinking about and using portfolios, I remembered the term "deep image" used several decades ago by Robert Bly. He had gone back to Pound's famous dictum about poetry. "The image," Pound said, "is a radiant node or cluster; it is what I can, and must perforce, call a VORTEX, from which and through which, and into which, ideas are constantly rushing" (106). What prompted my memory and what I am adapting to the portfolio is the idea of creative depth that is activity—the notion of a space where "ideas are constantly rushing."

The idea that the portfolio can be a creative resource for the student grew as we worked on choosing readings and creating classroom activities and writing tasks. We began with the commitment that all writing assignments would ask students to use their experiences and reflect on their literacies, building on and extending them in new directions. We felt it especially important in teaching open-admissions students that the classroom be student centered, not only in terms of group activities and peer/group workshops, but also in focusing on students' own languages and texts and in using published texts that connect to students' lives.

Although our starting assumptions were solidly based on our own teaching experiences, many others have stressed the importance of incorporating students' literacy practices into writing curriculum. Paul Bodmer, former chair of the National Two-Year College Council and now an associate executive director of NCTE, made this point in a 1994 interview: "Students' interactions with their own languages and their own texts become extremely important" in the two-year college (qtd. in Flanagan 3).

Mina Shaughnessy perhaps can be credited with beginning the movement to consider the student's own literacy as a starting point for teaching writing. Certainly Mike Rose's *Lives on the Boundary*, as well as his collaborative work with Hull, Fraser, and Castellano, argue persuasively for greater respect for and use of student literacies in the classroom. Likewise, in "The Interaction of Public and Private Literacies," Richard Courage, an assistant professor at a community college, advocates a "multiple literacies" approach in teaching basic writing. He explains how he integrates student literacy practices from "outside the context of the college classroom" (493), drawing upon students' diverse, nonacademic lives as "cultural resources" (494).

In creating a pedagogy that draws on students' multiple literacies, I now emphasize multivoiced writing—that is, collaborative writing activities, diarylike expressions of changed viewpoints, journals, and drafts (often unfinished)—and value them in themselves as components of a deep portfolio. I have taken Mary Louise Pratt's analysis of the "arts of the contact zone" to heart. Instead of making assignments in terms of single, unified papers, I now aim more for interconnected writing and reading activities that question, echo, parody, and reconsider previous writing from different perspectives. Instead of thinking of the paper as the whole unit, I now consider the deep portfolio as the zone where contact, contest, and mediation occur through reinvention. The portfolio contents may not be—in fact, usually are not—wholes, but pieces and parts of the stages in dialogue, development, questioning, critique.

Let me end with some actual examples of assignments that illustrate how the deep portfolio approach ties reading and writing activities together explicitly with group work and collaborative writing activities. One writing assignment based on a piece of magazine journalism, Monty Roessel's "The Long Walk: Navajo Family Remembers Tragic Time," asks students to respond to their reading collaboratively by doing a group analysis and then sends them back to their portfolio writings to apply what they have gained from the reading as they recast a previous draft of their own choosing:

> Oral history and storytelling are important forms of literacy. Even when written down, a story that comes from an oral tradition retains certain traits of the storytelling situation: a speaker in

front of a living audience using language that signifies the presence of speaker and listener. With your group, draw up a list of
storytelling characteristics in Roessel's selection. Then, look
through your portfolio for a narrative that you could recast as a
dramatic scene of storytelling using some of the techniques you
observed Roessel's mother using.

Other assignments ask students to go back to their portfolios, reconsider a draft, and adapt it in light of new information
or transform it to a new purpose. New writing assignments send
students back to the portfolio to generate a metacritical reflection on a particular topic. Some assignments ask students to write
a group paper, rather than an individually written one, or ask
them to write a paper of multiple viewpoints in several columns
or in separate parts. Assignments send students out of the classroom to look at and reflect on the culture of the world around
them and ask them to connect their reading to this cultural research. For example, after reading a selection entitled "Graffiti,"
by Patty Romanowski and Susan Flinker, students are asked to
search out graffiti and consider it as another form of history, in
addition to published and oral forms.[2] Journal writing prompts
further this dialogic, recursive activity. For example, one journal
prompt reads, "Return to an earlier journal entry you have done;
reread it, looking for a word, phrase, or key term that intrigues
you. Freewrite for five to ten minutes on that word, phrase, or
key term." Another journal writing prompt asks, "Skim your
portfolio looking for personal anecdotes you have used in other
journal entries or drafts. Read the anecdotes and then write a
'behind-the-scenes' description of those anecdotes. What have
you left out of the anecdotes? How have you 'modified' what
really happened? Why have you modified it? What impression of
you does the anecdote create?" Others ask students to make lists
or freewrite on topics connected to writing assignments and to
draw on their knowledge outside the classroom, for example on
their knowledge of the workplace (e.g., "Make a list of any specialized terms or language used in your workplace; define the
terms. Talk with long-time employees at your workplace about
how the workforce has changed over the years—who works there
now who previously did not? Who no longer works there? Reflect on these changes.").

For the final writing assignment, I ask students to write across these contending voices and disparate pieces by writing a reflective learning letter that serves as an introduction to their portfolio. I ask them to quote snippets of their various writings as they connect their learning and writing by linking the pieces in their introductory narrative. This final assignment has grown in importance. I now see it as central to the process of transculturation. Cheryl Geisler defines academic literacy as "the ability to negotiate among multiple worlds of discourse" (44), and she defines research as "a process of systematically acquiring experience from multiple perspectives at the site of a single 'practice' of literacy" (45). The deep portfolio, even when its contents are not conventionally academic, functions as a site where literacy is practiced, as a student assembles and constructs her or his own relations to multiple literacies.

What I have been describing as the deep portfolio approach is certainly not the only pedagogy that might reintroduce the rich heritage of literacies into a basic writing curriculum. Surely, there are many ways to foster an appreciation of the struggle and play of literacies. But what I like about the deep portfolio is that it is a space the student controls. It is a creative space. In rereading her or his writing and using drafts of journals and papers as the basis for new work, the student comes to understand the recursive nature of writing. Moreover, with a deep portfolio, revision is not tied to, nor is it a part of, a concept of error. Revision is also not a slowed-down process approach to remediate "deficient" students. Rather, with a deep portfolio, revision becomes reinvention, the recursive process of creativity, that produces writing.

Afterword: 2000 and Beyond

This essay was composed in 1993–94. Since then I have been mulling over the question of how, or whether, contact zone theory changed composition studies. I was attracted to Pratt's concept of contact zone theory because it seemed to offer a way to discuss two-year college students' languages, cultures, and experiences while positioning them in dialectical, rather than merely subordinate, relationships to the academy, to standard language codes, and to hegemonic culture. In the early to mid-nineties, however, the term "contact zone" seemed to pop up everywhere, and I began to question its use. I wondered whether all classrooms were potential "contact zones," and if so, why English classrooms, in particular, should be conceptualized as contact zones. In fact, I came to doubt that the term "contact zone" actually stands for a single concept. I think instead that it is a metonymy, "a figure of speech in which an idea is evoked . . . by means of a term designating some associated notion" ("Metonymy"). In this case, the site of contact (a classroom, a border area, an international zone) is associated with and invites analysis of the dialectical relations in play during contact itself.

I think the most interesting work that has been generated by contact zone theory are studies of instances of student discourse as displaced contact zones. Close reading and analysis of such texts reveal how differential relations of power are textually embedded and often appear as grammar and/or dialect problems. I do think such close reading practices have led to imaginative new ways of responding to student writing. Gayatri Spivak reminds us of "the staging of language as the production of agency" (189). In understanding students' usage and creating pedagogies that get them to analyze, examine, and rewrite how they have been shaped by asymmetrical relations of power, we can help students become agents. This application of contact zone theory sees language use not as passive reflection of or unimportant in regard to "real-world" activities but as a central practice for change. It conceptualizes the teaching of writing not as indoctrination into the mainstream by transmitting a fixed code but as exploration and negotiation of literacy practices, so that, as Raymond Williams states, "we can have full knowledge of what we can ourselves make or do" (23). While I worry that we have entered into a period of backlash against the kind of multicultural curricula Pratt championed, I am more optimistic that we have learned from Pratt's contact zone theory how to better understand and respond to students' texts as arts of the contact zone.

Note

1. One of the anonymous reviewers of this essay pointed out, quite correctly I believe, that there are potential tensions and political implications in bringing literacies like graffiti into the classroom. For a warning that such contact is not necessarily safe, see Richard Miller's "Fault Lines in the Contact Zone." For a recent positive view of creolized art forms like graffiti, see "Creolizing for Survival in the City" by Ivor Miller, who believes that graffiti "writers constantly reinterpret mainstream culture by using its images and its tools, such as spray cans and advertising, to express their own worldviews. The work of these artists demonstrates a wealth of cultural ingenuity and a capacity for resilience that keeps inner city youth culture a creative and enduring force" (185).

Works Cited

Bartholomae, David. "Inventing the University." *When a Writer Can't Write: Studies in Writer's Block and Other Composing-Process Problems*. Ed. Mike Rose. New York: Guilford, 1985. 134–65.

Courage, Richard. "The Interaction of Public and Private Literacies." *College Composition and Communication* 44.4 (1993): 484–96.

Flanagan, Anna. "Two-Year College English Teachers Face Many Challenges." *The Council Chronicle* Feb. 1994: 3.

Geisler, Cheryl. "Exploring Academic Literacy: An Experiment in Composing." *College Composition and Communication* 43.1 (1992): 39–54.

Hull, Glynda, Mike Rose, Kay Losey Fraser, and Marisa Castellano. "Remediation as Social Construct: Perspectives from an Analysis of Classroom Discourse." *College Composition and Communication* 42.3 (1991): 299–329.

Leeson, Mark (pseudonym). "The Homecoming." Student paper. 1992.

"Metonymy." *The American Heritage Dictionary of the English Language*. 3rd ed. Boston: Houghton, 1996.

Miller, Ivor. "Creolizing for Survival in the City." *Cultural Critique* 27 (Spring 1994): 153–88.

Miller, Richard E. "Fault Lines in the Contact Zone." *College English* 56.4 (1994): 389–408.

Pound, Ezra. *Gaudier-Brzeska: A Memoir*. New York: New Directions, 1960.

Pratt, Mary Louise. "Arts of the Contact Zone." *Profession 91*. New York: MLA, 1991. 33–40. (Originally presented as the keynote address at MLA's Responsibilities for Literacy conference in September 1990 in Pittsburgh.)

Roessel, Monty. "The Long Walk: Navajo Family Remembers Tragic Time." *New Mexico Magazine* Aug. 1993: 72–78.

Romanowski, Patty, and Susan Flinker. "Graffiti." *Fresh, Hip Hop Don't Stop*. Ed. Nelson George, Sally Banes, Susan Flinker, and Patty Romanowski. New York: Random, 1985. 29–53.

Rose, Mike. *Lives on the Boundary: A Moving Account of the Struggles and Achievements of America's Educational Underclass*. New York: Penguin, 1990.

Shaughnessy, Mina P. *Errors and Expectations: A Guide for the Teacher of Basic Writing*. New York: Oxford UP, 1977.

Spivak, Gayatri Chakravorty. *Outside in the Teaching Machine*. New York: Routledge, 1993.

Williams, Raymond. *Marxism and Literature*. Oxford: Oxford UP, 1977.

Writing Centers as Linguistic Contact Zones and Borderlands

CAROL SEVERINO
University of Iowa

The "contact zone" and "borderland" metaphors are excellent heuristics for analyzing writing center work. Both can help explain the position of the writing center vis-à-vis the larger academic community, although, as I'll show, this particular "spatial" application of the metaphors invites the temptation to romanticize the writing center and its staff and students as victims of the power structure. I will argue that both metaphors can be applied just as productively and without danger of exaggeration to analyze the written and oral texts of the writing center as contact literature and contact dialect—the "arts of the contact zone" (Pratt). After I explain the derivations and uses of "contact zone" and "borderland," and how the metaphors do and do not apply to the writing center's place, space, and mission in the academy, I will analyze the writing center's texts as contact zone creations, demonstrating how the center functions specifically as linguistic contact zone and borderland. Thus, I will show how the spatial applications of the metaphors may not be as helpful for revealing the nature of writing center work as are the linguistic applications.

Contact Zone Analogies

Mary Louise Pratt defines contact zones as spaces "where cultures meet, clash, and grapple with each other, often in contexts

This essay was originally published in *The Writing Lab Newsletter* 19.4 (1994): 1–5. Used with permission.

of highly asymmetrical relations of power such as colonialism, slavery, or their aftermaths" (34). Writing centers are contact zones because they serve and respect U.S. and international students and their diverse cultural, linguistic, and disciplinary backgrounds. Within the academy the writing center is the contact zone where diverse cultures, languages, literacies, and discourses "meet, clash, and grapple with each other." The center is a "disciplinary borderland" where the rhetorics of the humanities, social sciences, and natural sciences meet—to both intersect and conflict.

Thus, the writing center's mission is a borderland one—to help students articulate the cultural and rhetorical similarities and differences they observe and confront; to help them "grapple with" or negotiate between and among intersecting and clashing cultures, languages, literacies, discourses, and disciplines; to help them decide when to follow organizational and stylistic conventions (e.g., place thesis at the beginning, avoid using "I") and when to take risks and violate them—instead of being violated by them.

The "asymmetrical relations of power" that Pratt says often structure the contact zone contribute to the violence of language contact—the clashing, the colliding, the grating and grinding emphasized by J. Elspeth Stuckey in *The Violence of Literacy*. Using the United States–Mexico borderland as her point of reference, Gloria Anzaldúa also explores the violence of the contact zone when she calls it an open wound—"*la herida abierta*"— where the Third World grates against the first and bleeds. In the writing center as the site of struggle within the academic hierarchy of asymmetrical power relations, the more powerful discourses of the academy sometimes grate against the discourses students bring with them. Those who work in writing centers do indeed witness open wounds and bleeding, although the brutality is usually psychological and metaphorical; the students' wounds are psychic, their egos and papers are bleeding, their selves as readers and writers are violated. How often do writing center tutors hear tales of students who are "dissed" (disrespected), their work "trashed" (put down) by a harsh system of rewards and punishments? (More on writing center slang later.) Students' psychic pain could indeed become economic and physical if, for example, they lose financial aid, graduate school, or professional opportunities because of the effects of "academic hazing." The writing center invariably becomes a recovery room and trauma center where students come to heal the wounds inflicted on them most likely by those higher on the ladder.

On the other hand, if we carry the "open wound" aspect of the contact zone analogy too far in situating writing center work, we distort and trivialize the very real physical suffering and death in very real borderlands, the extermination of indigenous peoples in Latin America and the United States and the political situation to which Anzaldúa is referring: the economic and physical humiliation of undocumented Mexicans who give their life savings to coyotes to cross the Mexico-U.S. border only to be captured and deported. We must admit that the "highly asymmetrical relations of power such as colonialism, slavery, or their aftermaths" in Pratt's definition of contact zone are not as prevalent in U.S. institutions of higher education. U.S. colleges and universities are not purposefully and blatantly oppressive and colonial, as some of our governmental, penal, or mental institutions are, although universities certainly do have colonizing features, especially their intimate relationships with corporations and the state and their complicity in the more sinister endeavors of capitalism and imperialism such as defense and weapons research. Even though we and our students may feel exploited and violated at times by our institutions, we are not slaves, peasants, or undocumented workers. Writing about the politics of higher education, Flora Mancuso Edwards reminds us that even the term "disadvantaged college students" is an oxymoron when considered in the context of the urban underemployed underclass that did not even complete high school. In addition, most of us who staff writing centers have chosen to do so, preferring colleges to corporations or government agencies, consciously choosing the borderland site of the writing center over more "central" positions in our departments or units. Somehow I doubt that Frantz Fanon was referring to us or even to most of our students when he spoke of the "Wretched of the Earth."

Therefore, while we do acknowledge the psychic and economic violence in the writing center as site of struggle and site of recovery, taking care not to exaggerate our conditions of oppression and overanalogize the center as open wound, it is equally necessary to emphasize the creative, generative, and combinatory aspects of cultural and linguistic contact that occur within a writing center. When cultures and languages meet and rub against one another, deplorable things occur, but astonishing things do, too. Sparks fly, humor happens, surprising new combinations emerge; sometimes, out of open wounds, new texts and forms of consciousness are born, new genres of what Braj Kachru calls "contact literature," which, I would argue, should be added to Pratt's discussion of "arts of the contact zone." I don't want to pose a strict cause-effect relationship wherein one must have violent linguistic conflict and the accompanying pain and suffering in order to produce the contact zone arts, as in a painful and bloody labor that results in the birth of a child. Pain sometimes, but not always, accompanies the creation of contact zone arts. The writing center then is not only a site for the culture wars, but a site for the creation of contact literatures that result from languages and cultures in touch.

Contact Literature

Contact literature is often characterized by nativization of a non-native discourse, for example, varieties of world English such as Kachru's East Indian English and Achebe's Nigerian English—the language of the colonizer bearing the cultural stamp and personality of the colonized. Nativized content, organization, and style are also features of one of the arts of the contact zone that Pratt highlights—the "autoethnographic text," which should be included as a genre of contact literature. In this genre, second-dialect or second-language-influenced forms of the dominant power language are used to define or redefine one's identity, to describe one's culture for oneself and for members of the dominant culture who may hold simplistic views of it. Autoethnographic texts, says Pratt, are those "in which people undertake to describe themselves in ways that engage with representations others have made of them" (35). Such texts are quite common in writing centers, especially in centers in which students do a lot of writing, sometimes in response to the center's own assignments.

For example, in response to an assignment to tell about a time when students suffered an injustice, African American male students in our writing center and writing courses have told of their experiences with racial profiling and police brutality, using a borderland register that is not street English, but is not college sociologese either. For their writing center and rhetoric teachers of the dominant culture, they define themselves as people who experience fear, instead of those who inspire fear in others, their common stereotypical image in the dominant society, whether they are on the football field or on the streets.

In the following excerpt written in response to a writing center assignment "A Place Called Home" and then published in *Voices,* the writing center newsletter, an African American student engages with common representations of Africa and of "home."

"There is no place like home."

That is a saying that I have come to believe, for ironically, there is no place like a home that you've never been to. I've traveled to a lot of places in this country, but there is one place on this earth that I have not been yet. I carry it within me. I desperately long for it—HOME.

When I say "HOME," I'm not referring to my home in Davenport; in fact, I'm not referring to any place in America. The home I'm referring to is my spiritual home—the home of my ancestors. The home of mine is across the Atlantic. The name my ancestors gave to this home was ALKEBU-LAN. To the rest of the world, it's simply known as AFRICA.

I feel the need to go to Africa because I seek the knowledge of myself. I want to know how my ancestors lived and how they continue to live.

I did not always have such a desire to go to Africa; in fact, that was the last place on earth I would want to go, for I was taught that there was nothing there but a bunch of jungles and cannibalistic savages. I hated Africa. At that time of my life, as a mental slave, I would fight in an instant if I were called an African.

I reflected on why I had that attitude towards Africa and came to the understanding that the white man had taught the Black man—embedded within the Black mind here in America—the negativities of Africa. We as Black people have been systematically brainwashed into hating Africa and in the process we ended up hating ourselves. One cannot hate the roots of the tree and not hate the entire tree itself.

Because the student has redefined in writing the concepts of "home" and "Africa" for himself and for his more "mainstream" tutor, this piece can be read as an autoethnographic text created in the writing center as a contact zone.

Assignments such as former University of Iowa Writing Center Director Lou Kelly's "Where do you come from?" or "Special Place," in which students are asked by their tutor to describe in detail the physical and cultural properties of their hometown or of a meaningful place, often result in contact literature, especially when the writers are ESL/international students who are themselves in a borderland state—as Anzaldúa says, straddling two cultures and languages. The content of their writing is almost wholly related to the native culture, but their language (English) belongs to the new culture, except for nativized interlanguage syntax and lexical items (Selinker) that are either impossible to translate or that the writer would rather not translate to avoid distorting her meaning ("translator, traitor," as the Italian proverb goes). Or the writer consciously refuses to translate in order to teach those expressions to her or his writing center tutor. The resulting piece of writing often constitutes self- and cultural definition for the enlightenment of the tutor in particular and for representatives of the dominant culture in general—again, the autoethnographic text. Many pieces collected in the writing center newsletter, *Voices*, are examples of contact literature. In the following *Voices* essay called "Night Market," a Chinese student engages the representations that Americans have of foreigners eating strange meats such as snake. She points out that eating steak is equally exotic and bloody to people from Taiwan.

Every time I stay up all night, I miss my hometown, Taipei. It's hard to Americans to relate to my feelings because I never see a night market here. Night market, as the word directs, is a market only held at night. Taiwan's climate is warm all year round, so many people hold the market at night to entertain those day-working people. At the night market, you can buy real bargains, taste delicious food, and even watch free shows. Ever eat snakes or drink snake blood? Try it at the night market and the merchant will show you how "fresh" the snake meat is because he will kill the snake and take off the snake skin before you. I know this surprises Americans, but the first time I tried rare steak, I was also shocked by the bloody meat.

Every time I stayed up to study, I would take a break to the night market, enjoy the joyful air there and have some midnight snacks (not snake, I promise). When I came to the States, you know how disappointed I was because there is no place to go at night.

Another form of contact literature is the inadvertent ESL poetry of unique and surprising nativized phrasings that result from interlanguage processes (Severino). Forms of accidental or "found" poetic language can result from mistakenly adding extra word endings or from combining two words or meanings. Here is an example of an extra suffix added by an Asian student describing how she misses her husband: "The difficulty is that every time I feel upset or frustrated here, I cannot get his timely comfortness."

Another Asian student conflates the adjective "alarming" (threatening) with the sounding of an alarm clock: "When I was waken up by the alarming of the clock, I thought, 'How can time pass so fast?'" Both of these constructions are "mistakes" that evoke poetic effects of sound, rhythm, and multiple meaning.

When writers purposely use poetic forms, organizational patterns, and other rhetorical features from their native culture and language to write in English—for example, the indirect peeling-the-onion-form that Fan Shen describes as a way to introduce a topic (stating the "conditions of composition" first) or the proverbs and sayings more common in Chinese than in U.S. expository prose—the hybrid text that results is also an art of the contact zone, an instance of native rhetoric in the host culture's language, in this case, Chinese English rather than Kachru's Indian English or Achebe's Nigerian English. This process of rhetorical nativization can be considered a linguistic attempt to balance the "asymmetrical power relations" to which Pratt refers, such as the power relations that typically characterize the situation of ESL students in the host country. In our writing center, we even occasionally have students write in their native language. For example, last November before Thanksgiving break, writing center teacher Patricia Coy had her Chinese-speaking student who was familiar with Thanksgiving rituals write in Chinese to her other Chinese-speaking student, who was curious about pilgrims and turkeys, informing him about these exotic U.S. cultural practices. The result was a kind of "inverse" autoethnographic text: native (Chinese) code and nonnative (U.S.) cultural content—or pilgrims and turkeys.

Contact Dialects

The oral arts of the writing center as contact zone are as important as the written ones. Writing center talk—informal talk about writing—often happens in a borderland dialect, on the border of orality and literacy, what Judith Langer refers to as "literate talk," or what James Cummins would place in between BICS (basic interpersonal communication skills) and CALP (cognitive academic linguistic proficiency). In other words, as all writing teachers and tutors already know intuitively, basic interpersonal communication about texts and ideas is not very basic at all, especially if the text and the conversation are in the student's second language.

Although it is intellectually rigorous, writing center talk sometimes has a kitchen English rather than an academic English flavor—thus its borderland nature. Transcriptions of tutorials are full of "yeah," "you know," "uh huh," "for sure," and tutor comments such as, "That's a whole nother research paper." In the support program in Chicago where I tutored, we dropped the "g" at the ends of some words, influenced by our students' dialects: "How's it goin'?" "I'm runnin' late." However, we would not substitute "n" for "ng" on words that denoted academic activities, i.e., "I see you've been studying hard and reading carefully." When we listen to ourselves, we become aware of the Rocky-Balboa-esque style some of us use. About a student's options for revision, we might inquire: "So whaduya wanna do with this supporting stuff here? Ya wanna cut it, move it, or what?"

However, as Ilona Leki warns us, an informal register can confuse international students who learned a more formal style with a Latinate rather than an Anglo-Saxon-based vocabulary in their native countries.

Our tutoring "dialect" has features of the American students' language, but it is not the same as the students' language. It's a borderland register, a contact dialect. Otherwise, in tutoring younger students, we would use the youth expressions "awesome," "cool," "like," and "you know" a lot more than we do. For example, we would suggest: "Like your paper would be, like, really awesome, you know, if you, like, stuck in some cool quotes from some famous dudes." Writing center lore is also created and exchanged via informal language. Tutors speak of what Muriel Harris has called "assignments from hell" and of "dead essays," papers that teachers have given a final grade and returned to the student without the chance to revise. However, even though the features of tutor talk are informal and take place in a kind of contact dialect, the discourse's functions—to pose optional rhetorical operations and to discuss the complex ideas of the students' papers—are highly sophisticated, an example of what Judith Langer calls "literate thinking," as distinguished from literacy, the acts of reading and writing. "Literate thinkers," she says, "objectify subject matter, making it opaque and malleable, thereby permitting self-conscious distinctions to be made between language structure, discourse, meanings, and interpretations" (3). These self-conscious distinctions can be made in either an informal or a formal dialect. A formal dialect does not insure or guarantee literate thinking, and, as Peter Elbow has demonstrated, an academic dialect can mystify readers so that they are not even aware that literate thinking is missing.

To sum up, we need to guard against overanalogizing the colonial, oppositional, and violent aspects of the writing center as borderland and contact zone. If we avoid romanticizing our own institutional circumstances and thus distorting situations of more threatening, physical oppression and culture-clash, and if we emphasize the processes of creating arts of the contact zone, the borderland/contact zone metaphor can be a useful and productive heuristic for examining written and oral texts of the writing center as examples of contact literature and contact dialect.

Works Cited

Achebe, Chinua. *Things Fall Apart*. London: Heinemann, 1958.

Anzaldúa, Gloria. "Borderlands/La Frontera." *Ways of Reading: An Anthology for Writers*. 3rd ed. Ed. David Bartholomae and Anthony Petrosky. Boston: Bedford, 1993. 23–65. Rpt. from *Borderlands/La Frontera: The New Mestiza* by Gloria Anzaldúa. San Francisco: Spinsters/Aunt Lute, 1987.

Cummins, James. "The Entry and Exit Fallacy in Bilingual Education." *NABE Journal* 4.3 (1980): 25–59.

Edwards, Flora Mancuso. "Beyond the Open Door: Disadvantaged Students." *Higher Learning in America, 1980–2000*. Ed. Arthur Levine. Baltimore: Johns Hopkins UP, 1993. 309–21.

Elbow, Peter. "Reflections on Academic Discourse: How it Relates to Freshmen and Colleagues." *College English* 53.2 (1991): 135–55.

Fanon, Frantz. *The Wretched of the Earth*. Harmondsworth: Penguin, 1967.

Kachru, Braj B., ed. *The Other Tongue: English across Cultures*. Urbana: U of Illinois P, 1982.

Langer, Judith A. "A Sociocognitive Perspective of Literacy." *Language, Literacy and Culture: Issues of Society and Schooling*. Ed. Judith A. Langer. Norwood, NJ: Ablex, 1987. 1–20.

Leki, Ilona. *Understanding ESL Writers: A Guide for Teachers*. Portsmouth, NH: Heinemann/Boynton Cook, 1992.

Pratt, Mary Louise. "Arts of the Contact Zone." *Profession 91*. New York: MLA, 1991. 33–40. (Originally presented as the keynote address at MLA's Responsibilities for Literacy conference in September 1990 in Pittsburgh.)

Selinker, Larry. "Interlanguage." *International Review of Applied Linguistics* 10.3 (1972): 209–31.

Severino, Carol. "Inadvertently and Purposely Poetic ESL Writing." *Journal of Basic Writing* 13.2 (1994): 18–32.

Shen, Fan. "The Classroom and the Wider Culture: Identity as a Key to Learning English Composition." *College Composition and Communication* 40.4 (1989): 459–66.

Stuckey, J. Elspeth. *The Violence of Literacy*. Portsmouth, NH: Boynton/Cook, 1991.

Teaching in the Contact Zone: The Myth of Safe Houses

JANICE M. WOLFF
Saginaw Valley State University

some other where
alchemists mumble over pots.
their chemistry stirs
into science. their science
freezes into stone.
　　　　LUCILLE CLIFTON, from "Quilting"

As teachers, we sometimes see ourselves as alchemists, trying for the right mix; sometimes as scientists, classifying, typing, ordering the chaos of the classroom. But oftentimes the work in the laboratory places us in a most unsettling environment, attempting to produce good teaching. Lucille Clifton recognizes the dangers of such pseudoscience and points out the stony results of such endeavor. The story that follows is a journey of a teacher into alchemy, the search for gold, for a "contact zone," for a "safe house" in which to teach.

Three authorities have influenced and continue to influence my alchemy: Mary Louise Pratt's contact zone theory; Henry Giroux's critical pedagogy; and Toni Morrison's novel *Beloved*.

An earlier version of this essay was published in *Critical Theory and the Teaching of Literature: Politics, Curriculum, Pedagogy,* edited by James F. Slevin and Art Young (NCTE, 1996). Used by permission. Excerpt from Lucille Clifton's "Quilting" reprinted from *Quilting: Poems 1987–1990.* Copyright 1991 by Lucille Clifton. Used by permission.

Pratt has borrowed the anthropological term "contact zone" and made it a metaphor for the imaginary spaces where differing cultures meet. Very often the cultures have different languages and, certainly, different values, and very often one culture will dominate the other as it privileges itself. The "contact zone" is where the two come together, sometimes in situations of conquest and sometimes in conversation. Giroux outlines a project aimed at democratizing the classroom, a project enabled by a "critical pedagogy," one that is self-aware and self-critical, a pedagogy that talks about itself and is cognizant of the power relations in the classroom—the teacher has all power and students have none—and aims to rectify those inequalities. "Border pedagogy," too, comes into Giroux's project for the classroom: it is the sort of pedagogy that admits the ideological geography of the classroom—again, the arrangement that puts the teacher at the center and the students on the margins, on the border of the space for learning. Visions of Pratt, Giroux, the "contact zone," and "border pedagogy" were very active upon my teaching as I began a recent fall semester, as I began rereading *Beloved* for the term ahead. Contact zone and border theory and critical pedagogy made sense to me and taught me that

> where there are legacies of subordination, groups need places for healing and mutual recognition, safe houses in which to construct shared understandings, knowledges, claims on the world that they can then bring into the contact zone. (Pratt, "Arts" 40)

Constructing that "safe house" for learning, building an environment that would encourage knowledge making and risk taking, would be my alchemy.

Toni Morrison is a teacher herself, one who works at the intersection of print and oral cultures. As Joyce Irene Middleton has pointed out:

> Through her playful intermingling of an ancient, oral storytelling genre with a modern literate one, Toni Morrison draws on the creative dimensions of both oral and literate language, giving us new and stimulating perspectives on oral memory in her accomplished modern novel. (74)

Though Middleton writes of *Song of Solomon*, her point applies as well to *Beloved*. In the way that Morrison brings orality and literacy together and in the way that she blurs the distinctions between the two, she implies the presence of the "contact zone" for those interested in the relationship between theory and pedagogy. This essay explores the ways in which contact zone and border theory inform the teaching of a novel such as Toni Morrison's *Beloved* and, by extension, inform pedagogy.

After having immersed myself in reading Pratt's theory, I began to see her concept of the contact zone insinuating itself into my courses: in my American literature course, a survey spanning several hundred years of written material, a course that was all but unmanageable in its scope—pre-Columbian to 1900—I began by asking students to think about cultures in terms of orality and literacy. I am using concepts of oral and print cultures as Walter Ong has presented them for us: "orality" indicating a culture that is "innocent of writing," and "print" indicating culture that has an established chirographic representation of text (18). Admittedly, the idea of "oral cultures" and "print cultures" sets up a dichotomy, a system of binaries that will not necessarily hold, but one which seems to make the idea of "contact zone" knowable. The students and I spent some time listing the possible features of each, where they might overlap, and so on. (We returned to the notion of print versus oral cultures at the end of the semester when we read *Adventures of Huckleberry Finn*, so the concept never really went away.) When we read explorers' narratives, I asked students to write about which voices seemed most intent on conquest, which best exemplified the sense of being "Monarch of all I survey." We explored Eurocentrism as it manifested itself in the readings and looked for the naturalistic impulse to list and classify the flora and fauna. We recognized this impulse as we read Álvar Núñez Cabeza de Vaca and saw his tendency to place European comparisons on places and things in the new world: the newly "discovered" islands remind him of "springtime in Andalusia." Pratt asserts that science, particularly that Linnean brand of classification, had a central part in the colonization process, that natural history set in motion a secular, global labor that, among other things, made contact zones a site of intellectual as well as manual labor, and installed there the distinction between the two. (Pratt, "Science" 27).

At the same time that Pratt's contact zone theory was informing my pedagogy in the American literature class, her earlier work on natural narrative was informing my pedagogy in Literary Analysis, a general education course required of many of our majors. But contact zone theory coalesced when we came to the reading of *Beloved*. On the first day of discussion, students told me of their difficulty with reading the novel. The first sentence, "124 was spiteful," stopped their reading cold. Some pushed forward, allowing their reading to teach them that 124 was an address, a house, a metonymic accounting for a building. One student even asked me to lecture, to tell the book to the class. Two pages further on, students confronted yet another semantic stumbling block: the presentation of Sethe's sexual bartering for the letters on the tombstone: "Ten minutes for seven letters. With another ten could she have gotten 'Dearly' too?" (5). It seemed to me that this was the sort of textual fragment, unreadable though it was for students, that represented the meeting of print and oral cultures. It seemed, too, that Sethe was at the mercy of the individual who "had" print culture on his side.

Because contact zone theory informed my reading of Toni Morrison's *Beloved*, I thought that that reading would establish a "safe house" in which to discuss the novel. "Contact zone," as Mary Louise Pratt explains it, refers to

> social spaces where cultures meet, clash, and grapple with each other, often in contexts of highly asymmetrical relations of power, such as colonialism, slavery, or their aftermaths as they are lived out in many parts of the world today. (Pratt, "Arts" 34)

In *Beloved*, those asymmetrical relationships of power obtain in the confines of Sweet Home; the Blacks live a colonized existence under both the Garners and Schoolteacher. When Sethe's nonliterate "rememory" meets the Linnean print classification system of Schoolteacher, contact zone asymmetry is evident. He asserts power, and she, throughout the novel, rememories the violent events precipitated by the clash of cultures. Sweet Home is the first site of contact zone counterpedagogy, given the teaching methods of Schoolteacher that capitalize on the asymmetrical relationships of power, but the novel is punctuated with incidences of print cultures colliding with oral culture.

In addition to thinking in terms of the contact zone, my students and I agonized over some of the unsolvable narrative issues in the novel: Is the ghost real? Is Beloved real? How could a mother murder her child? But I kept returning to the idea of the contact zone, the site where print culture meets oral culture. Pratt provided us with language that allowed us to speak about the print culture as it reproduced the oral culture, as the one culture asserted its scientific, naturalistic, textual might, as the one culture appropriated the Other. Pratt's metaphor of the "safe house" allowed students to examine the political in light of the historical and the pseudoscientific. Morrison's already masterful subverting of the narrative, coupled with Pratt's questioning of the colonizing impulse, allowed for some thoughtful discussion of the insertion of the self into culture. Students began to see that out of the fragmented narrative, the recounting of slender threads, a tapestry of meaning might be woven.

Our reading, our impulse to create order out of seeming chaos, paralleled the naturalistic impulse in the novel. Nowhere is the "systematizing of nature," that impulse which supports the "authority of print, and . . . the class which control[s] it" (Pratt, "Science" 30), more evident than in the character and behaviors of Morrison's Schoolteacher. His presence at Sweet Home is the presence of the empiricist, the one who must make order out of the chaos of the plantation, the one who records and measures and writes, the one who privileges text and colonizes the unread. Schoolteacher becomes "the (lettered, male, European) eye that held the system [and thus] could familiarize ('naturalize') new sites/sights immediately upon contact, by incorporating them into the language of the system" (Pratt, "Science" 31). Pratt further characterizes the naturalist-collector-scientist as a "benign, often homely figure, whose transformative powers do their work in the domestic contexts of the garden or the collection room" (33).

In addition to spotting the evil that Schoolteacher engenders, my students identified his impulse as a scientific one, a way of producing "a lettered, bourgeois discourse about non-lettered, peasant worlds" (Pratt 34–35). Schoolteacher uses that lettered, narrative impulse to exert power and to create the slave class as Other. Ultimately, he enacts "our impulse to organize in power lines that create false distinctions and class/race hierarchies" (Barnett 2).

In order to "rememory" power lines and class/race hierarchies, Sethe tells Denver the story of Schoolteacher:

> Nothing to tell except schoolteacher. He was a little man. Short. Always wore a collar, even in the fields. A schoolteacher, she said. That made her [Mrs. Garner] feel good that her husband's sister's husband had book learning and was willing to come farm Sweet Home after Mr. Garner passed. The men could have done it, even with Paul F sold. But it was like Halle said. She didn't want to be the only white person on the farm and a woman too. . . . He brought two boys with him. Sons or nephews. I don't know. They called him Onka and had pretty manners, all of 'em. Talked soft and spit in handkerchiefs. Gentle in a lot of ways. (36–37)

But more than narrating the past, the "rememory" enables Sethe to continue with the job of living. After having been colonized, marginalized, and nearly erased, she narrates herself into a historical subject. It is as if characters must either narrate or resign themselves to a mute (or dead) state: consider that Denver, after being asked about her history by a schoolmate, becomes speechless for a number of years. Sethe sees that "book learning" is a privileged position; she also sees rightly that Mrs. Garner didn't want to be in the minority, on the margins of the farm community, even with the power of being White. Sethe's assessment of the culture as represented by Schoolteacher reveals gentility as a veneer. She "reads" him very well, indeed. The narrative goes on, though, and describes the site where the two cultures meet and blur:

> He liked the ink I made. It was her recipe, but he preferred how I mixed it and it was important to him because at night he sat down to write in his book. It was a book about us but we didn't

know that right away. We just thought it was his manner to ask us questions. He commenced to carry round a notebook and write down what we said. I still think it was them questions that tore Sixo up. Tore him up for all time. (37)

Schoolteacher's pedagogy is one neither Pratt nor Henry Giroux would support, thought it is consistent with the classifying, taxonomizing, naturalistic impulse. It is a pedagogy that is immoral, a false attempt at knowledge making, a counterpedagogy that exploits its subject even as it studies it—forcing Sethe to make the ink that produces the signifiers that render her family into text. Schoolteacher's methods make Sethe complicitous in her own objectification. Giroux proposes a pedagogy that undermines Schoolteacher's:

> At the heart of such a pedagogy is the recognition that it is important to stare into history in order to remember the suffering of the past and that out of this remembrance a theory of ethics should be developed in which solidarity, compassion, and care become central dimensions of an informed social practice. (Giroux 102)

Schoolteacher's methods may be historical, in the way that he inscribes and measures and records the subjects, but never ethical. Rather, his pedagogy constitutes a "narrative act of colonizing that is finally disabling and tyrannical" (Barnett 3). His science is pseudoscience and othering.

Bit by bit Sethe's remembered narrative returns to her: "Easily she stepped into the told story that lay before her eyes on the path she followed away from the window" (29). Remembering the pregnancy that was key to her run from Sweet Home, the bodily sensations, the swollen feet that nearly kept her from running, she recalls that

> she waited for the little antelope to protest, and why she thought of an antelope Sethe could not imagine since she had never seen one. She guessed it must have been an invention held on to from before Sweet Home, when she was very young. Of that place where she was born (Carolina maybe? or was it Louisiana?) she remembered only song and dance. (30)

She wonders about the choice of the metaphor "antelope," and it shapes more memories of the oral culture:

> Oh but when they sang. And oh but when they danced and some-times they dance the antelope. The men as well as the ma'ams, one of whom was certainly her own. They shifted shapes and became something other. Some unchained, demanding other whose feet knew her pulse better than she did. (31)

The clash of cultures has removed the young Sethe from her mother, an assertion of asymmetrical power.

As if the fading antelope metaphor isn't enough, as if the erasure of one's mother isn't enough, as if linguistic othering isn't enough, Sethe has a dim memory of the language that once was hers:

> The woman who cared for Sethe as a child was Nan who used different words. Words Sethe understood then but could neither recall nor repeat now. She believed that must be why she remem-bered so little before Sweet Home except singing and dancing and how crowded it was. What Nan told her she had forgotten, along with the language she told it in. The same language her ma'am spoke, and which would never come back. But the mes-sage—that was and had been there all along. Holding the damp white sheets against her chest, she was picking meaning out of code she no longer understood. (62)

The lived experience, her narrative, supplies the meaning even though the signifying system is all but gone. Hanging up damp sheets becomes the memory trigger that contains traces of the past.

There are other instances of the contact zone, where print culture privileges itself and colonizes those who are unread: the newspaper clipping that contains the picture and the account of Sethe's murder of her child sends Paul D out of the house and away from her. Even though he cannot read the alphabetic repre-sentation of the event, Paul D "reads" the implications of the text: for people of color to become textualized means something very bad indeed. When Beloved, or the incarnation of her, arrives at 124, she spells her name in a way that identifies her illiteracy.

But it is at Lady Jones's school that the more positive features of the contact zone are realized:

> For a nickel a month, Lady Jones did what whitepeople thought unnecessary if not illegal: crowded her little parlor with the colored children who had time for and interest in book learning. The nickel, tied to a handkerchief knot, tied to her [Denver's] belt, that she carried to Lady Jones, thrilled her. The effort to handle chalk expertly and avoid the scream it would make; the capital *W*, the little *i*, the beauty of the letters in her name, the deeply mournful sentences from the Bible Lady Jones used as a textbook. Denver practiced every morning; starred every afternoon. She was so happy. . . . (102)

In spite of the more common travesties found in the contact zone, Denver enjoys, for a short time, the "safe house" that Lady Jones provides, the safe house on the margins of the educational system. Prior to the "rage, incomprehension, and pain" that Denver ultimately experiences, she also finds "exhilarating moments of wonder and revelation, mutual understanding, and new wisdom— the joys of the contact zone" (Pratt, "Arts" 39).

In many ways, the contact zone and its inherent terrors and triumphs inform our reading of *Beloved*, and, in many ways, *Beloved* shapes our reading of contact zone theory. The more crucial question is where were my students in the quest for the contact zone? To be very honest, most were resistant to the reading, as was evident in many of their reading journals. Most could not abide the nonlinearity of the book. Many were shocked by the idea of bestiality, and shocked, too, at the suggestion of oral sex. Many wanted me to supply a plot summary; many, I suspect, wished for Cliffs Notes to accompany their reading. A few said that they stuck with the book, read as if they knew what was going on, powered through, and were rewarded around midpoint with meaning. Fragments were beginning to add up for them. It was with and through that fragmented reading experience—a reading that made demands on the students, a reading that disrupted their conventional notions about narrative patterns—that students began to see not only what was privileged in the 1850s slave culture, but also what sort of reading is privileged in the academy. Students admitted that their reading history included texts that progressed logically from point A to point B to point C; their reading experience did not include narrative fragments, out of time, out of sequence, just as their education did not include material out of time, out of logical sequence. The subverted narrative of *Beloved* confounded the conventional, orderly presentation of material to be learned, what the students had come to expect from the classroom environment.

Because they weren't ever sure of the "what occurs when" in the novel, students worked on fragments of knowledge—they had to. *Beloved* denies a reading that supports conventional reading behaviors. We had to invent some new tactics. Students worked in small groups to frame boundaries for the characters, that is, to define characters according to their relationships to one another. For instance, one group worked to define Sethe according to Paul D, another group defined her according to School-teacher, another group created Sethe through Denver's eyes, and others did so through Beloved's eyes, Amy's eyes, and so on. We filled in the gaps where we could; we wrote Halle's narrative, told his story. We talked about the novel in terms of cultural and political boundaries, too, seeing the moral and legal ramifications of a slave culture. But it was the day that the small groups were still at work on the identities of Sethe that I met with some contact zone resistance of my very own. I was circulating, listening in on the small groups, when I came to a group that seemed to be finished with the work at hand. After asking whether they were socializing—a valid thing to do in a "safe classroom"—a member of the group looked up at me in all sincerity and asked: "Why did you assign this book?" Embedded in her question was the resistance that both Giroux and Pratt speak of, but something else was at work, something that the journals evidenced, too. My style of teaching had changed, yes; no longer was I telling students the meaning of the novel through the medium of lecture. Small groups and initiatory writing (Elbow's concept) and journals were better ways for "constructing meaning." I imagined myself teaching in the "contact zone," where

> every single text we read stood in specific historical relationship to the students in the class, but the range and variety of historical relationships in play were enormous. . . . All the students in the

class had the experience, for example, of hearing their culture discussed and objectified in ways that horrified them; all the students saw their roots traced back to legacies of both glory and shame. . . . (Pratt, "Arts" 39)

Pratt is speaking specifically about a course she teaches, but it informed the way I heard the question from my student, the one about why I had them read *Beloved*.

Her resistance was honest and compelling for me. Why did I select that novel? What was my intent? Aside from the fact that *Beloved* is one of my favorite novels, and aside from the fact that my professional title gives me the power to put selections on the syllabus, I discovered that I depended upon the always already institutionalized reasons for my choice. *Beloved* became a part of the syllabus because the novel says both loud and subtle things about our history and our culture; it carries the literary and artistic features that English teachers relish; it is weighty enough to bear multiple readings (and needs rereading). Beyond those elements, it supports and exemplifies other literary structures that this Literary Analysis class had been reading about and testing out: natural narrative, literary anecdote, metaphor, intertextuality, and naming—all concepts mapped out for us in Scholes, Comley, and Ulmer's *Text Book*.

Text Book was a force to reckon with all semester, and it provided us with strategies for making meaning from *Beloved*. Knowing that the novel is a story woven from a nineteenth-century news account of a former slave who tried to kill her children rather than let them live a slave existence made the novel intertextual for the class. Metaphor, and our special attitude toward it, allowed us to see the figurative impulse of the writer. But more than seeing the historical or literary structures in the novel, my hope was that students might begin to see the boundaries that are so defined in Sethe's story, boundaries as they are presented to us in *Text Book*. The reading of *Beloved* uncovers cultural, legal, and institutional boundaries that support racism. Identifying those boundaries so apparent in the novel might allow us as a class to confront our own racist positions. The idea of the contact zone, the reading about historical contact zones, and the becoming part of a contact zone in the "safe house of the classroom"—if such a space is more than myth—allow students and teachers "the opportunity to engage in antiracist struggles in their effort to link schooling with real life, ethical discourse with political action, and classroom relations with a broader notion of cultural politics" (Giroux 141). I wanted students to recognize racism; I wanted "to make antiracist pedagogies central to the task of educating students to enliven a wider and more critically engaged public culture." I wanted "students not merely to take risks but also to push against the boundaries of an oppressive social order" (141). The irony seemed to be that the oppressive social order that students pushed against was me.

Teaching in the contact zone can be fraught with danger, and sometimes establishing a "safe house" is little more than myth. For every exhilaration, there seems to be a corresponding downward spiral. Using contact zone theory as a screen through which to read a complex novel was one thing, but realizing that the metaphor of the contact zone was also active upon the classroom itself was daunting. It was never clearer than the day I had the terms "print culture" and "oral culture"—those arbitrary and imaginary classifications—on the board. I was asking students to help me characterize the two, to list the features of a culture rich in print—libraries, newsstands, alphabetic writing, text of all sorts—and the features of oral culture: people without writing, people using oral language, people studied by anthropologists. We were doing fairly well, listing, pulling ideas from one another, when a student suggested a third category, that of "video culture." No problem. The twentieth century surely does make room for such a classification. Father Ong's notion of secondary orality was active upon me as I took the liberty of aligning myself with print culture as it appeared on the chalkboard, showing myself to be one with that culture. The rest is fragmented memory, somewhat repressed. Next, I asked students to align themselves with the appropriate category, making the assumption that video would be their choice, or possibly even oral culture. In effect, what I was doing was saying that I was representative of print culture and that students were something Other.

A discerning student responded with some petulance to the way I was constructing the categories, saying that he felt students straddled categories, had to, in fact, in a culture that demanded literacy. He went on, as I found later in a journal entry, to say, in effect: "I felt excluded when you said you were the print culture and students were oral. I read, lots. In fact, the word 'condescending' comes to mind. I felt cheated. Here, all semester you have been saying in 'Literary Analysis' you were going to give us access to literature, and in a very few minutes, you seemed to close doors to us."

What had I done? Up until that moment, I felt I had been working to give students access to literature, to allow them entry to that literate world. I felt that my pedagogy had been a critical one, a democratic one, one that Giroux espouses:

> pedagogy that replaces authoritative language of recitation with an approach that allows students to speak from their own histories, collective memories, and voices while simultaneously challenging the grounds on which knowledge and power are constructed and legitimated. (105)

But in the very telling of contact zone theory, I had centered myself and relegated students once more to the borders of knowledge making. By naming myself the representative of the print culture, I had emphasized the false dichotomy of print culture and oral culture; I had bought a bill of institutionalized goods. Instead of teaching against the grain, instead of practicing a critical pedagogy, I had subscribed to one that undermined what I had hoped to do.

As problematic as that moment was, and as perplexing as it was for someone interested in critical pedagogy, it became a real object lesson in what it said about contact zone and border theory. The moment we center ourselves and privilege our discourse, whatever narrative it may involve, we may be constructing counterpedagogy. Morrison's "Schoolteacher" is a metaphor for all of us working in the contact zone. Bringing theory to bear in the classroom is critical to our work. Researching ethnological approaches in the classroom must also teach us that we are "Schoolteacher"; we are the latter-day naturalists trying to produce texts about the reading and writing processes of our students. When we consider the work that we do, we must not forget the fact that theory that informs the way we read literature is also applicable to the classroom. Students know marginalization when they see it, and perhaps not even classrooms intended to be "safe houses" can be very safe, either for students or for teachers. Ethics is key to a discussion of critical pedagogy. Where Giroux outlines critical pedagogy, he stresses that "ethics must be seen as a central concern of critical pedagogy. . . . Ethics becomes a practice that broadly connotes one's personal and social sense of responsibility to the Other" (74). My alchemy for the classroom was getting a bit ahead of my ethics.

Perhaps the best that teachers can do, when concerned with matters of pedagogy and theory, is to read theory and then problematize it. For instance, reading Pratt's contact zone theory and seeing it as an account of the classroom is good. Thinking of the classroom as a "safe house" is also good. To read Giroux and to understand that one must maintain a self-critical pedagogy is another positive move. But then one must read them against the grain. We must, as readers and teachers, employ the "greatest gift of deconstruction: to question the authority of the investigating subject without paralyzing him [or her]" (Spivak 9). This deconstructionist gift allows the reader of Pratt to say, "Well, yes, she critiques the naturalistic impulse to classify and hierarchize, but doesn't she allow herself the same privilege of classification?" And might not Pratt create classifications that are purely imaginary? And is Giroux political enough? Might his narrative support the very authoritative hierarchies that he seems to oppose? My best advice is to read theory but refuse to privilege it. Read about the "contact zone," use it as a metaphor for the classroom, let it inform pedagogy, but always with a Derridean caveat: Use the term under erasure.

Reflections

Following are my thoughts on Section III of this volume, written a day after rereading the selections:

◆ In response to Cynthia Lewiecki-Wilson's essay, "Teaching in the Contact Zone: Multiple Literacies/Deep Portfolio": What do I like? The ease with which Lewiecki-Wilson brings Mike Rose,

Mary Louise Pratt, and Mina Shaughnessy into dialogue with each other, and the way she outlines her own development of pedagogy—how she moves from deficit model to contact zone and deep portfolios. What could use more development or more discussion: The way that Mike Rose's ideas about "generative struggle with ideas" and "play" could be even more closely aligned with "deep portfolio." "Deep portfolio" evokes for me Geertz's notions of "deep play"—and all that that implies for recursive and dynamic work in revision. Students could certainly be encouraged to play—to write parody and dialogue as they revisit the portfolios. Good advice for us, as well.

◆ In response to Carol Severino's essay: Here we have a very careful scholar, interested in the metaphor of contact zone, but wary about applying it to writing center dynamics. She wants to avoid trivializing real scenes of oppression and pain—the real blood of Third World contact. Severino prefers thinking of contact zone theory as heuristic for the writing center—a way to reconsider linguistic formations—a way to develop critical questions about writing center literacies. One small issue: As I read the student writing in her article, I wondered about the writing center newsletter *Voices*. I started to wonder about how these pieces are treated in the scheme of things—on the one hand it is good that there is a public place for writing produced in the writing center, but on the other I wondered whether *Voices* further marginalizes those students. It must be noted, however, that Severino brings those students' voices into her professional piece and, appropriately, dignifies their writing by naming it "contact literature."

◆ In response to Carole Yee's chapter, I find myself asking: What are Yee's "'desires, repressions, investments, and projections'"? I am impressed by her list of sources, her treatment of ethnography and how it is produced, but I would like to hear more about the process that her own humanities department has gone through. This may be a difficult subject, or she may be too close to it. If, in ethnography, "the observer frankly reveals his or her persona," I wonder why Yee has so carefully disguised her role in the study?

Has she encouraged colleagues to write autoethnography of their humanities department? Stories of their program and goals? Those would make compelling stories of contact.

◆ Jeanne Weiland Herrick's essay on narrative is a careful look at an inner city basic writing class. She might do well to keep narrative as an assignment but advise students to describe the components of narrative that are specific to their particular cultures—that is, do some theorizing about the nature of storytelling.

Works Cited

Barnett, Marianne. Response to an early draft of this chapter. January 1993.

Cabeza de Vaca, Álvar Núñez . Selections from his journals. *The Heath Anthology of American Literature I.* Ed. Paul Lauter (gen. ed.). Lexington, MA: Heath, 1990. 89–99.

Clifton, Lucille. "Quilting." *Quilting: Poems 1987–1990.* Brockport, NY: BOA Editions, 1991. 3.

Giroux, Henry A. *Border Crossings: Cultural Workers and the Politics of Education.* New York: Routledge, 1992.

Middleton, Joyce Irene. "Orality, Literacy, and Memory in Toni Morrison's *Song of Solomon.*" *College English* 55.1 (1993): 64–75.

Morrison, Toni. *Beloved: A Novel.* New York: Penguin, 1988.

———. *Song of Solomon.* New York: Knopf, 1977.

Ong, Walter J. *Interfaces of the Word: Studies in the Evolution of Consciousness and Culture.* Ithaca: Cornell UP, 1977.

Pratt, Mary Louise. "Arts of the Contact Zone." *Profession 91.* New York: MLA, 1991. 33–40. (Originally presented as the keynote address at MLA's Responsibilities for Literacy conference in September 1990 in Pittsburgh.)

———. "Science, Planetary Consciousness, Interiors." *Imperial Eyes: Travel Writing and Transculturation.* New York: Routledge, 1992. 15–37.

Scholes, Robert, Nancy R. Comley, and Gregory L. Ulmer. *Text Book: An Introduction to Literary Language*. New York: St. Martin's, 1988.

Spivak, Gayatri Chakravorty. "Subaltern Studies: Deconstructing Historiography." *Subaltern Studies* 4 (1985): 3–32.

CHAPTER THIRTEEN

Contact Zones in Institutional Culture: An Anthropological Approach to Academic Programs

CAROLE YEE
New Mexico Tech

M ary Louise Pratt's "Arts of the Contact Zone" provides an intriguing, perplexing, and rich reading experience. She makes clever use of various materials: her child Manuel's baseball card fetish, his wonderful writing titled "A grate adventchin," Felipe Guaman Poma de Ayala's twelve-hundred-page letter to King Philip III of Spain with its history and context. That Pratt's own examples are such a mixture of materials and cultures helps to make her point. My own appropriation of the notion of "contact zone" in this paper tries to use Pratt's metaphor to explain how the anthropological research methods that gave rise to contact zone theory can be used to describe academic cultures.

After providing a brief history of what prompted the study, this paper discusses some popular approaches to describing particular academic programs. Among these approaches, the "autoethnographic narrative" is discussed and then used to describe and analyze a small humanities department with a B.S. degree program in technical communication, where I teach and work. Finally, this paper provides some background and details on applying an autoethnographic narrative approach to describing and analyzing academic programs.

My own work on this paper began more than five years ago as an exploration of assessment, but it grew into something else entirely, an examination of the usefulness and methods of an autoethnographic approach for a description of a program or department. "Assessment" for me now pretty exclusively means outcomes assessment of student learning. Autoethnography has also come to have a different meaning for me than it did five years ago, although the seeds of that meaning can be found in this paper. In the New Mexico Tech Technical Communication Program, I have taught students to write ethnographies of institutions and other workplace and school cultures. An autoethnography, as Pratt and Lester Faigley use the term, is "a text in which people undertake to describe themselves in ways that engage with representations others have made of them" (Pratt 35). Faigley proposes that we assign autoethnography assignments in college composition classes to help students understand their own postmodern selves.

In conceiving this paper, I was most interested in the ways that departments and programs partake of the colonial metaphor, whereby colonized and colonizer parody one another. I saw a small humanities department replicating, despite itself, the attitudes, fears, and values of the larger institution that was our science and engineering state-supported college. Even within the humanities department itself, I saw the same colonial architecture at work, whereby the degree-granting Technical Communication Program and its home department of humanities related like colonizers and colonized, sometimes playing one role and sometimes the other, but always in a contact zone. That was what I saw to be Pratt's most significant point—that postmodern condition wherein the power relations are not equal but the parodies of one another are imaginative attempts to equalize the power structures, much like Henry Louis Gates's concept of "signifying" in *The Signifying Monkey*.

The contact zone is a complex concept. It is not a practice, a methodology, or an approach. It is instead a model of those in unequal power relations trying to equalize their power through self- and mutual parody. Contact zones are places where we yearn for the humility and wisdom to restrain our exercise of our own power, and yet our roles as teachers and colleagues force us to colonize our students, as well as our fellow teachers and administrators, just as they colonize us. We too seek "A grate adventchin," a panacea like Pratt's son Manuel proposes, in this case one that will level power relations between us and those we teach and work with. Alas, however, we can only parody one another in an endless shadow box of us and them.

Pratt's "Arts of the Contact Zone" uses a postmodern anthropological approach to understand what she calls "the pedagogical arts of the contact zone," or teaching multicultural literature in the multicultural classroom. Pratt's approach applies as well to the description of institutional cultures—specifically, academic programs and departments. Description can lead to assessment of faculty performance, student learning, or programs. All assessment seeks, ultimately, to evaluate. Pratt's approach provides a creative method to describe before we attempt to evaluate.

Concerning the assessment of faculty, for instance, experts agree about one consistent failure: higher education faculties generally possess a wider range of abilities, talents, and interests than our crude assessment tools can adequately measure or describe (see, for example, Richard Miller's *Evaluating Faculty Performance* and Ernest Boyer's *Scholarship Reconsidered*). As Miller suggests, the urgent academic and social issues of our time should force us to ask "how institutional diversity can be strengthened and how the rich array of faculty talent in our colleges and universities might be more effectively used and continuously renewed" (13).

Boyer's *Scholarship Reconsidered* also calls for a broad, creative, and flexible approach to faculty and, by implication, to program assessment. The message in this report is that our assessment tools are inadequate to measure and evaluate the unique abilities and contributions of a diverse faculty working in a wide variety of kinds of programs. In the final analysis, service and teaching are less valued than publishing, which all too often ends up as the single standard for evaluating many faculty, whose reputations often become the most important standard for assessing their programs and departments.

Miller argues that "an individually developed valuative grid— in line with the objectives of the institution and the department— provides optimum flexibility and individualization. The grid should consider three dimensions: the nature of the institution, the nature of the department, and individual interests and abilities" (12–13). Miller's emphasis on the uniqueness of any faculty, any program, and any institution suggests that program planning be driven by the goals most important to that particular academic culture. To arrive at those goals, however, we must be able to describe our particular academic culture.

A method for doing that—for describing a particular academic culture—is what I present here. When our academic programs begin planning change with a "thick description" of ourselves, as Clifford Geertz (1973) calls ethnographic description, our programs potentially learn much that is useful and meaningful. Ideally we can discover a direction and focus for our talents. Moreover, as Nancy Roundy Blyler points out, the pedagogy of helping students learn to critique institutional culture through learning to use a narrative framework allows us to "clarify for students both the workings of power and cultural reproduction and the nature of socially responsible communicative action" (293). Likewise, when we use a narrative framework to describe our own institutional culture, we clarify for ourselves the workings of power and cultural reproduction in our institutions, and we too can learn the nature of social action by learning to use a narrative framework. As Blyler says, "Understanding narrative, then, can give us insight into the ways people conceptualize their individual and communal lives and organize their existences in concert with others. . . . [Thus] narrative can provide a basis for reflection, critique, and dialogue." (295)

Alternatives to Autoethnography

Without question, there are other sorts of program description and assessment. A very familiar approach to program description is student assessment. Tests, theses, thesis defense presentations, and portfolios are some ways we evaluate our programs by evaluating what our students have learned and how they can perform.

Departments and programs also use outcome research to track their students' occupations, skills, beliefs, and attitudes. Graduates are asked to fill out questionnaires or are interviewed to learn whether and how they used their education in their work and their lives. Learning about the outcome of students who completed the program can reveal much about a program's strengths and weaknesses, and the results sometimes surprise those who operate the program.

Another—and probably the most familiar—sort of program assessment consists of outside reviews by professional societies and accrediting agencies, who visit the program and interview faculty, students, and administrators. These reviewers usually issue a report about the program that measures it against its past as well as against similar programs. Although these reviews begin with a "self-assessment," they are often tedious to undergo, and the report is sometimes a shocking inconvenience to the evaluated institution.

A third and altogether different approach is that of measuring programs on the basis of the sorts of social ends they try to produce. As Marilyn Cooper says, "The measure of our success is the kind of society our graduates make" (12). Cooper cautions that "all successful programs are site-specific" (3), meaning that success builds on local and unique features of that program. She defines our ultimate goal of teaching as the following: "The outcome of any endeavor is a positive good in society" (11). Cooper's argument, with which I basically agree, suggests that we evaluate the design of our programs by the criterion of the potential we help students develop for ethical social action.

Autoethnography: What Is It?

But the problem of program assessment often becomes the problem of program description. We may feel we know what sort of impact our graduates are making. We may feel we know our own faculty's abilities, talents, and interests. We may feel we know our program's strengths and weaknesses. Such a description, however, may not be as self-evident as it initially seems. Organizations—academic and corporate—consist generally of many subcultures rather than of one overarching megaculture, and, as researchers have demonstrated, the differences among those subcultures can be profound (Glaser, Hacker, and Zamanou). For example, top management or administration may have a significantly more positive climate, stronger communication, and more effective supervision and involvement in the organization or institution than do lower-level supervisors or faculty, who may feel decidedly less certain than those at the top that employee or faculty ideas and opinions are valued or considered, that departments and divisions interact, that meetings involve interaction and decision making, that employees or faculty know what they should be doing or where the organization is headed, or that supervisors provide feedback and recognition for good work. In short, people at different levels often work in vastly different organizational cultures. We recognize that institutions, contrary to the institutional culture myth, do not have a single, monolithic culture. As Helen B. Schwartzman explains, an institution's formal organization, or official rules and regulations, and its informal organization, or interpersonal relations, are often quite different from each other (12).

What is meant by an autoethnographic description of our programs is based upon Mary Louise Pratt's definition of autoethnographic texts, in which, she says, "people undertake to describe themselves in ways that engage with representations others have made of them" (35). These texts are constructs in what Pratt calls "contact zones," which are "social spaces where cultures meet, clash, and grapple with each other, often in contexts of highly asymmetrical relations of power, such as colonialism, slavery, or their aftermaths as they are lived out in many parts of the world today" (34).

Pratt's example is a 1613 text written in Peru by an indigenous Andean of Inca descent who wrote in "a mixture of Quechua and ungrammatical, expressive Spanish" (34). The manuscript is a twelve-hundred page letter addressed to King Philip III of Spain, but it apparently never reached him, its intended audience. Rather it was "discovered" in Copenhagen in 1908. Pratt says this text describes the Peruvian culture in terms that are a parody, an oppositional representation of the Castilian speech and rhetoric of Guaman Poma's Spanish conquerors.

We gain power over our differences when we describe ourselves, as Guaman Poma does, in the intercultural or informal organizational language of those in power and those on the margins, under, or beside, the point of power. Further, we look for the places where differences "meet, clash, and grapple with each other"—the contact zones of "highly asymmetrical relations of power." We want an approach to describing ourselves through the representations others have constructed of us. Informed by autoethnographic descriptions, we can see the culture of our program or department as a multidimensional complex, textured and layered. But we can also organize an interpretation, without denying the ruptures and clashes caused by difference.

An Autoethnography of a Small Department

A humanities department in a science and engineering college, situated in a small, remote town, provides the required courses in English, history, foreign languages, philosophy, political science, and other humanities areas for the general curriculum that all students at the college must take. The department has also offered a degree program in technical communication for the past dozen years. Being a small, nonscience, nonmath component of the school, the department seems to have perpetual identity problems.

When the local newspaper published a supplement about the college at the beginning of the new school year, the article about the humanities department began with the following narrative. The names in the narrative, and throughout this description, are fictional.

> Retired professor Jack Jones has a story about the college's then fledgling Humanities Department.
>
> An administrator came barreling into Jones's office, steaming. "He demanded an ethics course be added on," Jones recalled. "When I asked why, he replied, 'Because someone stole my slide rule.'" ("New Mexico Tech—1995")

This narrative, an autoethnographic description of the nature and identity of the department, answers many questions about the sort of organization the department sees itself to be. Nancy Roundy Blyler calls this sort of autoethnography, an "organizational saga" or "shared fantasy" (302). Stories such as these shape the reality of people working in the organization; they are, as Blyler says, "part of the workings of power" (303).

This story appears, at least on its surface, to describe a cozy, small, informal school where administrators and faculty share power in determining the curriculum. The humanities department is widely recognized as serving as a way to meet the human or "preparation for living" ("New Mexico Tech—1995") needs of science and engineering students, and as a result its offerings are required as part of their college education. Defining "humanities" may not be easy, but everyone recognizes that the humanities have value, especially when there's a social or human crisis. At first, then, the humanities appear to be perceived to have certain value within the community of educators that forms this institution.

At the same time, however, the story describes a beleaguered part of the institution, an alien community amidst strangers. The story describes how the authority figure of the administrator "barrels" into a faculty office, "steaming." The humanities faculty feel taken for granted, exploited, misunderstood by science faculty and administration. The humanities faculty, for their part, see the administration, and presumably the science faculty they represent, as uninformed about the humanities and about what people in the humanities do. Basically, the administrator sounds foolish and self-serving, wanting to provide an institutional course to compensate for his own personal loss of a slide rule and to rehabilitate students through knowledge. The story culturally reproduces the dynamic between faculty and administration, between the humanities and the rest of the institution. The humanities are unappreciated and misunderstood; yet when they must define and explain who they are and what they do, they are forced to rely upon traditional models and conventional descriptions, such as "enhancing the training" of a science education ("New Mexico Tech—1995").

All students at the college must take twenty-seven credit hours of social science, writing, literature, philosophy, fine arts, and political science in their entire curriculum. Students are required to take only nine hours of those twenty-seven as prescribed courses, choosing the remaining humanities courses themselves. Although these humanities courses are required of every student, many of the courses in the department were designed and conceived decades ago. Four or five years ago, most literature courses were historically organized surveys, most history courses were based on traditional models (such as "Western Civilization," "American History"), or course offerings were reflections of individual faculty interests.

Four years ago, mindful of the possibility of updating and redesigning the humanities offerings, the department chair asked a one-year visiting faculty member to act as a participant-observer and interview department members about the offerings in the general humanities areas. Could and should the courses be updated? How could faculty imagine changing the course offerings in humanities? Did the course titles have a race and gender bias (given that all the writers, philosophers, historical figures named in the course descriptions were White men)? The visiting faculty member/participant-observer interviewed the department faculty and produced a summary of those interviews for the department to consider.

What emerges from those interviews is that although the course descriptions in the catalog were characterized as "uninviting," most faculty said in one way or another that they were committed to continuing to offer surveys in literature and not allowing individual faculty too much leeway in designing new courses. Departmental guidelines for future directions were seen as necessary, but there was a general fear and mistrust of the idea of changing anything, except for allowing individuals to introduce new courses, always with the proviso that the department must constrain or direct those innovations. Some mentioned the traditional role of the department as a "service" department, although a popular and well-known degree had been offered by the department for nearly a dozen years. Several faculty worried about "divisiveness" if the course offerings were examined. Generally faculty longingly talked of courses in women's studies, cultural studies, minority literatures, and other ways of diversifying the offerings, but the overwhelming impression the interviews make is of a group of people fearful of losing a sense of direction or of seeing the curriculum succumb to a transitory "trendy" fashion.

The surveys and resulting summary describe the difficulty this group of people have in imagining change that won't threaten but will improve their sense of identity as a humanities department. The participant-observer described the department as "split" between those who wanted change and those who did not. Because faculty were in their "little niches," and uninterested in "discussing the direction of the humanities as a whole in that institution," the split between those who wanted change and those who resisted it would continue.

The cultural reproduction in the organizational saga about an administrator demanding the introduction of an ethics course tells of a discipline inadequately valued and misunderstood, but this culture is reproduced again in the faculty survey. The desire or need to update and renew the department's course offerings is offset by the greater need to follow time-worn, traditional models, for fear of cheapening the product or stirring up division within the culture.

Benefits and Difficulties

An autoethnographic description can provide many benefits. Ethnography has been used in anthropological, writing, and corporate contexts to provide insight into how people work together, what they value, and what beliefs they hold that cause conflicts.

The value of an autoethnographic approach is in the answers it provides to many of our program assessment concerns. From such a study, we arrive at our common values and goals—those of administrators, teachers, and students. Those values and goals consist, in this instance, in conserving and maintaining the sense of importance and identity inherited from a traditional approach to their disciplines. Other cultures might value and hold different goals: attracting better or different students, fostering more effective teaching, encouraging more faculty development, or attracting more or different funding. Through autoethnographic description, we arrive at a fuller and deeper understanding of our own unique talents and interests as a program, which can produce greater faculty motivation for development. Acknowledgment and recognition of faculty interests provides incentive for continued or renewed pursuit of those interests, whereas standards that devalue faculty uniqueness lead to frustration and eventual burnout.

Such obvious benefits are really secondary to the less obvious but more important value of autoethnographic program description: This sort of study does not produce a self-congratulating pep talk, which may make everyone feel happy but produces no real information. Autoethnographic description does not force us to pump ourselves up in order to evaluate what we are in the process of describing. Instead, an autoethnographic description can tell us what in fact to measure when we do eventually subject ourselves to evaluation.

There are, however, disadvantages of beginning with an autoethnographic description. Such a description should involve wide reading in the intricacies of ethnography, careful and time-consuming planning, perhaps months of observation, and a decided commitment to writing the autoethnographic description. We may encounter colleagues who seriously mistrust the process, refuse to cooperate, or oversimplify the strategy. All of these negative factors can become an obstacle too large to overcome. In practical terms, we may not know how to succeed in setting up the necessary conditions for a useful autoethnographic description of our program or department.

Central Features of Autoethnography

In this section, I will offer a summary of the major features presented in the literature about ethnography, followed by an evaluation of the possible applications to academic program description. Like descriptive cultural anthropology, the theory and method of ethnography attempt to address what James Clifford (1983) refers to as "the difficulty of grasping the world of alien peoples" (122). When we treat our own culture and its subcultures as "alien" for the purposes of observation and description, we are performing an autoethnographic study.

The basic philosophical premise of modern ethnography derives from Clifford Geertz's *The Interpretation of Cultures* (1973). Researchers seek to produce "thick description of contextual phenomena, based principally upon data collected by participant observation" (Kantor, Kirby, and Goetz 298). "No matter how exotic or familiar the group, researchers observe daily life, interview informants, keep field notes, review them, attend group functions, and examine whatever artifacts are manifest in the situation" (Brodkey 29). The "facts" in ethnography are constructions of the social context studied. We as researchers observe phenomena and reflect upon their significance. As autoethnographic researchers, we are aware of the inevitable contamination of our own projections on our constructions, and yet our "desires, repressions, investments, and projections" (Said 8) become an important part of the relationship between ourselves and the "representation" we create of ourselves.

Representation is the first central feature in ethnography. As ethnographers, we write down the observed social discourse, including what people say to us as observers and to each other, and from those "representations," we construct a possible meaning (Herndl 321). Representations are the things people say and do, the images they post, the spaces they occupy, and other "facts" about the daily life of the observed. Those representative facts are recorded by the observer, who makes interpretations of those representations.

"Even the most 'objective' interpretations are interpretive" (Doheny-Farina and Odell 506). So the first point to appreciate about our autoethnographic description is that the result does not deny our subjective point of view. Indeed, ethnography takes very seriously experience as knowledge.

At the same time, experience does not always lead to interpretation (Clifford 128), and this acknowledgment is the second central feature of autoethnography. Not all observation and experience produce meaning. Autoethnographic description begins with making observations—seeing is the preferred form of gathering data—and writing everything down, but the fieldwork becomes the representation from which we construct meaning. As James Clifford explains, the new style of representation developed by fieldworker-theorists in the 1920s (such as Malinowski and Mead) exhibits a number of new features that distinguish their style from previous fieldwork:

1. The observer frankly reveals his or her "persona."

2. The observer does not need to master the language of the native culture but can spend only weeks learning some means of communication.

3. The visual is made primary because "interpretation [is] tied to description."

4. A formulated point of view or theory helps more in understanding an alien culture than does an exhaustive compilation of cultural beliefs and ceremonies.

5. The research takes a "predominately synecdochic rhetorical stance" and parts can and do stand for the whole of the culture. (124–25)

As Geertz does with the Balinese cockfight, the observer hopes to find the particular thing that tells the story of this culture and allows the ethnographer to construct meaning. For example, when I visit high schools, as I often do, recruiting for my college, I am always struck by the difference between my own college culture and the secondary school culture. Those differences consist in the very nature of our buildings. High schools are large buildings with huge parking lots and silent corridors during classes. I'm always aware that when I visit a high school I don't know where to park, where to enter, where to find help. The physical culture is foreign to me. I try to impress upon high school teachers and students that when students come to a college or university, the same cultural differences will strike them. Those differences are not just physical, of course, and many new college students underestimate the overwhelming cultural differences between high school and college.

The ethnographic study, then, grants the subjective theoretical point of view and seeks to discover a "model" (Doheny-Farina and Odell 528) or "fields of synecdoches" (Clifford 131) through which to see and understand how the culture works.

The third feature of an ethnographic description, however, is to maintain the otherness of the culture under observation. The question of authority is crucial here. As observers, we want, as Clifford says, to "resist the pull toward authoritative representation of the other," and in a Bakhtinian sense, the ethnographer may need to develop a fictional dialogue "to maintain the strangeness of the other voice" (135). In sum, our autoethnographic description, like literary production and analysis, sees the culture under observation as a text to be read and analyzed, but we must construct a meaning that is respectful of the otherness of the textual culture and its many voices.

The fourth feature of an autoethnographic study is that we may begin with several theories of how the culture holds together but we will seek in the end to know how a part of our material can confirm a theory about the whole. If we choose the ethnographic approach, we must have more than one method of collecting information. If we take notes on observations and interviews, for example, we could also conduct surveys or questionnaires, such as annual review forms and student evaluations of faculty. Whatever the specifics, we must use alternative ways of collecting information. Ethnographers call this process "triangulation."

After setting up the necessary conditions, making the necessary observations and notes, and recording the necessary conversations, we then write our ethnography. That is, as Clifford says, after much observation and study, the ethnographer must construct meaning from experience by choosing some particular "intensely significant locus of the culture" (131) that tells the truth for the whole. This interpretation can be obtained only by writing up the ethnographic description. Such a description may become a valuable document for later decisions about goals and direction, but unless the participant-observer constructs a meaning that substantiates a theory about the culture, the description could be an unwieldy, boring, and useless document.

Applications to Understanding Academic Programs

To apply autoethnographic description to understanding academic programs, we can begin by listening to people's narratives about the program under observation. Narratives are rare in scholarly writing "because the academy is inclined to disdain narratives as anecdotes, that is, as unevaluated experience" (Brodkey 46). But if we wish to understand others on their own terms, we need to ask, "Who tells stories? Who listens to them? What stories are being told? What stories are being heard? When and where are stories told?" (Brodkey 47). The point here is that if we wish to "write down" experience, as ethnography tries to do, then we must narrate it. Narrative becomes a method for hearing the truth. Assessment of a program begins with the voices of those in the program narrating their histories.

What is the purpose of assessment? It is to evaluate our stories and experiences. To begin, then, we write down the stories our faculties, administrators, and students tell. We note where and when these stories are told. We ask people to write out their descriptions of the program under study. We can observe the forging of a program- or department-specific document, for example a policy statement, an annual report for the program's corporate board, or a departmental form for annual merit review. As an anthropologist observes a foreign or corporate culture and records behaviors and speech observed at a ritual or ceremony, a participant-observer of an academic culture can note the behavior and speech at a meeting. As people collaborate on writing a group document, working and discussing, a member of the group can act as observer and write an individual record of his or her observations.

In summary, I recommend that we appropriate the theory and methods of ethnography to forge a description of our academic programs as a basis for establishing goals and determining direction for those programs. Following the procedures of contemporary ethnography offers some distinct advantages for program description, despite the commitments of time and focus that such procedures require. By using such methods, we may arrive at a deeper, richer, more accurate understanding of our program's goals, talents, interests, and abilities. Despite the possibility that we may sometimes feel we're spending too much time noting everything, the ethnographic process fundamentally holds the potential to reveal secrets, to inform colleagues of others' perceptions, and even to describe the crucial cultural concerns of a program or department, concerns which may operate only at the subconscious level. We may learn what the important heroes and heroines, ceremonies, goals, rewards, values, and communication networks in our organization really are, as opposed to seeing only what we think they are. In the end, we can base our decisions on the program's culture, not on an abstract set of standards that tell us nothing of value about our own program. In the final analysis, we use program assessment to help set our goals and direction, based upon who we really are.

Works Cited

Blyler, Nancy Roundy. "Pedagogy and Social Action: A Role for Narrative in Professional Communication." *Journal of Business and Technical Communication* 9.3 (1995): 289–320.

Boyer, Ernest L. *Scholarship Reconsidered: Priorities of the Professoriate*. Princeton: The Carnegie Foundation for the Advancement of Teaching, 1990.

Brodkey, Linda. "Writing Ethnographic Narratives." *Written Communication* 4.1 (1987): 25–50.

Clifford, James. "On Ethnographic Authority." *Representations* 1.2 (1983): 118–46.

Cooper, Marilyn M. "Model(s) for Educating Professional Communicators." *Proceedings of the 1990 CPTSC Meeting* (1990): 3–13.

Doheny-Farina, Stephen, and Lee Odell. "Ethnographic Research in Writing: Assumptions and Methodology." *Writing in Nonacademic Settings*. Ed. Lee Odell and Dixie Goswami. New York: Guilford, 1985. 503–35.

Faigley, Lester. *Fragments of Rationality: Postmodernity and the Subject of Composition*. Pittsburgh: U of Pittsburgh P, 1992.

Gates, Henry Louis. *The Signifying Monkey: A Theory of African-American Literary Criticism*. Oxford: Oxford UP, 1988.

Geertz, Clifford. *The Interpretation of Cultures*. New York: Basic, 1973.

Glaser, Susan R., Sonia Zamanou, and Kenneth Hacker. "Measuring and Interpreting Organizational Culture." *Management Communication Quarterly* 1.2 (1987): 173–98.

Herndl, Carl G. "Writing Ethnography: Representation, Rhetoric, and Institutional Practices." *College English* 53.3 (1991): 320–32.

Kantor, Kenneth, Dan Kirby, and Judith Goetz. "Research in Context: Ethnographic Studies in English Education." *Research in the Teaching of English* 15.4 (1981): 293–309.

Miller, Richard I. *Evaluating Faculty Performance*. San Francisco: Jossey, 1972.

"New Mexico Tech—1995." Supplement in *El Defensor Chieftain* (Socorro, New Mexico) 16–17 Aug. 1995.

Pratt, Mary Louise. "Arts of the Contact Zone." *Profession 91*. New York: MLA, 1991. 33–40. (Originally presented as the keynote address at MLA's Responsibilities for Literacy conference in September 1990 in Pittsburgh.)

Said, Edward W. *Orientalism*. New York: Pantheon, 1978.

Schwartzman, Helen B. *Ethnography in Organizations*. Newbury Park, CA: Sage, 1993.

CHAPTER FOURTEEN

Telling Stories: Rethinking the Personal Narrative in the Contact Zone of a Multicultural Classroom

JEANNE WEILAND HERRICK
Northwestern University
University of Illinois at Chicago

One day after class, Joanie, a rather truculent yet engaging student, stopped me to ask about an assignment, a fairly benign assignment, I thought, that asks the students to write a narrative based on a personal experience of theirs. With a twinkle in her eye, she said, "I've got you figured out. I know what you like. You want to find out about students' personal lives, learn our secrets. That's what you English teachers really like. You want us to spill our guts." Somewhat taken aback by Joanie's directness, I chuckled and replied, "No, not necessarily, but we do like learning about people. That's probably one reason we became teachers."

That was my immediate reply, but my reaction didn't stop there. Joanie's charge lingered in my mind. There was both the ring of truth and the sting of an indictment in her shrewd observation. The personal narrative assignment seems innocent enough. After all, we have all heard stories and told stories almost from the moment we entered into language. And what do students know better than their own lives? On this topic, they are the undisputed authorities. *Write what you know.* Isn't that the common dictum for all novice writers? However, my experience in teaching composition to a class of radically diverse students at a large, urban university has convinced me that in the contact zone we need to rethink this assignment and the forms we allow and expect students' narratives to take.

In truth, it is probably impossible to exclude storytelling from the composition classroom, or any classroom for that matter. Cognitive psychologists like Jerome Bruner make a compelling argument for narrative as a ubiquitous cognitive means for making knowledge. Humans, Bruner contends, have a "readiness or predisposition to organize experience into narrative forms (Bruner, *Acts* 45). In fact, says Bruner, "we organize our experience and our memory of human happenings *mainly* in the form of narrative—stories, excuses, myths, reasons for doing and not doing and so on" (Bruner, "Narrative" 4). And this holds true not just in the personal and social domains. In "Ecological Theories as Cultural Narratives: F. E. Clements's and H. A. Gleason's 'Stories' of Community Succession," Debra Journet makes a convincing case for narrative as the organizing principle of knowledge construction in the scientific domain as well. Narratives do not just enable humans to represent reality to themselves or others; narratives are also the primary, universal means by which we humans construct what passes for reality itself (Bruner, "Narrative" 4).

All this would seem to be cozy comfort for those of us who as composition teachers routinely include a personal narrative as one of our assignments, frequently the first, when teaching students in a multicultural and, therefore, often multilingual and multidialectal classroom. Although the term "multicultural" has been so appropriated and misappropriated that it may no longer have any stable, clear-cut meaning for us, I would like to use the term "multicultural classrooms" here to mean those classrooms where we find what Min-Zhan Lu calls "border residents." Taking an image from Gloria Anzaldúa's *Borderlands/La Frontera*, Lu uses "border residents" to refer to those students who straddle the border(s) between at least two different cultures or subcultures. This would include native-born U.S. residents who are members of marginalized subcultures, such as Native Americans, or inner-city African Americans, who have been historically subordinated by the dominant culture, as well as immigrants new to the United States. It would also include those students from social classes, such as the working class, who have also been subordinated by hegemonic social, economic, and political practices. This is the kind of classroom Mary Louise Pratt calls a "contact zone," and this term has gained much currency within composition studies to designate those "social spaces where cultures meet, clash, and grapple with each other, often in contexts of highly asymmetrical relations of power" (34).

Although these students may come from diverse cultures, if narrative is a universal cognitive tool for making meaning found in every culture's tool kit, as Bruner describes it, then we are surely on solid theoretical and pedagogical ground in asking *all* our students to write narratives. In fact, Mary Louise Pratt lists "exercises in storytelling" first in her catalogue of the pedagogical arts of the contact zone. Therefore, it would seem that we do not put these students at a rhetorical or cultural disadvantage by requiring them to write a narrative. Or do we?

The assumption, I believe, warrants a closer look, for two reasons. First, if all speech genres, as Mikhail Bakhtin makes us aware, are socioculturally specific, then the forms that narratives take are necessarily shaped by the particular culture that produces them. Students from different cultures would, then, be likely to have differing narrative forms operating within their linguistic and rhetorical repertoires. Second, while the ethics of the personal narrative are questionable for all our students, it is potentially even more dangerous for our nonmainstream students. For these reasons, we need to rethink the place of the personal narrative assignment in the classrooms of the contact zone.

While hardly a first-year composition syllabus is written that doesn't begin with, or at least include, a narrative assignment, this commonly means, as Anne DiPardo points out, not just any narrative but a narrative of the student's personal experience. "While the narrative form can assume guises ranging from the scientific to the poetics," says DiPardo, "among composition teachers *narrative* and personal experience essays are generally regarded as the same, largely suspect phenomenon" (61). At an NCTE research conference on the use of narrative to make meaning (held in Chicago in 1993), I was struck by the unspoken and obviously widespread assumption on the part of the participants that when we speak of narrative in composition studies, we mean *personal narrative*, a speech genre that is widely used in our American popular culture as well as in the culture of the composition classroom. The predominance of tell-all and kiss-and-tell books and television shows—such as the *Jerry Springer Show* or the *Jenny Jones Show,* where ordinary people routinely reveal intimate and often humiliating details from their private lives for public consumption in exchange for their fifteen minutes of fame—is evidence of the appeal of and fascination with personal stories. We may publicly decry shabby books and exploitative programs, but the books sell and the shows garner high ratings. Regardless of whether or not confession is good for the soul, it sells. Self-revelation is deeply embedded in the American culture.

The privileging of self-revelation may influence our evaluation of student writing more than we are comfortable admitting. As composition teachers, not only do we commonly require one kind of narrative, a narrative of personal experience, we also frequently reward one kind of personal narrative—that of self-revelation. Moreover, we tend to reward those essays in which one kind of self is revealed. As with Steven Schreiner's claim that our tradition of composition-as-process pedagogy rests upon an assumption that our students share, or should share, "a sameness of student experience, ambition, and ability" based on a Western literary model (102), we may also assume and expect all students, even those from different cultural backgrounds, to approach narrative with the same self-reflexive, self-revelatory impulse of a literary author. In "Judging Writing, Judging Selves," Lester Faigley argues that we are looking for a writer who presents a traditionally Western, humanistic self, one who has achieved "rationality and unity by characterizing former selves as objects for analysis" (411). Faigley supports his contention by examining *What Makes Writing Good*, a collection of student essays solicited by William Coles and James Vopat from a wide range of leading composition theorists and teachers, essays these teachers believe demonstrate "excellence" (404).

Of forty-eight essays submitted, thirty were personal narratives, and twenty of those were autobiographical. Although Faigley admits, "I have no simple explanation for the strong preference for autobiographical essays," (404) he observes that many teachers are quite willing to overlook surface-level errors of mechanics if they consider that the student writer has been "honest," written in an "authentic voice," or demonstrated "integrity." What constitutes honest writing, says Faigley, seems to be the student's willingness to reveal painful aspects of her or his own life. He points to a terminal comment written on a student's paper by Erika Lindemann. "'Good writing is most effective when we tell the truth about who we are and what we think.'" "Why," asks Faigley, "is writing about potentially embarrassing and painful aspects of one's life considered more honest than, say, the efforts of Joe Williams's student, Greg Shaefer, who tries to figure out what Thucydides was up to in writing about the Peloponnesian War" (404–5). Why indeed?

One answer may be that while, as Bruner argues, narrative itself may be a universal process in the human cognitive tool kit for making meaning and constructing knowledge, the *forms* that narratives take are shaped by the culture that produces them. In "The Problem of Speech Genres," Mikhail Bakhtin says that utterances, his basic linguistic unit, fall into "relatively stable types," which he calls "speech genres." These speech genres are socially constructed, shared, and replicated in the same way all languages are—national languages and all their variant forms (60). "Thus," says Bakhtin, "a speaker is given not only mandatory forms of the national language (lexical composition and grammatical structures), but also forms of utterances that are mandatory, that is, speech genres" (80). Because "they are not created by him but given to him," the process of becoming acculturated within a specific social domain or speech community means in part becoming familiar with and learning the speech genres specific to that domain or community (80–81). Or, as Jerome Bruner would put it, each of us acquires those narrative structures that are part of our culture's tool kit.

In "Writers and Their Subjects: Ethnologic and Chinese Composition," David A. Jolliffe asserts that "composition is always ethnocomposition" (265). In other words, because the teaching of composition is always and inevitably "situated within a specific cultural domain, it is always and inevitably culturally specific, not just language but also the forms that language may permissibly and predictably take" (265). Jolliffe points out that "students in every college and university composition classroom [in the United States] are taught to participate in a kind of discipline; they are led to enter an intellectual community where certain subject matters are privileged, certain intellectual and logical operations are appropriate for them to employ, and certain discourse, syntactic, and stylistic conventions are 'correct' for them to use" (265).

As Pratt puts it, because the teacher has the upper hand in the classroom, it is the teacher who decides what constitutes a "legitimate move." "Teacher-pupil language," says Pratt, "is defined from the point of view of the teacher and teaching, not from the point of view of pupils and pupiling." In fact, Pratt goes on, "whatever students do other than what the teacher specifies is invisible or anomalous to the analysis" (38).

The personal narrative, then, is just such a "legitimate move," to use Pratt's words, or a "correct" and "privileged" kind of discourse, to use Jolliffe's, and too often it plays out that the more personal and revealing these student essays are, the better the grade they receive. This fact presents some very troubling problems when our students are not from the Western European–derived American middle-class, whose values and assumptions, literary and cultural, have long been the foundation of our pedagogy.

Nowhere did this become more apparent to me than in my own classroom several years ago. On the first day, I realized that this class of so-called basic writers (a naming practice that needs to be done away with) constituted a veritable mini United Nations. This is not unusual on the campus where I was then teaching, the University of Illinois at Chicago, an institution whose history and character Carol Severino ably describes in "An Urban University and Its Academic Support Program: Teaching Basic Writing in the Context of an 'Urban Mission.'" Most students commute to school from homes within the city boundaries, work at least one job, and are the first members of their family to attend college. Of the approximately sixteen thousand undergraduates at this time (1993), 10 percent were African American, 13 percent were Latino or Latina, 17 percent were Asian American, and 6 percent were international students, meaning that nearly half of the undergraduates came from nonmainstream home cultures. When one adds in the many immigrants from Eastern Bloc countries, especially those immigrating from the former Soviet Union, who retain much of their home culture as well as their home language(s), it is easy to see that, more likely than not, one finds Pratt's contact zone waiting for them in the classroom. Each semester, I have informally polled my students and have found that approximately 65 percent of them, even those who are business majors in business writing courses, speak a language other than English at home. Students at UIC are placed in courses designed for basic writers on the grounds of a placement test that includes a writing sample, which causes the diversity of students in these courses to be even greater than that in other first-year composition courses—a fairly common situation.

Of a total of sixteen students in my class that semester, only two were U.S.-born European Americans, and they were both from the working class of Chicago's South Side. Five of the sixteen had been in the United States less than three months: three women from the former Soviet Union, a Chinese woman from Taiwan, and a young woman who had recently completed her service in the Israeli army and whose father was attached to the Israeli consulate in Chicago. In addition, there was another Chinese woman from the People's Republic, two Filipino Americans, two African American men from the nearby projects, three Latina women, and a young man born and raised on the West Bank of Palestine, who had immigrated to the United States just three years before. This was the contact zone manifest in the flesh and lives of actual students.

In this class:

> All the students . . . had the experience, for example, of hearing their culture discussed and objectified in ways that horrified them; all the students saw their roots traced back to legacies of both glory and shame; all the students experienced face-to-face the ignorance and incomprehension, and occasionally the hostility, of others. (Pratt 39)

Nowhere was this more evident than in the interaction, or, to be more precise, the avoidance of interaction between the Israeli woman and the Palestinian man. They literally sat as far apart physically as possible, the Israeli sitting in the front row to my far right and the Palestinian sitting in the last row to my far left. Both repeatedly confided to me that they were afraid to speak in front of the other and actually stated that they feared for their lives. When I assured each of them, separately of course, that they were being unnecessarily suspicious, they both were quick to assure me that they knew their situations and its risks far better than I. For my own part, not being a part of either of their cultures, I could not be totally certain they were not correct. Therefore, I respected their requests and tried to never put either of them in a position where they would be compelled to speak in front of the other.

Given this classroom environment, how could I rely on my usual, standard pedagogy of assigning a personal experience narrative and putting the students in small groups to workshop their drafts? What other fears lurked unspoken in this contact zone of strangers? It didn't take me long to learn that workshopping wouldn't work in a classroom where the varieties of English, complete with all their different and dialectal styles and accents, made it a struggle for students to understand each others' words, let alone each others' meanings. If necessity is the mother of invention, it is also the mother of experimentation.

I began the semester's assignments with the writing of a narrative, as usual, but this time I decided to experiment. I intentionally left the definition of what constitutes a narrative open to each student's interpretation, so the students could write any kind of a story they wished; I simply asked that their essays tell a story and that the story make a point. In class together, we brainstormed about various ways they might approach this assignment, including the writing of a story of personal experience as one of the options—just not the only option. I was curious to discover how these students would define the assignment for themselves, how each would conceptualize what a narrative is.

The day I collected their essays, this is what I found in their opening sentences.

Judy, the woman who had recently immigrated from Taiwan, told a love story in the form of a fairy tale of a young Chinese girl who disguises herself as a young man in order to get an education. "Once upon a time, there is a man named Liang Shan-po. He'd like to go to the capital for the examination which decided people could be a governor or not." Similarly Irena, a recent immigrant from Belarus, formerly of the Soviet Union, told her story about the folly of greed in the form of a traditional Russian folktale. "Once upon a time lived a young woman, an honest wife of an honest man. All her life Masha was very modest and quiet and loved her husband devotedly."

Svetlana, from the Ukraine, wrote a true story about her grandfather but told it as if she were presenting an oral tale. "I want to tell you a tragic story about my family. That story is about a brutal Civil Ware in Russia when one brother could kill another."

Marisol, a young Puerto Rican woman, also wrote a family myth, a ghost story evoking some of the lyrical surrealism of her Latin heritage. Her opening paragraph, however, was personal in style and tone. "Every summer I would fly to Puerto Rico, to visit my family in the country. One summer night my uncle Jose told me the story of a ghost that roams the roadsides at night."

Meanwhile, Donald, a thirty-three-year-old African American military veteran, wrote about an incident of his own personal public humiliation, but he wrote it in the style of a short fiction, obscuring his identity by taking the voice of a fictional first-person narrator, but not his own voice. "This particular morning, I had awakened from a dead sleep to the rays of sun that beamed through my barrack room window because the curtain was partially closed. 'Damn,' I said to myself in a low tone. 'Another hangover.'"

Larry, a working-class White, began his fiction about domestic violence with a dialogue. Consistent with the dictums of American fiction writing, Larry jumps right into the action. "'You bitch,' he shouted, 'I can't believe you slept with him!'" When Larry read a draft of his story to the class, Ibraheim, the Palestinian, objected not only to Larry's use of the word "bitch," but also to Larry's jumping right into his story. "He needs to tell the reader what his story is going to be about in his first sentence," advised Ibraheim, who believes that writers should set up the story they are about to tell. Indeed that is precisely how Ibraheim opened his own narrative. "The story I am about to tell you is a real story, which happened in the south side of Chicago in September of 1992 and indangered the life of my best friend during a brutal shooting."

This representative sample of how these culturally diverse students opened their narratives demonstrates that students from differing social loci bring to the classroom differing models of what a narrative is and can be, models that expand the range of narrative possibilities beyond the monologic speech genre of a narrative of personal experience. Discussing these essays together in class provided these students with a way to engage each other and their cultural backgrounds and assumptions, in some instances uncovering differences separating them and in others finding common ground linking them. These essays, then, became the springboard for a semester-long discussion of cultural and rhetorical differences and similarities. Not only were we discussing the differences between languages or dialects, but also we had expanded the terrain of our exploration of language practices beyond the range of word differences to include those of genre and, more specifically, narrative genres.

Yes, there were conflicts, among the students and sometimes between the students and myself. In the beginning of the course, the three young women from the former Soviet Union sat together, as a bloc. They kept up a steady undercurrent of chatter among themselves, no matter who was speaking, including me. It was almost the kind of behavior that happens too often these days in movie theaters when the audience keeps up a steady current of talk throughout the film, as if those about them are as deaf to their talk as those on the screen. One day I confronted the three of them after class. They apologized and made an obvious, though not entirely successful, attempt to curb their distracting conversations. As they slowly grew to feel some trust in me, they confided to me that in Russian schools, students and their teachers were locked in an adversarial relationship. Teachers functioned more as examiners than as teachers, determining who would go on and who would be flushed out of the educational system. As a consequence, students typically banded together to help each other. They told me that if students were left alone in an examination room, they would usually share answers and help each other. They neither trusted nor respected their teachers.

By the end of the semester, they appeared to have very slowly come to know and trust me. On the final day of class, the four of us shared a picnic together on one of the few patches of grass on UIC's urban campus. I learned much from them as they talked about their lives in the former Soviet Union and their experiences in coming to the United States. They learned, I hope, that teachers are not always the enemy.

There were other conflicts. For example, when we workshopped a draft of one of Judy's, the Taiwanese woman's, essays, Irena wrote as a suggestion to Judy, "Learn more words in English so your essay is not so boring, boring, boring." Because I collected the students' written suggestions before giving them to the writer, I discussed Irena's suggestion with her. I told her that not only was this comment likely to hurt Judy's feelings but also it might even discourage her as she tentatively learned to write in English. Irena appeared to understand, and was more sensitive in the comments and suggestions she wrote to other students after that.

There were moments of hope. One of the most amazing moments was when Ibraheim, the Palestinian, was struggling to show the class how verb tense in his native Arabic is determined by punctuation marks. As he struggled to explain, writing samples on the blackboard, Becca, the Israeli, momentarily forgetting their animosity, raced up to the board to help him. Although their unity lasted only a brief moment, they did connect.

There were also moments of disappointment. Not a week or two after the classroom incident just described, I was working one-on-one with Becca. Again the topic of the Palestinians arose in our conversations. I mentioned how helpful she had been to Ibraheim in the classroom. She stared resolutely into my eyes and said, "They [meaning the Palestinians] are animals. They are not even human. There is nothing bad enough that it shouldn't happen to them. I hate them all and wish them all to die like dogs." I made a feeble attempt to engage her in a discussion that would shift her opinion, but the steeliness of her gaze and the metallic clip of her speech made me recognize that her feelings and beliefs were far too intractable to be shifted, let alone changed, in the course of one semester of composition. Whenever I hear news from the Middle East, I recall and am chilled by Becca's stare. The contact zone is often uncomfortable and can be disheartening.

Another source of my own discomfort was my recognition of my almost automatic response to try to acculturate the students and their writing to standard composition essayist prose. I confess that in responding to their rough drafts, I had to consciously fight an impulse to pull these heterogeneous texts toward some kind of unitary narrative center, informed by the literary standard of the culturally "correct" or "legitimate" narrative style I brought with me: the active voice, strong verbs and evocative nouns, concrete imagery, a sense of immediacy, and a strong personal voice; in other words, the voice of Lester Faigley's rational and unified "self."

Faigley is, I think, correct in saying that the voice of this kind of self is the hallmark of the personal narrative genre in most composition classes. Because we value this kind of voice, we often reward it in our grade books. Yet, this concept of the "self" is ethnocentric to the hegemonic American culture. As Jolliffe learned when he taught in China, the relationship between the individual and the community varies with culture. "The ideal Chinese writer is a cooperative member of a collective, not a novel, independent, individual" (268). Not, in other words, the autonomous, rational, unified, isolated "self" of the idealized composition student here. This is true for other more communal cultures as well. What this means for composition teachers is that assignments requiring students to write personal narratives in the mode of a self reflecting upon past personal experience in order to make some sense of it may put some students in our multicultural classrooms at a disadvantage. Serving as their guides into the realm of hegemonic academic discourse (and in some cases, such as Irena's, behavior), we may acquaint them with this new form, the personal narrative essay, but do we have the right to base their grade on their ability to write in a form that may be not only alien to them but often even threatening to their own cultural sense of "self" and who they are? This is particularly troubling when we know that the genres considered *correct* and *legitimate* in other disciplines, while they may include narratives, will rarely honor or even include narratives of a personal nature. One can be a successful scientist without mastering the personal narrative.

At the very least, we must expand our definition of what constitutes a narrative to allow our students to hybridize their varieties of narrative with those they receive from the dominant culture. The terms that Pratt uses for this process, a term borrowed from anthropology, is *transculturation*, those "processes whereby members of subordinated or marginal groups select and invent from materials transmitted by a dominant or metropolitan culture" (36). How might our own conception of narrative be invigorated and refreshed by creative reshaping and recasting according to perspectives that many of us can hardly imagine? Is this not the source of much creative activity—to take what is familiar and give it new life with a fresh and original perspective? As Lu points outs, border residents not only *struggle* with the conflicts; sometimes their "attempts to cope with conflict also bring 'compensation,' 'joys,' and 'exhilarations'" (Lu 888). Rather than simply marching our students through an activity in which they recreate the same genre, offering new wine in old skins, what if we allowed—no, even encouraged—our students to remake the casks themselves.

But all of this really circumvents an even more troubling concern: What of the ethics of this assignment? In an article in the *Chronicle of Higher Education*, authors Susan Swartzlander, Diana Pace, and Virginia Lee Stamler express concerns about the ethics of requiring a personal narrative of any composition student. While opposition to this speech genre has centered on whether or not personal narratives really help students acquire the critical thinking and writing skills they will need in order to function and succeed in academic and professional domains, the ethical dimension of this question has been largely overlooked. Swartzlander, Pace, and Stamler question whether grades should be tied to self-revelation. Like Faigley, they observe that the most "moving" essays "are often given the highest ratings; most notably papers usually about emotionally charged topics such as the death of a parent or the suicide of a teen-aged friend" (B1). Composition teachers frequently agonize over how to grade a poorly written essay about a traumatic personal experience. "We have to ask ourselves, are we grading writing or grading lives?" (B1).

Swartzlander, Pace, and Stamler also contend that those very students who are already at emotional risk because their personal boundaries have been transgressed are put at risk again by composition teachers who are violating those same boundaries. "Requirements that demand self-disclosure can intensify a student's feelings of abuse and powerlessness" (B1). Because "women students are more likely to have horrid tales to tell in their writing, since women are more often than men the victims of rape, incest, and sexual abuse," the personal narrative assignment may put female students at greater risk than male students.

If this is true for female students, what does that mean for students who come from cultures that have been historically and traditionally oppressed? bell hooks cautions us that for minority students, making the private public often entails risks, risks that students may not want to incur (39). Indeed, when there is a clearly perceived discrepancy between our social power outside of the classroom and that of our students, our students may be even more reluctant to reveal any information about their extra-curricular lives.

For example, during this same semester, one of my students, Donald, the thirty-three-year-old African American GI from the inner city of Chicago, had agreed to do a case study with me. My aim was to discover how a student who, like me, was a native speaker of English and was born and raised in the United States—but from a social and economic background very different from my own—would understand and make use of my comments on the drafts of his writing. I specifically wanted to find out whether dialectal differences played a role in how he understood my meaning or, more important, how he understood my meaning to be something other than what I intended. We met weekly to discuss Donald's reactions to my comments and to allow me to gather some detailed, in-depth information about him and his background, all of which was to serve in establishing the contours of the social context of Donald's various literacy practices, as distinguished from my own White, middle-class, Anglo-Saxon practices.

Although Donald had agreed to participate in the study—in fact, he had been quite eager—he was suspicious of me and my motives from the beginning. Donald had many family members, older brothers and uncles, who had been and possibly still were active members of a street gang. Assuming that I was married, Donald repeatedly asked me if my husband were a cop. "Just what does my family background have to do with my writing?" he continually and persistently asked. While I tried to explain that one's family and social background influences what and how one learns, I am not sure Donald was ever completely convinced that he wasn't putting those he cared about, even himself, at some risk. Yet, he willingly and even diligently worked with me throughout the entire semester. However, in his writing for class assignments, he always wrote about personal experiences from the detached position of a third party outside of the action, as if he were writing about someone else.

We may want to believe that we don't require students to reveal anything they don't want to, but experience has made our students savvy about what gets rewarded. In the words of Joanie, many of our students believe that what we want is a revelation, and the more dramatic the better: "You want us to spill our guts." The personal narrative assignment may unwittingly place our students in the dilemma of having to choose between wanting, on one hand, to please the teacher, play the school game, and get a good grade, and wanting, on the other hand, to protect their privacy and that of those they care about.

So, am I recommending that we eliminate the teaching of the personal narrative in the contact zone? No. "We are not suggesting that all writing about personal experience should be abandoned," say Swartzlander, Pace, and Stamler (B1), and neither am I. In fact, this essay itself is a form of a personal narrative, the narrative of one of my personal teaching experiences. Swartzlander, Pace, and Stamler recommend that when we teach and assign the personal narrative essay we do so with caution, carefully respecting our students' rights to privacy. At the practical level, they suggest that we not require students to read their personal narratives to the class or take them to a tutor, and that we orient these narratives to the future, asking students to write about their plans, hopes, and dreams for the future, rather than to their past.

I would go still further. We need to expand the range of narrative forms our students can "legitimately" write, allowing space for them to bring in narrative speech genres from their own cultures and transculturate the speech genres of the dominant culture. As Pratt says, "While subordinate peoples do not usually control what emanates from the dominant culture, they do determine to varying extents what gets absorbed into their own and what it gets used for" (36). The contact zone must be a site of greater choice; the range of legitimate moves must be expanded. Anzaldúa's "new *mestiza,*" her prototypical border resident, must be free to roam within flexible boundaries if she or he is to create, or even survive.

This expansion serves theoretical as well as practical purposes. If, as Jerome Bruner contends, the narrative models we use shape and determine the configuration of our epistemologies, a more expansive range of narrative forms would allow for and even stimulate diverse kinds of knowledge rather than regularizing and delimiting the construction of knowledge by the imposition of a standard, hegemonic narrative form or even standard genres. Differing ways of telling stories mean differing ways of knowing, and there ought to be room in our classrooms for a rich variety of people, styles, stories, and knowledge—including those that coexist and grapple with each other in contact zones. "Because," as Anzaldúa says, "the future depends on the breaking down of paradigms, it depends on the straddling of two or more cultures" (80). Border residents, with their *mestiza* consciousness, those very students we find in the contact zone of our multicultural classrooms, can lead us to new ways of seeing and experiencing the world, instead of their having to always follow another's old way. We can only benefit from such inclusion, and so can our students, who have the right to choose *not* to reveal their personal lives to their classmates and to their teachers. How we composition teachers rethink and redefine the use of personal narratives and the personal narrative assignment in the contact zone of our classrooms will, in the end, tell a revealing story about us.

Works Cited

Anzaldúa, Gloria. *Borderlands/La Frontera: The New Mestiza.* San Francisco: Spinsters/Aunt Lute, 1987.

Bakhtin, Mikhail. "The Problem of Speech Genres." *Speech Genres and Other Late Essays.* Ed. Caryl Emerson and Michael Holquist. Trans. Vern McGee. Austin: U of Texas P, 1986.

Bruner, Jerome. *Acts of Meaning.* Cambridge, MA: Harvard UP, 1990.

———. "The Narrative Construction of Reality." *Critical Inquiry* 18.1 (1991): 1–21.

DiPardo, Anne. "Narrative Knowers, Expository Knowledge: Discourse as a Dialectic." *Written Communication* 7.1 (1990): 59–95.

Faigley, Lester. "Judging Writing, Judging Selves." *College Composition and Communication* 40.4 (1989): 395–412.

hooks, bell. *Teaching to Transgress: Education as the Practice of Freedom.* New York: Routledge, 1994.

Jolliffe, David A. "Writers and Their Subjects: Ethnologic and Chinese Composition." *A Rhetoric of Doing: Essays on Written Discourse in Honor of James L. Kinneavy.* Ed. Stephen P. Witte, Neil Nakadate, and Roger D. Cherry. Carbondale: Southern Illinois UP, 1992. 261–75.

Journet, Debra. "Ecological Theories as Cultural Narratives: F. E. Clements's and H. A. Gleason's 'Stories' of Community Succession." *Written Communication* 8.4 (1991): 446–72.

Lu, Min-Zhan. "Conflict and Struggle: The Enemies or Preconditions of Basic Writing?" *College English* 54.8 (1992): 887–913.

Pratt, Mary Louise. "Arts of the Contact Zone." *Profession 91.* New York: MLA, 1991. 33–40. (Originally presented as the keynote address at MLA's Responsibilities for Literacy conference in September 1990 in Pittsburgh.)

Schreiner, Steven. "A Portrait of the Student as a Young Writer: Reevaluating Emig and the Process Movement." *College Composition and Communication* 48.1 (1997): 86–104.

Severino, Carol. "An Urban University and Its Academic Support Program: Teaching Basic Writing in the Context of an 'Urban Mission.'" *Journal of Basic Writing* 15.1 (1996): 39+.

Swartzlander, Susan, Diana Pace, and Virginia Lee Stamler. "The Ethics of Requiring Students to Write about Their Personal Lives." *Chronicle of Higher Education* (17 Feb. 1993): B1–B2.

AFTERWORD: ON THE TEACHER'S ZONE OF EFFECTIVITY

RICHARD E. MILLER
Rutgers University

When I finished writing "Fault Lines in the Contact Zone" (included here as Chapter 6) nearly a decade ago, I opened a file called, "Son of Fault Lines," where material for a future essay would be stored. Over the years, my file has grown fatter and fatter with stories about how lives are lived and lost at moments when power relations are inequitably distributed or deployed. In the New York area, these examples are everywhere ready to hand:

- On August 9, 1997, Abner Louima, unarmed, is assaulted, then sodomized with a stick, by police officers while in custody.

- On February 4, 1999, Amadou Diallo, unarmed, is killed by police officers in a hail of forty-one bullets after reaching for his wallet. All four officers are later acquitted.

- On March 17, 2000, Patrick Dorismond, unarmed, is shot and killed in a scuffle with undercover police officers. Dorismond, the target of a sting operation, had refused to buy drugs from the undercover officers.

Then, there's O.J. and the "Crime of the Century"; Colin Ferguson strolling through the Long Island Railroad commuter, shooting thirty passengers and killing six on December 7, 1993; the three Texans, Lawrence Russell Brewer, Shawn Allen Berry, and John William King, chaining James Byrd to the back of their pickup truck and then dragging him two miles until he was ripped to pieces in June 1998; and Eric Harris and Dylan Klebold killing twelve fellow students and a teacher before killing themselves at Columbine High in April 1999.

This list, which we might just as well label, "Men (mostly white) killing the defenseless," could be extended almost indefinitely. In the world defined by these events, fear of contact and its consequences regularly results in violent outbursts, murderous rage, death, and destruction. It is a world, it seems, always on the verge of apocalyptic collapse.

There's no reason to assume, of course, that the violence that has found such regular and full expression in the high schools during the past decade won't eventually make its way into our lecture halls, seminar rooms, and college dorms, but for the moment it is safe to say that most of us who teach in higher education do not inhabit this space of homicidal violence *while at work*. Indeed, the injustices that occur outside the academy are so clear and so great that they perpetually demand our full attention: we write about and get our students to write about the world *out there*, a world which roils with racism, prejudice of every kind, economic injustice, irrationality, and bureaucratic indifference. We write and because we feel this experience has transformed us we feel that it can and will transform our students so that, someday, there will never again be spaces of exclusion.

This is a noble goal, one that serves to enchant the work of teaching and make it appealing to those of us who have committed our working lives to helping others learn to read and write expository essays. But as I make my way through this hulking file, it is hard for me to see what this goal has to do with the daily workings of the educational system. There are the stories about the Greenwich High students who embedded the phrase "Kill All Niggers" in their yearbook; the Manhattan High School students who left notes for their teachers saying, "Kill All the Jewish People;" the student who was denied his role as class president because he had inserted the word "crematoriums" in a list that appeared beneath his yearbook photo; the Louisiana State University administrator who awarded forty-nine of fifty-four minority fellowships to White students; the university president who was quoted as saying that minority students lack the "genetic hereditary background" to score well on college entrance tests.

Public and private schools, colleges and universities: despite being inhabited with so many people of such good will, these institutions routinely create situations where power is abused by teachers, administrators, and students alike. The contact zones, thus, aren't just "out there," or just at the interface between school and the world outside the school yard; they also could be said to saturate and to define the educational environment, influencing all that gets said and done in these spaces.

The value of the "contact zone" concept rests with its ability to make these abuses into objects of study, thereby helping to bring to light the complex social and cultural histories that allow such abuses to go from being imaginable to being permissible. Unfortunately, this analytic concept is so perfectly suited to the work of identifying areas of conflict for analysis and critique that it can seduce us all into believing that producing such analyses or critiques (or lists of abuses for that matter) is of some consequence in and of itself. The danger in being so seduced is that giving ourselves over to the business of producing critique can serve to forever divert attention from the one zone where we have the best chance of exercising some real, sustained influence: our home institutions.

My growing dissatisfaction with the gap between the production of critique and the generation of viable plans of action is the reason that "Son of Fault Lines" never got written: I now feel that the stories that fill the headlines come from worlds where I am unlikely ever to exercise any significant influence and that continuing to write about them only serves to divert my attention from the areas where I have some hope of effecting a measure of change. So, I grieve over these events that dominate the headlines, I can't get them out of my head, but I focus my attention on the work that can be done by a writing teacher—work on the curriculum at my institution, on our retention policies, on our support services, on teacher training, on accumulating the resources necessary for other teachers in our program to do a good job. These areas constitute the academic's primary zone of effectivity, and by concentrating my attention on this zone, I am able to engage more productively with the forces that are exerting an ever-increasing control over the form and content of higher education—local, state, and corporate funding streams, demands for greater teacher accountability and more accurate testing and placement of students, merit-based performance assessment, and the allocation of all available resources to technological initiatives. The notion of the "contact zone" helped me to see these forces and to name them for what they are, and this has value as long as it is a preliminary step in the process of learning how to act in the conflicted, contestatory curricular spaces that surround us all.

Focusing on curricular matters may seem quite distant from—and even trivial in comparison to—the racially charged events discussed above or the violent acts I wrote about in "Fault Lines." I would argue, though, that when we devote our energies to the curriculum, to better understanding the funding of higher education, to taking control of testing at our home institutions, and to plunging ourselves headlong into the technological revolution, we are working in direct and concrete ways to determine who gets access to higher education and what experience awaits them when they arrive. We are moving, in other words, from studying the contact zone to creating a zone of effectivity, a pragmatic space where our actions have discernable consequences. To commit to such work is to acknowledge that there is no academic space that is not a "contact zone" and thus that there are no battles—curricular or otherwise—that are ever over. In the end, all we have is the constant struggle to realize the elusive goal of creating wider, more supportive communities.

The formation and dissolution of communities—at least academic communities—is not the stuff that headlines are made of. Stanford's Culture, Identities, and Values (CIV) course, which serves as the background of Pratt's article, was, of course, an exception to this rule: its introduction into the curriculum a decade ago made the front pages of newspapers around the country. There just seemed to be something particularly newsworthy in the image of students chanting, "Hey, hey, ho, ho, Western Civilization's got to go." But when the CIV course was dismantled and replaced with a series of more traditional humanities courses a few years back, hardly anyone took notice. Indeed, when, at the General Education in the Research University conference held in June 1999 at New York University, John Bravman, vice pro-vost at Stanford University, offered the assessment that the CIV course was "a relic of our PC past," the statement sparked no response at all. And so, the curricular space that Pratt describes with such pleasure at the end of "Arts of the Contact Zone," that space of joy and peril, has been eclipsed by a competing vision of what first-year students should be reading and writing about.

How that came about is a longer story, but this much should be obvious to us all: across the country, the first-year curriculum suddenly has the interest of administrators and funding organi-zations concerned with attracting and retaining students. For those who have learned how to work and live in the contact zone, this should not be perceived as a disaster, but as an opportunity that we cannot afford to let pass us by. Having learned the arts of the contact zone, it's time we put them to use building curricula that not only assist our students in assessing what's wrong with the world at present but also provide them with training in how to construct and plan for better futures for us all.

INDEX

EDITOR

Janice M. Wolff, professor of English at Saginaw Valley State University, where she has taught since 1992, also directs the university's Honors Program. She has published in *College Composition and Communication* and contributed to various NCTE books. She teaches both lower division and upper division writing courses, general education literature classes, gender studies, and theory courses. In winter 1999, she taught at Umeå University, Sweden, on a Fulbright appointment.

CONTRIBUTORS

Paul Jude Beauvais is associate professor of English and coordinator of First-Year Composition at Salem State College. Before returning home to Massachusetts in 2000, he worked for many years in Ohio at the University of Findlay, where he directed the writing program and developed courses in e-rhetoric and e-poetics. He has served on the editorial staff of *College Composition and Communication,* working as assistant editor from 1987 to 1990 and as associate editor from 1991 to 1993. His articles on rhetoric, composition, and linguistics have appeared in *Pre/Text, Written Communication, Text and Performance Quarterly,* and other publications.

Patricia Bizzell is professor and chair of the English department at the College of the Holy Cross. She founded and directed a writing-across-the-curriculum program and a peer tutorial workshop at the school, and also directed honors programs for the college and the English department. She teaches American literature, rhetoric, and first-year composition. Among her recent publications are the fifth edition of *The Bedford Bibliography for Teachers of Writing* (2000), co-authored with Bruce Herzberg and Nedra Reynolds, and the second edition of *The Rhetorical Tradition: Readings from Classical to Contemporary Times* (2001), edited and authored with Herzberg.

Katherine K. Gottschalk is the Walter C. Teagle Director of First-Year Writing Seminars in the John S. Knight Institute for Writing in the Disciplines at Cornell University, where she coordinates the first-year writing seminar program and the preparatory program for new instructors, as well as assisting in other projects. She is coeditor and author of *Teaching Prose: A Guide for Writing Instructors* (1988) and publishes on writing in the disciplines and writing program administration in such publications as *ADE Bulletin* and *Preparing College Teachers of Writing: Histories, Theories, Programs, and Practices,* edited by Sarah Liggett and Betty P. Pytlik (2001).

Mary R. Harmon, an award-winning English teacher in grades 7 through 12 for twenty-three years, now teaches in the English Education

Program at Saginaw Valley State University, where she coordinates the Freshman Writing Program. She has been president of the Michigan Council of Teachers of English, serves as associate chair of NCTE's Women in Literacy and Life Assembly, and has been active on various Michigan Department of Education committees. Especially interested in issues surrounding language use, power, and classroom discourse, she publishes and presents frequently on multicultural, gender-related, and sociolinguistic topics and is co-author of the forthcoming *Beyond Grammar: Language, Power, and the Classroom—Resources for Teachers.*

Jeanne Weiland Herrick is a lecturer with the Writing Program and with the McCormick School of Engineering at Northwestern University, where she teaches technical writing, teamwork, and composition, and in the M.B.A. programs at the University of Illinois at Chicago, where she teaches cultural diversity and business communication. Her research areas include the uses of narrative, composition and composition theory, and intercultural communication, especially in the contact zone of the workplace. She has published in the *Journal of Business and Technical Communication* and serves as a consultant to corporations on issues of cultural diversity and intercultural and professional communication.

Daphne Key currently supervises student teachers at Peru State College in Nebraska. Being a military spouse, she has traveled extensively and has had the opportunity to teach grades 4 through college across America. Also, she has begun literacy groups in Alabama, Virginia, and Nebraska. She is the author of *Literacy Shutdown* and has been published in *English Journal.*

Cynthia Lewiecki-Wilson is professor of English and affiliate of the Women's Studies Program at Miami University and teaches at the Middletown campus. She is interested in theories of writing and difference, and is the author of books and articles on writing, rhetoric, and literature. Her most recent book, co-edited with James C. Wilson, is *Embodied Rhetorics: Disability in Language and Culture* (2001).

Richard E. Miller is associate professor of English and associate director of the Writing Program at Rutgers University. He is the author of *As If Learning Mattered: Reforming Higher Education* (1998) and writes regularly about how intellectual labor and bureaucratic institutions are inextricably intertwined. His current project, *The Hope Machine,* is a series of essays on education and violence.

Robert D. Murray is assistant professor of English, assistant chairperson of the Humanities Division, and director of the College Writing Program at St. Thomas Aquinas College in Sparkill, New York. He is currently working on a collection of essays entitled *Reworking Classroom Authority* about the ways race and gender issues in the classroom can lead to a more complex understanding of the concept of textual authority. He is also interested in labor and social class issues as they are represented in the earliest texts of nineteenth-century American realism.

Diane Penrod is associate professor in the Department of Composition and Rhetoric at Rowan University, Glassboro, New Jersey, where she is also graduate program advisor for the Master of Arts in Writing. She publishes in the areas of popular culture, media literacy and ethics, discourse analysis of the Internet, and social justice issues in composition. She has edited two books and authored or co-authored nine articles. She is at work on two books, *Composition in Convergence* and *Web Talk*.

Thomas Philion is director of the Chicago Area Writing Project and associate professor in the College of Education at Roosevelt University, where he teaches courses on young adult literature, methods of teaching English, and reading and writing across the curriculum. Currently, he is working on a research project about the oppositional practices of urban literacy educators.

Mary Louise Pratt holds the Olive H. Palmer Chair in Humanities as professor in both the Spanish and Portuguese and the Comparative Literature departments at Stanford University. Her research and teaching encompass linguistics, literature, history, and anthropology to explore issues such as feminism, postcolonial theory, sociolinguistics, and literary analysis. She is co-author of *Linguistics for Students of Literature* and *Women, Culture, and Politics in Latin America* and author of *Imperial Eyes: Travel Writing and Transculturation*. She is currently working on another book, *Mujer y ciudadanía: historia de discursos, 1820–1997*.

Carol Severino is associate professor and associate chair in the Rhetoric Department at the University of Iowa, where she directs the Writing Center and teaches undergraduate rhetoric courses and graduate courses in writing research and pedagogy. With Juan C. Guerra and Johnnella E. Butler, she co-edited *Writing in Multicultural Settings* (1997). She is interested in contrastive rhetorics and cultural and linguistic issues in second language writing, especially ESL writing, and has an article in the recent collection *On Second Language Writing,* edited by Tony Silva and Paul Kei Matsuda (2001).

Carole Yee is professor of English at New Mexico Institute of Mining and Technology (New Mexico Tech), where she also serves as associate vice president for academic affairs. She was chair of the Humanities Department for seven years, 1991–98. She teaches literature and advanced undergraduate courses in the New Mexico Tech B.S. degree program in Technical Communication, housed in the Humanities Department. Her many publications in books and journals include studies on women writers in late twentieth-century American drama and in Victorian literature (George Eliot), as well as publications in technical communication and in organizational culture.

This book was typeset in Sabon by Electronic Imaging.
Typefaces used on the cover were ITC Fenice and Futura.
The book was printed on 50-lb. Lynx Opaque by
IPC Communication Services.